Altered Mates

Tom Morton works for ABC Radio National and ABC-TV as a journalist and broadcaster. In 1995 he presented the popular Radio National series 'Male Matters', and was a national Walkley Award finalist. Tom grew up in Adelaide, has lived, travelled and worked in Europe, and now lives in Sydney.

Altered Mates

The man question

Tom Morton

ALLEN & UNWIN

This project has been assisted by the Commonwealth Government through the Australia Council, its arts funding and advisory body.

First published in 1997 by
Allen & Unwin
9 Atchison Street
St Leonards NSW 2065
Australia
Phone: (61 2) 9901 4088
Fax: (61 2) 9906 2218
E-mail: frontdesk@allen-unwin.com.au
URL: http//www.allen-unwin.com.au

National Library of Australia
Cataloguing-in-Publication entry:

Morton, Tom, 1959– .
Altered mates: the man question.

ISBN 1 86448 333 4

1. Masculinity (Psychology). 2. Men—Psychology.
I. Title.

305.31

Set in 10.5/12 pt Sabon by DOCUPRO, Sydney
Printed by McPhersons Printing Group, Victoria

10 9 8 7 6 5 4 3 2 1

For Eurydice

Contents

Acknowledgements

The original idea for this book came from the *Male Matters* series, broadcast on ABC Radio National in January 1995. I wish particularly to thank everyone involved in the inception, planning and production of the series—Ann Arnold, Eurydice Aroney, Juanita Crowley, Roi Huberman, Kerrie Ross, Nick Rushworth and Jo Upham—for their inspiration and generosity in allowing me to draw on and quote material on which they worked.

My thanks go also to Richard Smart, of Richard Smart Publishing, for hearing a book in the radio series, and having the confidence in an untried author to find author and idea a home with Allen & Unwin. Richard also read the first draft of the manuscript and made a number of useful and perceptive suggestions for improving it.

I am grateful to Stephen Alward, Sarah Benjamin, Kirsten Garrett, Peter Manning and Jeune Pritchard of Radio National, both for encouraging me to write this book and for making it possible for me to take leave in order to work on it.

A number of people gave generously of their time and advice during the early stages of my research; among them were Michael Bittman, Bill Crews, Kate Funder, Helen Glezer, Bruce Hawthorn, Eric Hudson, Peter Jordan, Graeme Russell, Steve Sutton, Bill Wheeler and Ilene Wolcott.

I am particularly grateful to Grant Dempsey of Lifecare Counselling and Family Services and the members of the Campbelltown Men's Domestic Violence Group for permission to attend and observe the group on a number of occasions and to conduct interviews, and to Nick Bliss and the residents of Phoenix House for allowing me to visit and interview them. I also wish to thank Rod Greenaway and the members of the Doveton Men's Violence Support Group for allowing me to attend and record a session in January 1994 for the Radio National documentary *Disarming Daddy.* Some material from *Disarming Daddy* is quoted in this book.

The 'Circle of Men' welcomed me as an observer and participant at the 'Standing Up Alive' gathering near Lismore in November 1995. To Rein van de Ruit and Rob Fleetwood, to all the men who attended the gathering and especially to Martin, Bill, Peter, Alan and Bart, who agreed to be interviewed, I extend my warm thanks.

I also wish to thank Paul Matters, of the South Coast Labor Council, in Wollongong; Phil Cleary, formerly Independent Member of federal parliament in the seat of Wills; Erika Haubold of the University of Wollongong, for permission to quote from unpublished papers and research material from her PhD thesis; and Dr Anthony McMahon of Monash University for permission to quote from his PhD thesis.

I am grateful to Con Anemogiannis, Adrienne Burgess, Joanne Finlay, Carol Grbich, Elaine Stratford and Robyn Williams for enabling me to test my ideas, and providing me with many useful suggestions.

I owe a special debt of thanks to my publisher, Sophie Cunningham, who has consistently encouraged me to follow my instincts and convictions and given me valuable guidance where I was unsure. Rowena Lennox edited my manuscript with care and engagement, and Emma Cotter prepared it for publication while dealing patiently with an author as anxious as a first-time parent.

This book owes a great deal to the lively interest, support, and good humour of my friends, and to the many conversations I have had with them over the last two years. I especially wish to thank Rohan Bastin, Alison

Lewis, and Bill Loftus for their close and careful reading of a number of chapters and their many vigorous and productive criticisms; Marc Wohling and Roberta Perkins for their comments and responses to my drafts at various stages of writing; Kerrie Ross, Robert Dessaix and Glenda Sluga for illuminating discussions and useful advice; Tony Stephens, for his continuing intellectual encouragement over many years; and George Klein, who would have written a much better book about men than I have, but, nonetheless, was unstintingly generous with his ideas and insights.

Like me, my family—Bill, Zanna and Gordy—never imagined I would write a book about men, but they have followed its growth, listened, discussed, read my drafts and brought me back to earth. As with all my other projects and passions, their love and support has been a strength and an inspiration to me.

I—and this, my first book—owe most of all to Eurydice Aroney, my most exacting critic and my strongest supporter. Much of this book has grown out of our many conversations—and occasional disagreements—about men, while walking on the clifftops at Clovelly. Without her patience, care and confidence in me, *Altered Mates* could not have been written.

Preface

Why write a book about men? What is there to say about them? These two questions were waiting for me at the very beginning of the process which led to the writing of this book, and have accompanied me all the way through, like a pair of silent guides on a journey.

This book grew out of a series of programs broadcast on ABC Radio National in January 1995, under the title *Male Matters*. *Male Matters* was an experiment, put together and produced by a very enthusiastic team working above and beyond the call of duty. In the weeks before the series went to air, the word spread around Radio National that we were doing a whole two weeks of programs on men (for an hour a day in the *Life Matters* timeslot). 'What on earth would you want to do that for?' was a common response, or 'Isn't that what's on the radio all the time anyway?'

Despite our own doubts and the dire predictions of our colleagues, the series was very successful. The talkback lines buzzed and we were showered with phone calls, letters and faxes. Interestingly, some of the most positive responses came from women; many of them said they were glad and relieved that men were finally starting to talk about themselves and their problems openly and in the public arena.

Responses from men were more varied and more extreme. Some accused the series of being 'anti-male' and dominated by a feminist agenda. Others wanted it to continue every week. One thing was clear, however, from the range and intensity of the feedback: *Male Matters* had touched a nerve. People wanted to talk about men.

In the course of writing this book, that impression has been reinforced again and again. In the early months of my research, I felt a little embarrassed when people asked me what I was working on. 'Oh, I'm writing a book about men', I would say, and try to change the subject. To my surprise, more often than not my interlocutors, both male and female, would actually want to talk about men—sometimes for hours and hours. I am grateful to those many men and women who gave me their views and ideas and enabled me to test mine in conversation. They also encouraged me to believe that there really is something to say about men, and that the time is ripe to say it.

Another of my initial reservations about this enterprise has also vanished over the last two years. I was sceptical about the 'men's movement' and the public discussion of 'men's issues' (what little of it there was), before I worked on *Male Matters* or this book, being under the impression that both were dominated by middle-class men from comfortable inner-suburban backgrounds feeling sorry for themselves. Whatever it was that these men felt they needed to discuss, I thought, it could not be of much relevance or concern to the majority of Australian men.

I soon realised how wrong I'd been. The men I've met and talked to over the last two years in the course of my research—some two hundred in all—come from a very broad range of ages, backgrounds, income groups and educational levels. If anything, men from working-class and lower-income groups occupy more of the spotlight in *Altered Mates*, because it seemed to me that these men experience particularly acutely the problems and dilemmas faced more broadly by men in Australia now. Many of these men told me their stories, often difficult and painful ones to tell, and their own words from some of those stories have found their way into the text you are about to read.

Out of those words, and my own reflections on them,

grows a portrait and an analysis. The principal theme of this book is that men are facing a number of important challenges to their sense of themselves and their place in the world, challenges posed primarily by the changing nature of their relations with women. These challenges have arisen in part from the impact of feminism on our intellectual and moral life as a society, and the choices and possibilities which feminism has opened up for women. Yet, as I try to show, the changes men are facing grow also out of what we might call a 'paradigm shift' in the nature and structure of our economy, a shift which is producing its own far-reaching effects on men's everyday relations with women, both in the 'public' world of work and the 'private' world of the family and intimate relationships. Indeed, I argue, if we want to understand what is happening to men, we need to see these worlds as linked very closely to one another.

In one sense, *Altered Mates* does chart the experience of a particular group of men: typically, heterosexual men somewhere between the ages of 30 and 50 who have encountered a crisis in their relationships with wives or partners, or in their sense of identity as men, and who have tried to come to terms with or make sense of that crisis. Often, their experiences represent an extreme or heightened form of problems and conflicts which many men confront on a regular basis in their interactions with women, even when their marriages or relationships are not in crisis. These men belong to the first generation that has had to grapple with the practical impact of feminism on their everyday lives.

Though the principal focus of the book is on men's relations with women, the later chapters explore men's attempts to create new forms of solidarity with other men in the 'men's movement' and new patterns and possibilities in their relationships with children. In this sense, I argue, men's attempts to re-invent themselves arise not only out of a reaction to feminism, or because their female partners are telling them that they need to do so, but out of a deeply-felt need to do so on their own account; a conviction that the 'script' of conventional masculinity is something that they no longer wish to go on acting out.

As a journalist, I've tried to write a book accessible to a general audience, one which I hope the men and women I've talked to, argued with and listened to over the last two years might want to read. At the same time, I've tried to put our present dilemmas as a society about gender relations into a broader historical context and to provide a critical and analytical framework within which we might get a clearer appreciation of what is at stake in those dilemmas. Much of what I say is, of necessity, speculative and exploratory, and I make no apologies for this. As I've hinted, it is only very recently that we have begun, as a society, to talk about men, to analyse and theorize about them—though it's been encouraging and illuminating for me to observe how quickly men and 'men's issues' have moved into the media mainstream in the two years since we broadcast *Male Matters*. People caught up in the currents of profound historical change—as I believe we are in the relations between the sexes—are often not best-equipped to see and understand what is happening around them. My account of that change is partial, speculative and polemical. I expect, and hope, that it will provoke comment and correction from both men and women.

A century ago, intellectuals in Europe and North America were much-occupied with what they called 'the woman question', a vigorous and often acrimonious debate about the rights and status of women, and the obstacles to their social and sexual autonomy. Over the last 30 years, feminism has put the 'woman question' in such a way that it is no longer simply a matter of intellectual debate, but a powerful force for change and greater equality between the sexes in their everyday lives. At the end of our century, the time has come to ask the 'man question'; and that is what this book is about.

1

The men's revolution

> I think women had their revolution in the sixties—and their revolution was from being submissive. Men have been having their revolution from the mid-eighties, and theirs is from being aggressive and oppressive. We're having ours now and early in the next century we'll all be equal. Sometime in the next five or ten years the revolution will be over and we'll all be the same.
>
> Ron, Doveton Men's Violence Support Group

Ron is not everyone's picture of a revolutionary. He's a big, powerfully built bloke pushing 40, neatly dressed in slacks and an open-neck shirt, and he's worked a lot of his adult life in the meat-packing industry. He's got a friendly smile and a sense of humour as dry as the Nullarbor. Ron is not a big talker, until you get him started on the men's revolution. But if you told him he was part of a 'men's movement', he'd probably say you'd got the wrong bloke, or something less polite.

Every Monday night for about 18 months, Ron has been coming along to a men's group at the Doveton Community Centre. Doveton is an outer eastern suburb of Melbourne. It's a good 30 kilometres from the inner city. Middle Australia doesn't get much more middle than this.

Ron's here because he has a problem. He used to beat up his wife. When she finally left him, he thought his world had fallen apart. He pleaded with her to come back, promised he'd never hit her again. She told him no chance.

Ron became depressed and teetered on the brink of a breakdown. One of his relatives had heard a segment on talkback radio about community groups that helped men who were violent and wanted to stop. Ron found out about the Doveton group and joined.

Doveton seems a strange place to stumble across the stirrings of a revolution. Yet that's what Ron believes is being born in groups like this one. He and the eight other men present—all 'regulars'—make up the usual suburban Australian mosaic of occupations, class and ethnic backgrounds. They'd never met before they joined the group. The only common ground they share is a history of domestic violence. Yet tonight, in the course of a two-hour meeting, they've said things they'd never dream of saying to other men at the pub or club, things they often wouldn't tell their partners, either.

Groups similar to the Doveton group have sprung up in the suburbs of most Australian cities in the past decade. There are around 30 in Melbourne alone. They've received little coverage in the mainstream media, and for some years their very existence was the subject of bitter controversy. Women—and men—who'd spent years working with the victims of domestic violence in the courts and the women's shelters dismissed the groups as a cop-out, a soft option for violent men who ought to be in prison. But some of the wives of men in the groups reported that something was happening: their husbands were changing. Arguments no longer inevitably ended in blows. They no longer had to live in constant fear.

Today, the groups are well established in three states—Victoria, South Australia and Western Australia—and are growing in number in most others. Hundreds of men join them every year. They are one small but important sign that something is happening to men in Australia, something that would have been unimaginable 30, perhaps even 20 years ago. Whether or not this something amounts to a revolution, as Ron believes, is one of the questions this book sets out to answer. What *is* certain is that men are living through the beginnings of a very fundamental transformation of their sense of themselves and their place in the world—a transformation that will affect every aspect of what it means to be a man in Australia in the twenty-first century.

My purpose in writing this book is to try to understand how and why that transformation is happening. Like all great changes in history, I believe, it revolves around power. The balance of power between men and women, which for much of Western history has been weighted firmly in men's favour, is starting to shift. In many different areas of their daily lives, both public and private, men are seeing their power or predominance challenged: in the workplace and the home, in the boardroom and the bedroom, on the sportsfield, the stock-exchange floor and the military parade-ground. Sometimes men meet these challenges with openness and co-operation; sometimes they resist them bitterly. As the foundations of men's power begin to quiver, a great and complex struggle is going on. Its consequences reach into the most intimate recesses of our emotional experience, and resound on the front pages of our national newspapers.

The furious public debates that surrounded Helen Garner's book *The First Stone* bear witness to the intensity of this struggle; yet it is a struggle that is being fought out not only in the world of ideas, but in the everyday lives of ordinary men and women, with painful and sometimes deadly results. Many men do not like the way the world is changing. They are angry about it and some, in stark contrast to the group at Doveton, will use threats, abuse, harassment, violence or murder to try to turn the wheel back the other way.

Just after nine in the morning on 21 March 1996, while I was writing this book, Hoss Majdalawi walked up to his estranged wife Jean outside the Family Court in the Sydney suburb of Parramatta and shot her five times with a pistol, killing her with a final shot to the head at point-blank range. Jean Majdalawi had taken out an apprehended violence order against him the previous year. She and her children had been living in women's shelters for two years.

In February 1996, her husband applied for custody of the children through the Family Court. On the morning he shot her, he and his wife were due to appear in court for his application to be heard. But the hearing never took place. Majdalawi is reported to have put the gun into his pocket, smiled, and given himself up to a security guard after killing his wife.

The case of Hoss Majdalawi is an extreme one. In 95 per cent of marriage break-ups, disputes between husbands and wives over who gets custody of their children are resolved without the matter ever going to a final judicial hearing. Only a very small proportion of men resort to violence in cases where custody is contested. Yet many men who've been involved in custody disputes express feelings of powerlessness and loss of control over their lives, and tend to see women and institutions such as the Family Court, which they believe are biased towards women, as the villains. There are now fathers' rights groups in every Australian state that lobby actively to broaden the legal rights of separated fathers. Often these groups argue strongly that men can 'parent' just as well as, if not better than, women.

However, it's not only angry fathers who have organized themselves into groups to fight for their rights. Men's rights groups devoted to everything—from ending male circumcision (and encouraging men to regrow their foreskins) to combating what they see as 'propaganda' from the Office of the Status of Women—have sprung up all over Australia in the last ten years. Often these groups speak the language of the victim, arguing that men are discriminated against or vilified in a 'pro-feminist' society. They have even coined a word for this: 'misandry', the equivalent of misogyny when applied to men.

It could not be said that groups such as these have

attracted a large following among the male population in Australia. However, many of the men I spoke to in the course of writing *Altered Mates* voiced a sense of disquiet and uncertainty about their relations with women, a feeling that they did not know how to respond to the desires and aspirations of the women in their lives and were on the back foot in their dealings with them. For many men, this amounts to a feeling of embattlement and powerlessness, often accompanied by extreme insecurity. As Tim, a 35-year-old plumber and veteran of one of the anti-violence groups, put it to me:

> Women have changed their expectations. They know what they want out of a relationship and they go and get it. Men I think are a little bit slow—more set in their ways. I haven't got a right role model to say that's right and that's wrong. That's the scary part. You've thrown it all up in the air, and you've got to pick up the right models, leave the ones on the floor that are wrong.

Tim's sentiments are very common, and are by no means restricted to men who, like him, have been violent to their wives. They point to a fundamental paradox in the state of power relations between men and women. On the one hand, men continue to control the levers of power in Australian society. They dominate most of the powerful institutions in our society: the political parties, the banks, the churches, the television stations, the sporting clubs, the bureaucracies and organized crime. Until the 1996 federal election, on a world ranking of percentages of women in parliament Australia came in at number 65—well behind all of the European countries (except Britain), most of the African nations and a number of Islamic countries. Since the Coalition landslide in the 1996 election, Australia has moved up a few notches—but one senior Coalition source has acknowledged that many of the women who were elected as Coalition members of parliament were put up as candidates in what were considered unwinnable seats. In 1996, only 23 per cent of managers in Australia were women (this figure has actually decreased in recent years), and in senior management the number was a paltry 3 per cent. At current rates of change, it will take 170 years before women occupy half of the management jobs in Australian companies and institutions.[1]

There are plenty of other similar examples in Australian public life. Women have made very few inroads into the upper echelons of power and, if they have, they tend to be isolated and exposed. Why is it that men feel so insecure about their loss of power to women, when the concrete evidence of entrenched and intransigent male power is all around them? Getting to the roots of this paradox is the key to understanding what is happening to men in Australia in the late 1990s, and to evaluating their responses to the changing roles and aspirations of women. However perplexing their sense of insecurity may seem, as a part of the lived experience of many men in Australia today, it can't be made to vanish by waving the wand of reason.

On the surface, it would seem that we are talking about a simple split between the public and private lives of men—between a public world in which they still maintain a sense of purpose, control and confidence, and a private world of relationships and feelings in which they have lost their bearings, and are no longer certain of what it is their female partners want from them, or what it is they want themselves. Yet one of the key themes of this book is that these private and public worlds are—if the reader will forgive me an unfortunate but necessary pun—intimately intertwined. In the chapters that follow, I try to draw connections between large and far-reaching changes taking place in the economy and the structures of our society, and a gradual but fundamental shift in what we might call the dynamics of power in men's relationships with women.

Over the last two decades, Australian society has undergone a rapid and far-reaching process of economic and social change. We have relentlessly modernized, globalized and rationalized. The result of this process has been to shift our economy decisively from an industrial to a post-industrial mode of production. We are familiar with some of the social consequences of this shift: increased inequality, decreased job security and intractable structural unemployment. On the whole, however, we have tended to miss the fact that these changes are having a powerful impact on the family and the relations between men and women within families.

However much our socially conservative leaders of the 1990s—from John Howard to Tony Blair—might like to pretend otherwise, the family is not an immutable constant. Families take many different forms across human societies, and the shape and function of the family changes over time. The family model that we take for granted—Mum, Dad and the 2.2 kids—is largely a product of the Industrial Revolution. As we pass out of the industrial age, the family, too, is changing. Perhaps the most striking aspect of this change is the extent to which women are no longer economically dependent on men, and are able to make choices in their lives that would have been extremely difficult even 30 years ago. Over the 'life cycle', as statisticians like to call it, the patterns of Australian men's and women's working lives are becoming more and more similar.

The consequence of these changes is that women have less and less of an investment in conventional forms of marriage and family life, in which Dad is the breadwinner and Mum is the homemaker. This model of the family simply does not conform to the actual experience of the majority of women. Moreover, women freed of the shackles of economic dependence have fewer reasons to stay in marriages or relationships which do not satisfy them emotionally. Even though women are often worse off financially after divorce, they initiate nearly two-thirds of all divorces in Australia.

Men, however, have failed to grasp the implications of what is happening. Many men are still locked into attitudes and patterns of behaviour that were appropriate in the 1950s, but are out of step with women's needs and aspirations in the 1990s. They continue to have a powerful emotional investment in a form of the family which is fast becoming obsolete—and, as we'll see in Chapter 3, men tend to cope worse with divorce or separation and have fewer emotional resources for dealing with them than do women. In this respect, at least, men appear to need women now more than women need men.

This is one manifestation of a shift in the balance of power which is occurring in men's and women's intimate relationships with one another—a shift which I attempt to chart in more detail in the course of this book and which, I argue, is making itself felt not only in our private lives, but also in the public world of workplaces, businesses and institutions.

However, many men in Australia are beginning to grapple with the consequences of this shift. For some, this means a day-to-day process of negotiation with the woman in their lives about sharing work, housework and the care of children. Others join men's groups of varying descriptions and engage in organized action on 'men's issues'. As a result of violence in their relationships, others are forced to confront their attitudes and behaviour towards women and participate in anti-violence groups. Often, however, there is very little connection between men involved in these diverse forms of activity. One of the questions I attempt to answer in this book is whether or not there is such a thing as a 'men's movement' in Australia, and if so, what its goals are, what kind of men are involved in it, and whether it is likely to become a broadly based movement for social change, which can benefit both men and women.

This is a time of conflicts between men and women in which individuals often become the focus for much larger resentments. Julieanne Ashton, an assistant futures trader with Bankers Trust, was victimised and abused for daring to venture onto the trading floor at the Sydney Futures Exchange. She was one of the few women to enter this almost exclusively male territory. Ashton was called a 'slut' and asked for a 'head job' by her male colleagues, who also suggested 'bending her over' in her presence. Ashton subsequently took her employer to court for failing to act on her complaints of sexual harassment and received an out-of-court settlement. Clearly, it was not Ashton herself, but what she represented, that caused the men on the trading floor to react in the way they did. She represented a threat to their dominance, an intruder. However, their hostile reactions and attempts to humiliate her betray the true extent of these men's insecurity. How tenuous must their sense of themselves and their masculinity be, we must ask, if a single woman in her early twenties was such a threat?

Throughout this book, I try to stress that conflict of this kind arises out of a contest for power, which is often bitter and vituperative, and which is not likely to be resolved in the near future—especially if men and women begin to regard themselves as having fundamentally different concerns and interests. As individuals, we are both caught up in this contest, and contribute to it as we act it out in our own lives—with the added complication that we often find ourselves at odds with those for whom we care most deeply. For the majority of people we will meet in the course of this book, this is not an abstract ideological battle about women's or men's rights. It is a concrete, everyday struggle, and it is going on in the suburban living-rooms, kitchens and bedrooms of what John Howard likes to call 'mainstream Australia'.

For men like Ron, whom we met at the beginning of this chapter, and the other members of the Doveton men's group, the process of giving up violence in their relationships also means giving up power—or a certain way of exercising power. This is a terrifying prospect for many of the men, since their use of physical violence or psychological manipulation often conceals a deep and compulsive dependence on the woman they both love and abuse. Ron puts his finger on a problematic aspect of the 'men's revolution' when he describes it as a 'revolution from being aggressive and oppressive'. Not many revolutions have been made by those who hold power willingly surrendering it. Ron's case is an extreme one, but even for the vast majority of men who are not violent, responding to the changing desires, demands and aspirations of women and entering into more equal and democratic relationships with women will still mean surrendering certain kinds of power. Men are unlikely to do this unless they can see that there is something in it for them, that their lives will be made richer and more rewarding. They will almost certainly not be persuaded to make these changes by being shamed or admonished. Nevertheless, I think there is good evidence that men in Australia are beginning to move in a more progressive direction.

The next chapter looks more closely at the range of men's responses to the 'women's revolution', and at the questions of power which underlie those responses.

2

The power paradox

SONS OF EGALIA

> 'At the end of the day it's still men who have the children,' observed Director Bram, looking sternly over the top of her newspaper at her son. One could see that she was about to lose her self-possession.
>
> 'But I want to be a sailor! I'll take the children with me to sea!' replied Petronius with a flash of inspiration.
>
> 'And just what do you think the mother of the children will say to that? No, my dear boy, I'm afraid there are some things in life you'll just have to accept. Even in an egalitarian society like ours not everyone can do everything . . . It's time you stopped reading all of those girls' adventure stories about women who go away to sea, and read some boys' novels instead . . . And remember: a mother, Petronius, can never take the place of a father with his child!'
>
> Gerd Brantenberg, *The Daughters of Egalia*, p. 7

Picture a prosperous, well-ordered city of tree-lined streets and graceful buildings, a city without poverty, homelessness or street crime—a Stockholm or Copenhagen of the imagination, or the city Canberra was meant to be. As evening falls, men in all parts of this city wait for the sound of their wives' keys turning in the front-door lock, signalling the women's return from a stressful and demanding day in the office, boardroom or caucus room. He will have a drink waiting for her, and dinner on the stove, and perhaps he'll have changed into something special just to let her know how much he cares. Later, perhaps, if he's particularly lucky and she's not too tired from a long day's work, she may feel like making love to him.

This is the world that Gerd Brantenburg, a Swedish writer, describes in her novel *The Daughters of Egalia*, published in 1977.[1] In the imaginary country of Egalia, women run the parliament, the economy, the schools, the churches and the police force, and men are chiefly homemakers. Once boys attain puberty, they must begin wearing a PH or penis holder, an assemblage of straps and flaps that moors the male organ firmly in place and discourages it from developing a mind of its own. The novel tells the story of a group of men who begin to resent their lives of domestic drudgery and the limits imposed on them by Egalian society. They form a group to discuss their feelings and ideas. As the story progresses, they begin to ask more and more questions about their place in the world, and the power that women exercise over their lives. At the close of the novel, some of the men have decided to form a breakaway community consisting only of men, a community in which they will have the freedom to grow and change in the company and comfort of their own kind.

The Daughters of Egalia is a journey through the looking-glass, a satire in the best tradition of Utopian literature. It creates a topsy-turvy world, in which the roles and status of men and women in our own society are turned upside down. The more we read, the more the order of things in Egalia seems to us absurd, its arbitrary distinctions between the sexes a grotesque travesty. At the same time, we're confronted more and more forcefully with the absurdity of the way things are in our own world. It's the 'unthinkable' configuration of Egalian society—its total domination by women—that makes us realize just how pervasive the power and privilege of men in our own society really is.

Brandenburg's novel is a classic feminist satire, yet there's a certain irony in reading it today, nearly 20 years after it was written. Many of the speeches the male characters make about the injustices and oppression they experience at the hands of women sound not dissimilar to the views men are expressing today on talkback radio, and in books and newspaper articles. They feel embattled, beleaguered, borne down upon by what they see as the power and new-found confidence of women. In the more extreme versions of this sentiment, there's a strong element of male separatism, a feeling that men would be better off and happier without women. All of these men are caught up in a version of the power paradox: believing that somehow they have lost control over their lives and are on the losing end of a tug-of-war with women in both their working and their personal lives.

'Men's rights' groups seek to transform this perception into a platform for political action. The Men's Rights Agency in Queensland, for example, seeks, among other things, to 'correct the gender bias which is now occurring in government, the judiciary, police forces and the general public'.[2] Like many of the men's rights groups, the Men's Rights Agency focuses particularly on issues related to access to and custody of children after divorce. This is certainly the most controversial and emotionally charged issue for men's rights activists, as many of them believe there is now a systemic bias against men in the Family Court and in welfare agencies that deal with separated couples and their children. Interestingly, many of these groups include women among their members—usually women who are the partners of non-custodial fathers. However, the Men's Rights Agency also has broader aims, including lobbying government to fund men's organizations and to provide services for men in the same way and at the same level that it does for women.

Strangely enough, swimming pools seems to hold a particular fascination for the proponents of equal rights for men. In the northern Melbourne suburb of Brunswick in 1992, Brunswick baths decided to offer two women-only swimming sessions a week. Brunswick has a large number of Muslim residents and Brunswick City Council, which operated the baths, believed that women-only sessions would cater for the special needs of women of Islamic background, who could not use the pool if men were present. However, a male councillor opposed the sessions on the grounds that they were discriminatory and received support from a number of male Brunswick residents. Brunswick Council took the matter to the Equal Opportunity Board, seeking an exemption from the *Equal Opportunity Act* which would allow it to run the women-only sessions. The case was hotly contested: one resident who appeared before the Board argued that the sessions 'discriminated against men and were a return to the days of segregation'.[3] In March 1992, the Board refused to grant Brunswick Council the exemption and the sessions were discontinued.

Men's rights, however, have not always been upheld in matters aquatic. In another case in New South Wales in 1992, a man attempted to gain access to the McIvers baths at Coogee, which have been run on a women-only basis for around 50 years by the Randwick and Coogee Ladies Swimming Club. After the president of the club refused to allow the man to enter, he took the matter to the NSW Equal Opportunity Tribunal. The Tribunal referred his complaint to the Anti-Discrimination Board, which eventually granted the McIvers baths a special dispensation to continue as a women-only facility—in perpetuity.[4]

What's interesting about these cases is the way men have appropriated the language of the women's movement in arguing against 'discrimination' on the basis of their sex. Twenty years ago, women used many of the same arguments to gain access to public spaces that were off-limits to them—from the front bars of pubs to the lounges of exclusive gentlemen's clubs. Yet it's precisely this rhetoric of equal access and equal opportunity that is now being employed by men, who believe that the mere existence of separate services or facilities for women in some way deprives men of their rights or entitlements.

The 'men's rights' movement is still in its infancy, but already it is entering the mainstream political arena. Activists are calling for men's health centres, men's officers in student unions and the establishment of a Men's Electoral Lobby. It's difficult to resist the impression that there is a strong 'copycat' element to these calls. This part of the nascent men's movement appears to be emulating the tactics of the women's movement 30 years on. What's notable, though, is that the advocates of men's rights see men as caught up in a race with women, without paying much attention to the relative starting points of the contestants. Theirs is a version of egalitarianism that has broken away from its social and historical moorings. In this version, anyone who has something that I don't have has automatically become more equal than me, regardless of the larger distribution of power and privilege in society and our relative places within this bigger picture.

There is one simple but striking feature of this view of gender relations that is so obvious it's easy to miss. Until now, men have never thought of themselves as an 'interest group' defined by their gender, with a set of aims and interests particular to that group. They may have seen themselves as belonging to a particular class, or geographical region, or religious denomination, or subculture of some kind; but it's only in the late twentieth century that the possession of a Y chromosome has come to be a source of group indentity. The early Christian ascetics who foreswore the company of women and all other temptations of the flesh, and went into the desert to fast and sit on pillars in the blazing sun for 20 years did not see themselves as belonging to a men's movement. Nor did the ragtag armies of the Crusades, the agents of European colonialism, the Freemasons, the Mafia, the moving spirits behind early trade unionism, or any other male-dominated social or political movement. In this sense, Dr Paul van Buynder, one of the pioneers in promoting men's health in Australia, is not being facetious when he argues that if the men's movement exists at all, it does so in the RSL and Rotary Clubs and other existing all-male institutions in our society.

In fact, there would seem to be few compelling arguments against men having men's health centres or social services devoted to their special needs. It has now become almost a commonplace in the Australian media to depict men as congenitally unhealthy, dying earlier than women and saddled with a range of male-specific maladies from heart disease to prostate cancer. In late 1994, the *Bulletin* ran a cover story on men entitled 'The Weaker Sex', whose basic tenor was that having testosterone in one's body was a sure ticket to an early grave. There is a good deal of hyperbole in these depictions of men's health, but it remains true that men are prone to particular health problems, often connected with lifestyle and, in a broader sense, with the nature of Australian masculinity itself. It is also true that our health system has not dealt particularly well with preventing or treating these problems, despite the fact that it has been, and continues to be largely dominated by men.

Men's health is now a mainstream political issue. As health minister in the Keating government, Dr Carmen Lawrence was responsible for instituting the first federal men's health policy, an initiative that has been retained by the Coalition. Inevitably, there will be competition for money between men's and women's health services, though not necessarily any more than between other sectors of the health system, where aged care competes with paediatrics and high-tech cancer treatments vie with community health for resources. Funding a men's health centre does not automatically mean that resources will be taken away from a women's centre. Moreover, seeing this particular question purely in terms of competition between men and women ignores the fact that many of the men who might benefit from such services have wives, partners, mothers and daughters who want them to remain healthy.

The case is not so clear in the other area which has

become a major focus for the proponents of 'affirmative action for men', namely the education of boys in schools. This issue is now something of a cause célèbre in New South Wales, where the figures for students completing their Higher School Certificate (the school leaving-certificate in that state) show girls consistently out-performing boys in key subjects, but not mathematics. In response to this trend, a number of academics, journalists, and parents began lobbying for a 'Boys' Education Strategy', to match the Girls' Education Strategy introduced by the NSW Department of Education in 1989. After some pressure from the NSW Parents and Citizens Federation, the then state government set up an inquiry into boys' education, under Liberal MP Stephen O'Doherty.[5]

One of the contributors to the inquiry was Richard Fletcher, a lecturer in health sciences at the University of Newcastle. Along with some other Newcastle men, Fletcher was responsible for setting up a group called Fathers Against Rape, formed after the rape and murder of a young woman by a number of boys outside a Newcastle surf club. Fletcher's submission to the inquiry argued that a boys' education strategy would need to look at a whole range of questions, from why boys don't tend to choose subjects such as English, biology, history and languages, to why they tend to leave school earlier and in larger numbers than girls. The problems boys experience in schools, says Fletcher, are a consequence of the broader ways in which they are socialized, and the ways in which they come to understand what it is to be masculine.

There are many good arguments for looking closely at the way boys are socialized both in schools and outside them. There's no doubt that schooling tends to close off whole areas of emotional experience to boys. As a small boy attending a boys' school in Adelaide, I and my fellow pupils spent our first years of schooling, from age five onwards, being encouraged by the teachers—all women—to read, write stories, act out plays and make up games—as well as racing around the oval pretending to be jet fighters. On the first day of our arrival in the middle school, aged eight, we were informed by our male teacher that there would be no more of that woman's nonsense, which would be knocked out of us if necessary. Not all boys want to read novels or write plays, but not acquiring a facility with language, which often goes with reading, imposes a disability on boys. It's one of the truisms of research in child psychology and learning that girls tend to have better verbal skills and are better at telling stories about themselves than boys. Boys pay a price for this as men, when they are called on to articulate feelings and negotiate conflicts in their relationships with adult women, and often find it extremely difficult to do so. Both men and women have a stake in giving boys the opportunity to learn to communicate.

Unfortunately, not all of the advocates for boys' education are as sensible or sophisticated in their approach as Richard Fletcher. Too often, boys are depicted as having been neglected by an education system dominated by feminists. The success of girls is seen as somehow threatening to boys, and the schools and examination system are characterized as a battleground for gender warfare. This seems all the more curious in light of the fact that many parents have both sons and daughters, and are unlikely to begrudge the success of one if the other is not doing so well. Moreover, those who argue that boys are in some way disadvantaged tend to ignore a crucial factor: the collapse of the youth job market in the 1980s. Until the 1980s, young men who had no inclination to stay at school or go on to tertiary education could be reasonably certain of getting a job or apprenticeship at the age of 15 or 16. That certainty has now disappeared, probably forever. What work there is available for under-18s tends to be short-term and casual, with no prospect that it will lead to secure employment in the future. One of the mainstays of young male identity, and one of the principal ways in which young men could demonstrate that they were entering the adult world, has vanished in the space of a generation. It is hardly surprising that many boys aged 15 and above who are now required to remain at school for longer without any real motivation to do so, do not do well academically, and become bored and troublesome.

This ought to lead us to think more carefully about our notions of disadvantage. Not everyone in our society can be disadvantaged; the very meaning of the word rests on the idea that some of us have more advantages than others. 'Boys' and 'girls' cannot, by definition, both be disadvantaged groups, since then all children would be so. It makes more sense to talk about the ways in which particular groups of boys and girls or men and women may have more or less advantages than others—and this inevitably involves us in talking about class, a very unpopular notion in the 1990s, but one to which I shall be returning throughout this book, as it is absolutely crucial to understanding what's happening to men in Australia today.

The examples of men's health and boys' education show us clearly how men have begun to use the rhetoric of equality in much the same way as the women's movement did 20 years ago to argue that they are disadvantaged, and have special and distinct needs. In its more strident forms, this rhetoric tends to carry with it the implicit belief that men have somehow slipped backwards as women have advanced, that women's gain has been men's loss. 'Victim Masculinism' is the best way I can think of to characterize this position: an assertion of men's rights based on the belief that men have somehow become the victims of a feminist conspiracy, a clandestine seizure of power by women in our major institutions, our legislatures, and the domestic battleground of the family home. 'Victim Masculinism' can be seen as part of a broader trend in our society, which Eva Cox characterises as 'competing victims syndrome'; a desire to claim the position of victim for oneself so as to be able to compete for a share of the increasingly meagre resources of the public purse.[6]

Probably the best-known proponent of this view outside Australia is Warren Farrell, an American who was active in support of the women's movement in the 1970s, before he rebelled against what he calls the 'political cowardice of PC' and wrote a series of books arguing against the view that women are oppressed by men. *The Myth of Male Power*, published in 1993, propounds the view that men have let themselves be conned by feminism into believing that they hold all the power in modern industrial societies. In fact, says Farrell, men have been slaves to women in the home, condemned to spending a lifetime providing for a woman and her offspring and then dying before her. Moreover, women have actually held more power historically than men: 'almost every woman had a primary role in the female-dominated family structure; only a small percentage of men had a primary role in the male-dominated governmental and religious structures'.[7]

Farrell is never one to let historical fact get in the way of a good piece of polemic. Much of his book is downright inaccurate or just plain silly, but his portrait of 'male powerlessness' has plenty in common with views popular in certain sections of the men's movement in Australia. The men's movement, however, is by no means homogenous, and other groups active on 'men's issues' are diametrically opposed to the position of Victim Masculinists such as Farrell. Before we return to the question of men and power, it will be useful to get an idea of the diversity of men's activism in Australia, and what the different groups involved in it believe and strive for.

MEN IN MOTION

In Chapter 1, I raised the question of whether or not there really is a men's movement in Australia. One simple answer is that there is certainly a loose network of groups of men around the country who see themselves as part of a men's movement and who are active on 'men's issues'. With the desire to be playful rather than pejorative, I shall call these men the Born-Again Blokes, since they are united in the desire to create a strong, positive masculine identity, and because there is a certain, almost religious element of personal renewal and regeneration in their rhetoric.

The Born-Again Blokes believe that there is indeed something that men have lost, but they are less likely to blame women for the loss than the Victim Masculinists. What men have lost, say the Born-Agains, is a connection with some essential elements of our masculinity, powerful male archetypes, which are celebrated in traditional societies but are redundant or reviled in ours: the Wild Man, the Warrior, the King. The Born-Agains are deeply influenced by Robert Bly—author of *Iron John*—and often by Jung, New Age psychology and a form of romantic eco-primitivism. They see the loss of a strong, positive masculinity more as a product of industrialization, modern technology and global mass culture than as a result of the depredations of feminism (though feminism does not escape criticism). Masculinity, as they see it, is undergoing a deep crisis. It has become oppressive both to women and to men, who are profoundly alienated, cut off from any positive sources of identity in themselves. But these men also tend to see the roots of alienation in the nature of the modern world itself. The crisis of masculinity, for them, is a crisis of modernity.

Iron John has been enormously influential in the men's movement in both North America and Australia. It is the key text of what is referred to in the United States as the 'mythopoetic' men's movement—so-called because it draws heavily on the mythology of a large range of cultures, Western, non-Western and indigenous. Bly offers us—in the form of a series of fireside chats—a poetics of masculinity, a composite map of the mythical journeys of male heroes drawn from a range of cultures and literatures. His premise is a very simple one: in contemporary Western societies, dominated by industrial and post-industrial capitalism, consumerism and the mass media, we have lost touch with the myths and rituals that guided males from boyhood into manhood. He insists that there are important differences between men and women, and that the answer to the crisis of masculinity does not lie in making men more like women:

> It's important to be able to say the word masculine without imagining that we are saying a sexist word . . . Some say, 'Well, let's just be human, and not talk about masculine or feminine at all'. People who say that imagine they are occupying the moral high ground. I say that we have to be a little gentle here, and allow the word masculine and the word feminine to be spoken, and not be afraid that some moral carpenter will make boxes of those words and imprison us in them. We are all afraid of boxes, and rightly so.[8]

Throughout *Iron John*, Bly oscillates between the folksy tone of the paragraph just quoted, and a much more allusive, metaphorical style, replete with references to history, mythology, the Bible and the poetry of Rilke, D.H. Lawrence, Lorca and any number of others. This sometimes makes Bly's own position hard to get a fix on—something that he doubtless intended. There are some bizarre and puzzling moments in *Iron John*, such as the passage in which Bly suggests that therapists should do their work with a cow in the room. But what is lacking from the book is the kind of vindictive misogyny that runs through the tracts of the Victim Masculinists. On the face of it, it is hard to support the view that Bly is anti-feminist, if we accept that there is nothing antifeminist in arguing that the work of changing men is a task for men, and not the responsibility of women. But, as we will see in Chapters 8 and 9, there is a strongly conservative sub-text to *Iron John*, which seeks to reassert male authority over children (and by implication, women too).

In Australia, the most popular and articulate representative of the Born-Again Blokes is Steve Biddulph, author of *Manhood*. Biddulph himself has been strongly influenced by Bly. *Manhood* is full of quotes from *Iron John*, and echoes of Bly's voice can be heard throughout the book. Biddulph and his book have proved extremely popular in Australia. Interestingly, Biddulph's publisher, Rex Finch, believes that the greater part of the first edition of *Manhood* was bought by women, though he says the second edition is selling much more to men. Whatever the case, Biddulph is now much in demand as a public speaker and newspaper columnist, and his book is used widely in men's groups and schools. *Manhood* has plainly touched a nerve with the Australian public, both male and female, though, as I'll be arguing later, as a manual for bringing about real and effective social change it leaves a lot to be desired.

Later in this book we will meet some Born-Again Blokes who are actively involved in the men's movement. They come from all around Australia, and every year they converge on a site in the rainforest near Lismore in northern New South Wales for a meeting of the Circle of Men. These men bring a uniquely Australian perspective to the mythopoetic men's movement, and they have a strong interest in bringing elements of traditional Aboriginal culture into play in re-invigorating Australian masculinity.

What the Born-Again Blokes very definitely do not give us, and what neither Bly nor Biddulph supply, is any kind of analysis of the power relations between men and women in the broader society. It is here that the two major currents in the men's movement diverge most clearly. The first, which consists primarily of Born-Again Blokes, has what I'd call a 'redemptive' approach to the condition of men; it concentrates on men healing themselves through a process of personal tranformation.

The second has a broader agenda. For the men in this group, the principal goal is not personal redemption, but changing the power balance between men and women, challenging and dismantling a whole range of social structures and assumptions that allow men, as they see it, to take their power and privilege for granted.

Within this branch of the men's movement, there are a number of sub-branches. The most extreme consists of what I'd call the Sackcloth-and-Ashes Brigade. The men in this category more or less wholeheartedly embrace a feminist analysis of the power relations between men and women. They argue that men can only liberate themselves from the straightjacket of traditional masculinity if they are first prepared to dismantle patriarchy. For many of the early proponents of this view, such as the American Michael Kimmel (best known for his book *Refusing to Be a Man*), the only authentic way for men to fight against sexism and transform themselves was to support the struggles of women. It became fashionable for men to describe themselves as pro-feminist, a term adopted by many men's groups in Australia and the men's magazine *XY* (published in Canberra), which describes itself as 'pro-feminist, male-positive and gay-affirmative'. Men's pro-feminist protestations have not always been welcomed by feminists, who have sometimes wondered if they are not simply a sign that men can't bear to be left out of anything, even the women's movement.

There's often also a strong tendency in the public rhetoric of these groups to ask men to do penance for their masculinity, to wear sackcloth and ashes for the sins of men as a group. There's little reason to doubt that men who take this line are genuine in their desire to end the oppression of women and own up to men's part in that oppression. But whether their penitential approach to social change is likely to be effective in speaking to and convincing the broad mass of men in Australia is another matter.[9] While shame can be an important and socially productive emotion, it cannot be the primary source of an individual's or a group's identity. Nor will donning a sexual sackcloth and ashes be of much practical help and benefit to women. Too often the Sackcloth-and-Ashes Brigade is content to hand over the moral authority and the initiative in the struggle against sexism to women—a strategy that comes perilously close to handing over responsibility also.[10]

Having said this, pro-feminist men have made an extremely important and concrete contribution to the anti-domestic violence movement in Australia, and the setting up of anti-violence groups for men in the community. Though they are not usually characterized as a movement, these groups work in a very concrete and practical way with hundreds of men from a wide range of class and ethnic backgrounds. Many of the men who come to the groups to try to give up their own violent or abusive behaviour end up being trained to become group leaders themselves. Much of the initiative for setting up the groups has come from counsellors, social workers and other members of the 'caring professions', who often ran the groups unpaid in their own time. Pro-feminist men and men's groups such as MASA (Men Against Sexual Assault) have also played an important role in setting up and helping to support anti-violence programs for men. In New South Wales, MASA runs groups for men in prisons who have been convicted of violent crimes, and similar groups have been set up in South Australia and Victoria. I've chosen to refer to the men who work in these groups as 'Trailblazers'—a term borrowed from Alison Newton, a social worker in Adelaide who's worked with female victims of domestic violence for 15 years. She sees the men who join anti-violence groups as blazing a trail for other men to follow, showing by example how it's possible to renounce violence and learn new ways of relating to their female partners more equally.

However, the Trailblazers—whom we'll get to know in Chapter 4—have not been without their critics, from both within the men's movement and outside it. Some pro-feminist men believe the anti-violence groups are a cop-out. Domestic violence, they say, is a crime like any other violent assault, and should face the full force of the law. They say men who want to combat sexism should be supporting the victims of violence—that is, women—and not helping the perpetrators. However, many women whose husbands are violent don't want to leave them, and don't want them punished: they want them to stop hitting and abusing, and often take the initiative in finding help for the man by contacting one of the groups.

The Trailblazers, and in particular groups such as MASA, also tend to cop it from the other side of the trenches—from Born-Again Blokes who believe they give men a bad name by concentrating too much on the negative aspects of masculinity, such as violence and aggression, while not giving men enough positive reinforcement. Let's concentrate on re-building a healthy, strong and sensitive masculinity, they say, rather than shaming and punishing men. The Trailblazers reply that it's impossible to begin talking about healing or redeeming masculinity until these issues of power and violence have been addressed. They believe that the Born-Again Blokes have their heads in the sand, or more accurately in their own navels, and that deep down they're anti-women.

These conflicts are unlikely to go away. They're likely to intensify as men's activism expands and members of the different groups begin to jockey for territory. However, by far the largest group of men affected by the stirrings of the 'men's revolution' is one that hovers around the fringes of the men's movement and has no particular ideological affiliation. I call this group the 'Abashed Men'. The description comes from Michael Ondaatje's novel *In the Skin of a Lion*. Ondaatje's story begins with Patrick, the son of a timber-cutter and dynamiter growing up in the backwoods of Canada at the turn of the century 'in a region which did not even appear on a map until 1910'. Widowed early, Patrick's father leads a solitary life, speaking little to his fellow workers or neighbours, absorbed in his own world of work and struggle with the elements, and the upbringing of his small son. Ondaatje describes him as 'an abashed man, withdrawn from the world around him, uninterested in the habits of civilisation outside his own focus'.[11]

The *Macquarie Dictionary* defines abashment as 'a state of loss of self-possession'. Just as Patrick's father is abashed in his relations with other men, a large number of Australian men are, it seems to me, abashed in their relations with women—men like Gary, a member of a men's group in Shoalhaven, on the south coast of New South Wales:

> Some women . . . when I go out with them, I don't know how they want me to act . . . I don't know if they want me to kiss them or whatever . . . others will go as far as they want. The girls today don't like being paid for . . . especially the one I'm going with now, I've only been going out with her for a couple of weeks, but she really lays down the law. Women are getting a lot more independent.

If we turn from contemporary Canadian to Australian fiction, we come face to face with a whole tribe of abashed men—epitomized by Scully, the hero of Tim Winton's 1994 novel *The Riders*. Early in the book, Scully is abandoned by his wife, who's supposed to join him with their daughter in the house he's been renovating for the three of them in rural Ireland. When Scully goes to meet the plane, his daughter emerges from the arrivals gate minus her mother, who never reappears except in Scully's anguished imagination. Scully is a Decent Bloke: hardworking, kind, resourceful, absolutely devoted to his wife and daughter. He spends the rest of the novel trying to understand what he's done wrong, what he missed, how he failed. In a way, his perplexity is emblematic of that of a large group of Australian men who simply don't understand what is happening to them and how they're supposed to respond to the changes women are making in their lines and their range of new expectations and demands. The Abashed Men are not organized into groups, and they haven't yet become Victim Masculinists. They sense the stirrings of revolution, but still aren't sure where, if anywhere, they should line up.

It's worth mentioning one further group, who are not highly organized in Australia, but who certainly exist and have some representatives within our major and minor political parties. These are the men who believe that the moral fabric of our society has unravelled as a result of a decline in 'family values'. This is a kind of code: what they really mean is that as a result of women's greater participation in the workforce, more easily available divorce and greater sexual freedom for both women and men, the bonds of authority that held the nuclear family together have begun to loosen. A husband's authority over his wife, a father's authority over his children, society's control of the sexuality of children and adults: all these have weakened considerably over the last 30 years. Few men in Anglo-Australian families can expect to be regarded as 'head of the household' any longer, or if they do, to have their claim to authority go unchallenged. For a certain group of men, this is profoundly threatening. In the United States, these men have become politically active in an organization called the Promise Keepers, devoted to restoring strong families with strong men at the head of them. The Promise Keepers hold regular rallies and claim to have over 100 000 members. Like many groups outside the political mainstream in the United States, they are also active on the Internet.[12] A large part of their membership comes from traditional working-class and blue-collar backgrounds: men who have been disenfranchised by the erosion of America's traditional manufacturing base. As we'll see in Chapter 3, there is a large group of men from similar backgrounds in Australia, who have also been the losers in the restructuring of our economy during the 1980s. An Australian branch of the Promise Keepers has already been set up in Victoria.

ARE MEN OPPRESSED?

> I think that women are becoming the more dominant race, more so than men now, and I think that men subconsciously are letting them do it, letting them be the dominant person. Perhaps we don't want the responsibility. I think in a lot of households women are taking control.[13]
>
> Arthur, Shoalhaven Men's Group

In one way or another, all of the different groups of men we met in the previous section, from the Born-Again Blokes to the Abashed Men, are responding to a sense that power, both in the public and the private world, is somehow shifting away from men, that they have lost their place in the world and are struggling to find a new one. We're faced with two questions here: Is this simply a *perception* on the part of these men, since, on the face of it, it appears to have little foundation in the big picture of economic and political power, where men still hold most of the cards? Or are there good reasons for believing that in a number of important areas, men actually are losing power or being forced to give it up? The following chapters attempt to answer these questions from a number of different perspectives. It's important, though, to have a clear understanding of what we mean when we talk about power, and in the final part of this chapter, I'll try to clarify this somewhat.

One useful way of putting the 'power paradox' in perspective is to look at it in a historical context. Crises in masculinity are nothing new. When Lord Baden-Powell founded the Boy Scouts in 1907, it was his express aim to 'redeem boys from the rot of urban civilisation' and make them into manly men.[14] Beginning in the last decade of the nineteenth century—the *fin de siècle*—and gathering strength in the early years of our own, a strong current of cultural anxiety about the state of masculinity suffused both European and North American society. In the United States, this was attributed in part to the decline of the manly virtues of frontier life and what was seen as the creeping 'Europeanization' of American culture. A dramatic increase in the rate of divorce and a decline in the birthrate prompted Theodore Roosevelt to declare in 1903 that the American race was committing suicide. According to the French writer and philosopher Elisabeth Badinter, 'with his masculine role uncertain, with his fear of panicky fear of feminization, the average American man of the early 1900s no longer knew how to be a man worthy of the name'.[15] In Europe, the 'effete' aestheticism of the Decadent movement and its cult of the dandy—exemplified by Oscar Wilde—were blamed for fostering effeminacy in young men and encouraging homosexuality.

However, the real cause of men's anxiety on both continents was women. The growing confidence of the first wave of feminists, whom we know best as the suffragettes, with their demands for women's rights to vote, to work outside the home, and to be educated presented a powerful challenge to men. Male intellectuals in France gloomily prophesied the day when women would control the universities and academies and men would be reduced to making the jam and 'nursing the brats'.[16] In Britain, the Oxford Union voted overwhelmingly against admitting women to the Bachelor of Arts degree in 1896, and there were riots at Cambridge in opposition to allowing women to study at the university. Male scientists, doctors and writers were terrified of the educated, articulate 'New Woman', fearing that she would no longer be prepared to bear their childen or do their bidding. The president of the British Medical Association warned that educated women would become 'more or less sexless', while two of his scientific colleagues declared that such women might have highly developed brains, but most of them would die young.[17]

A satirical novel entitled *The Revolt of Man*, published anonymously in 1882, described a future England in which 'women have become the judges, doctors, lawyers and artists, while men are kept in complete subordination, taught to cultivate their beauty in order to be chosen in marriage by successful matrons'.[18] In the course of the novel—written by Walter Besant, founder of the Society of Authors and a staunch anti-feminist—men rebel against this unnatural state of affairs and bring down the matriarchy, much to the relief of women, who can give up the drudgery of work and study and devote themselves exclusively to haute couture and the 'sweet feminine gift of coquetry'.[19] Women's new assertiveness plainly had men badly rattled: 'to many late nineteenth and early twentieth century men . . . women seemed to be agents of an alien world that evoked anger and anguish, while to women in those years, men appeared as aggrieved defenders of an indefensible order'.[20]

In many ways, the crisis of masculinity in our own *fin de siècle* mirrors the crisis of a hundred years ago. Yet, as the feminist historian and literary critic Elaine Showalter points out, the anxious men of the late-nineteenth century were reacting to what were in fact extremely modest gains made by the opposite sex. In was only in 1882, for example, that English women gained the right to guardianship of their children after divorce or separation. Until then, custody of the children was automatically awarded to the husband. In France, women did not win the right to divorce until 1884. Women in the workforce earned 50 per cent of what men earned—and, most importantly to the suffragettes, women did not yet have the vote. Full female suffrage did not come in the United States until 1920, and in Britain until 1928—although one of the colonies, South Australia, had given women the vote as early as 1894. Plainly, the 'power paradox' was a feature of changing gender relations a century ago and this recognition could lead us to ask just what is different about our own time. If men at the end of the nineteenth century were over-reacting to women's very limited gains in independence and social freedom, could it be that men in our own time are over-reacting too?

The advances made by women over the last 30 years have been very striking, measured even by the standards of the 1950s, let alone the 1890s. Two out of three Australian women in the prime child-bearing years between 25 and 45 work either part-time or full-time. Women now make up roughly half of university students—and there is as yet no sign that their reproductive capacities have declined as a result, or that they are dying young in large numbers. Thanks to the post-war welfare state, and the existence of sole parents' benefits and other family allowances, it has become possible for women to bear and raise children on their own, or to support themselves and their children if a marriage breaks up. Moreover, the social and sexual stigma attached to falling pregnant out of wedlock has almost completely vanished, in Anglo-Australian culture at least. The shotgun wedding quietly disappeared long before we thought of banning shotguns. One in four children in Australia is now born out of wedlock.[21]

However fashionable it may be now to decry the excesses of the rock'n'rolling, acid-dropping, free-loving 1960s (especially among those who participated at the time but are now Older and Wiser), one thing remains absolutely true: the so-called sexual revolution, along with the advent of safe and reliable contraception and the freeing-up of abortion laws, has given women a degree of sexual freedom that they have probably never experienced before, in documented Western history at least. Perhaps most fundamentally of all, our ideas about women's rights and what they ought to be able to expect from their lives have been radically transformed. However much social realities may lag behind what is now written into our laws, few 'mainstream Australians' would argue with the view that women ought to be able to expect the same opportunities and entitlements as men, whether at work, in the education system, or in political life.

For all of these reasons, women's range of choices in life has expanded dramatically as their economic dependence on men has lessened. It's this perception of choice that gives women greater bargaining power in their relationships with men, power that some men find deeply threatening. Once a woman is no longer dependent on a man to bring home the bacon and pay for the roof over her and their children's heads, the man's role as breadwinner becomes redundant. But what will replace it? How will a man keep a mate if being a good provider is no longer enough? Will he have to become a raunchier, more skilful, sensitive lover? A better communicator? A sparkling conversationalist? Will he have to participate more in child-care and homemaking? All of these questions bubble away in the subconscious minds of many Australian men, and generate a good deal of anxiety.

It's this anxiety that is at the root of the power paradox. Of course, it would be nonsense to argue that all relationships between men and women in the past have been based primarily on economics. We know that there have been loving, companionable and sexually passionate marriages for hundreds of years, and there is a huge legacy of poetry, drama and novels, as well as the diaries and letters of married (and unmarried) couples to prove it. It remains true, though, that at least since the Industrial Revolution, a husband's authority as head of the household and his contribution to the family have been linked closely to his role as breadwinner. Even today, in Australia in the 1990s, when a marriage breaks up a man's first reaction may often be to revert to the breadwinner mentality and wonder with a mixture of anger and anguish, like Scully in *The Riders*, why his wife has left him after he has done everything right, paid all the bills, given her a nice home and looked after her and the kids.

However, men's feeling of powerlessness extends far beyond the demise of the breadwinner role and the vacuum it has left behind. It's fashionable now in certain sections of the men's movement to regard this feeling—sometimes referred to as 'men's pain'—as somehow existential, a product of the very nature of men's existence in modern, technological society. Coupled with this is the belief that men themselves are oppressed. In fact, so the argument goes, we are all oppressed, male and female, young and old, black and white, rich and poor—by 'society'. At a men's conference in New South Wales, I heard a man who is a prominent member of the men's movement and the founder of a number of men's groups solemnly espouse the view that people belonging to the 'owner class' were oppressed too—by their wealth.

A somewhat more muscular exposition of men's oppression comes from Warren Farrell. Farrell argues that because men on average die younger than women, are employed in by far the largest number of jobs in dangerous occupations, die more frequently in industrial accidents, go away to war and are killed and wounded on a far greater scale than women, they in reality suffer more at the hands of the social order than women. 'Male power', says Farrell, is a myth, assiduously maintained by women in order that men will continue to do the dirty work of maintaining society, protecting them from the assaults of other men, and providing them and their children with all of their material needs. The breadwinner thus becomes, in Farrell's eyes, a pitiable slave.[22]

Unfortunately, the uncomfortable fact remains that where there is oppression, there has to be someone doing the oppressing. If indeed some groups of men are oppressed in Australian society—which I would argue they are—they are oppressed primarily by other men. It is facile to suggest that men suffer domination by some impersonal entity called 'society' or 'post-industrial capitalism' without acknowledging that the structures of power and economic inequality in both are administered, manipulated and maintained largely by men. We need only look at the composition of governments, the boards of large companies, the judiciary and the senior levels of the public service to see that this is so. With the notable exception of Margaret Thatcher, the economic policies that have destroyed traditional areas of male employment in countries such as Australia, Britain and the United States have been put in place by men. These policies have led to an increase in average weekly working hours for men over the last decade, much greater insecurity of employment, and a staggering increase in the rate of male (and female) youth unemployment.

The same arguments can be extended to other areas where men suffer disadvantage. There is a great deal of sociological and statistical data to support the view, for example, that there is a close relationship between being poor and being in poor health. Being a man may predispose me to heart disease, high blood pressure, alchoholism and a number of other lifestyle diseases. However, being middle class, professional, with a relatively high income and from a non-Aboriginal background are all factors that, statistically speaking, mean my overall chances of being in good health are much better than those of an unemployed Aboriginal man or a working-class Anglo-Australian male living in the outer suburbs of any of our major cities. There is a link between economic and social inequality and the conditions of our lives, and this link can be seen explicitly in the fact that some men continue to work in dirty, dangerous jobs, the same jobs their fathers and grandfathers before them worked in, while other men work in air-conditioned offices and, like their fathers and grandfathers before them, may never need to do manual labour in order to earn a living. The inescapable conclusion that we are obliged to draw from this is that some men are oppressed—or at least disadvantaged—by structures from which other men benefit. Yet this is not primarily a result of gender, but of class and inequality.

Blaming men's pain or powerlessness on women, or on some nebulous entity such as 'society', is simply a way of palming off on to someone else the responsibility for the dilemma in which men find themselves. If men wish to do something about this dilemma, it is they who have the power to do so.

By the same token, it would be a mistake to assume that, simply because men control the commanding heights of our economic and political structures, all men are more powerful than all women, or that any individual man will automatically hold the power in his relationships with women. Nor does power in the public world of work, business or politics necessarily mean power on the home front. This is a point made by Eva Cox in her book *Leading Women*. Cox argues that even women in quite traditional nuclear families have some degree of power within the household—usually over 'incompetent males'. These men's 'incompetence' in the domestic sphere is the other side of their 'competence' in the public world of work and business. By the same token, women who have been largely excluded from exercising any kind of meaningful power in the public world have exercised a different kind of power in the private world of the family; as Cox puts it 'most women have some, if perhaps limited, power rather than being entirely powerless'.[23]

This is a circumstance recognized also by Meat Man, the narrator of David Ireland's great tragicomic novel of working-class masculinity *The Glass Canoe*:

> I worked out a theory about marriage after watching guys and knowing something about their women and home life.
>
> The bum at work is usually the boss at home. The boss at work is most often a bum at home, picked on, vulnerable . . .
>
> The theory is: Status in marriage is inversely proportional to the surrender value of the marriage. That's for the men.
>
> For women, it's the reverse. Their status is directly proportional to what they'd get from a surrender of the marriage policy.[24]

There's a healthy dose of intended old-fashioned sexism in Meat Man's pronouncement. What this quote helps to underline is what we know from our own experience of relationships and from watching our friends, parents, workmates and relations: that the distribution of power in people's intimate relationships is complex and varied, and that women often do hold the upper hand within the family. We might argue that this is the price both men and women have paid, or the bargain they made in the past when they formed families: women gave up any claim on power in the public sphere and in return gained power in the private sphere—the care and raising of children, the running of the household, even the management of the family finances. Just how pervasive this division of power has been, and continues to be, came to light recently when Stan Wallis, the head of the highly influential Wallis Inquiry into the regulation of Australia's financial system, admitted that his wife does all of the family's banking.

Conversely, in return for power in the public sphere, as worker, wage-earner, unionist, businessman or politician, the man surrendered power in the private sphere. He gave over the running of his intimate life and the responsibility for raising his children to his wife, and at the same time he gave up (often quite willingly) the possibility of a close emotional relationship with his children in their formative years.

Most feminists—and a growing number of men—would argue that this bargain was not an equal or fair exchange. But this is not the primary issue any more, because the bargain itself has passed its use-by date. The 'gender contract' on which the industrial nuclear family was based, to use a term coined by George Klein,[25] has run its course and is in the process of being abolished or, perhaps more accurately, unilaterally re-negotiated by women.

In this chapter I have tried to suggest some of the issues that are at stake in the shifting balance of power relations between men and women. I have also hinted at the necessity for us to look at both the private, 'intimate' world of men's and women's interactions with one another, as well as the larger structures of power in our society, if we want to understand exactly how this shift in the balance of power is occurring. I shall have more to say about the question of power in a number of different contexts throughout this book. In the next chapter, I shall explore more closely the intersection between men's and women's public and private worlds. By looking at how deep structural changes in the economy have brought about changes in the whole nature and meaning of the family over the last 200 years, we will get a clearer picture of what it means for men when their role as breadwinner becomes obsolete and they have to re-negotiate the 'gender contract' from a position of declining power.

3

The end of the gender contract

> Marriage is a contract between two persons for the mutual use of the sex organs.
>
> Immanuel Kant

During the 1996 election campaign, both the Coalition and the Labor Party claimed to be offering policies that would strengthen the position of Australian families and ease their financial burdens. John Howard makes frequent appeals to 'family values' in his speeches, and likes to portray himself as a champion of all that is good and wholesome about the mainstream Australian family. A preoccupation with the family is, however, by no means confined to the conservative side of politics. In Britain, Tony Blair likes to talk about the decline of the family and the need to restore it to its pre-eminent place as the basic building block of a healthy society. Bill Clinton stole the firm ground of family values from under the Republicans' feet in the 1996 US election campaign. Perhaps the most famous political pronouncement on the family in recent years came from Margaret Thatcher, however, who declared that 'there is no such thing as society: there are only individuals and their families'.

What all of these politicians have in common is an unspoken conviction that the family is something constant and unchanging, the rock upon which our social order is built, in short, something that has always been there and always will be. It might come as a surprise to them to learn that the kind of family we think of as the norm—Mum,

Dad, a couple of kids and maybe a dog or a budgie—has only been common in Western societies for around 200 years. It was largely a product of the Industrial Revolution, and the enormous social and economic changes that swept through Europe during the late eighteenth and early nineteenth centuries. The birth of the nuclear family brought with it a rigid division of male and female gender roles. Men became breadwinners, women homemakers.

Countries such as Australia in the late twentieth century are passing out of the industrial age into a post-industrial world in which information and services rather than manufacturing are becoming the driving force in the economy. My argument in this chapter is that the nuclear family as we know it is rapidly becoming as obsolete as the rusting factories of the industrial age. Just as the Industrial Revolution gave birth to a new form of the family 200 years ago, the shift from an industrial to a post-industrial society—sometimes called the information revolution—is loosening the ties that bind the nuclear family and creating a 'post-industrial family' in its place. The shape of this post-industrial family is still unclear: it is 'under construction', provisional, an experiment. But whatever it ends up looking like, it will have a profound impact on men and their place not only in the family, but in the broader society. In order to try to get some idea of where we are going, to chart the course of the family on its voyage from the industrial to the post-industrial world, we need to know where we have come from. This will involve some time travel.

THE BIRTH OF THE NUCLEAR FAMILY

Imagine you have just stepped out of a time machine sometime around the end of the seventeenth century in rural England. You wander across tilled fields and through woodlands, and eventually come upon a small village. Night is drawing on and you need somewhere to sleep, but there's no sign of an inn. Being an experienced time traveller you have disguised yourself in the costume of the period to avoid attracting attention—so eventually you knock on the door of a thatched cottage with a well-kept garden and ask if the family has a spare bed you could sleep in for the night.

You get a few odd looks on account of your accent, but the people are friendly enough, and show you the bed you'll be sharing with John the shepherd. (Even in inns in those days it was commonplace to share the bed with at least one or two other travellers.) If you happen to be a female time traveller, you're in a spot of trouble, as women travelling on their own are likely to be viewed with some curiosity, to say the least. You might pretend you're on your way to see your married sister in the next county—in which case you'll be given a bed with Ann the milkmaid. Ann is a girl of around 12 or 13, the daughter of a family in the market town some ten miles away. As you chat with Ann before the evening meal, you learn that her family are distant relations of the Gartrells, the family whose cottage you're staying in, and that the Gartrells are kindly and treat her as their own daughter.

When you sit down to supper it's with Jack and Beth Gartrell, Ann, John, and Beth's aged mother, Joan. The Gartrells' infant son, James, is already asleep in his cot. During supper, you learn that James was something of an afterthought. The Gartrells' two elder children, Michael and Sally, are both away in service, one on a farm some two hours' walk over the moors, and the other apprenticed to a bootmaker in town.

Not being impolite, you don't ask too many questions. But if you were to ask Beth Gartrell who her family are, she might look a little puzzled, and reply that they are her husband Jack, her mother Joan, young James and John and Ann. And, of course, Michael and Sally.

Would you be surprised by this description? As an experienced time traveller, probably not. It might seem odd, though, to a twentieth-century person who has never had the opportunity to step into a Tardis. The fact of the matter is that family meant something very different in late seventeenth-century England—or France, or Spain, or Germany—to what it means today. People were much more likely to think of their families as being the people they lived with in a household (including servants, farm labourers and artisans, tutors for their children and so on) rather than their blood relations exclusively. So, for example, the famous English diarist Samuel Pepys could write 'I lived in Axe Yard, having my wife and servant Jane, and no more in family than us three', while the first English dictionary published by Samuel Johnson in 1755 gave family as a synonym for 'household'.[1]

Historians first became seriously interested in the family around the middle of the twentieth century. In a sense, the mere fact that they have only relatively recently begun to see the family as a proper object of study is telling in itself. Historians are concerned first and foremost with how and why things change, and in many ways, the family has been seen as being without history because it was assumed to be changeless, a 'natural' form of human social organization that has always existed and always would.

Half a century of historical research has unearthed a very different picture. What it tells us about families in Europe alone is that the form of families, who people regarded as members of their family, and how they felt about them, varied considerably across time and space. Moreover, the household where people lived did not have quite the same significance in the world of the feelings as the family does for us today. In late twentieth-century Australia, we are used to thinking of the 'family home' as housing people who are connected to each other by special ties of emotional affiliation, as well as ties of direct kinship. We tend to think of the people with whom we cohabit—wives, husbands, partners, children, parents—as those who are closest and dearest to us, or at least ought to be. In other words, the family has a particular emotional meaning to us, which derives at least in part from the idea that there is a clear boundary around the family which marks off our relations with family members as being qualitatively different from those we have with other human beings. But in the past, and especially in the pre-industrial era (or the pre-modern period, as it is also known) this boundary was by no means so sharply defined, and the family itself did not have the emotional meaning that we tend to take for granted today. Households were a great deal more varied in their composition. So, for example, in early fifteenth-century Tuscany, one documented rural household, which was by no means wealthy, contained no fewer than 47 people, all apparently related by blood or marriage. This, however, was an exception, and most households were much smaller. The average size of households in France and England from the late sixteenth through to the early nineteenth century was about five to six persons.[2] However, members of these households were not necessarily parents and children, or even related by blood. Under the umbrella of the household came elderly relatives or unmarried brothers or sisters. It was also very likely to include anyone who depended on it for their livelihood. The household was essentially an economic unit, united by priorities of survival and domestic production. It might have been a farm, an artisan's workshop, a merchant's shop or warehouse, or a parsonage. In this sense, it was much more like what we might today call a 'collective' than the modern nuclear family.

Most households, even quite poor ones, also contained servants. This was as true of rural households such as the Gartrells' as it was of households in the cities. (We should remember that until the latter part of the eighteenth century, the vast majority of people lived in the country.) Being a servant in someone's household was not a mark of belonging to a lower class. Servants tended to come from the same economic circumstances as their masters. Perhaps most surprising for us is the fact that they were young, sometimes only eight or nine, though most did not go into service until their teens. Generally, children did not spend their teenage years in the same household as their parents, and they remained in service until they married, which might not be until their mid- or even late twenties.

The other striking feature of the pre-industrial 'household' was that women played an important and sometimes relatively autonomous role in its economic activities. The breadwinner/homemaker division of labour which, until recently, people in Western societies have taken for granted was much less clear-cut. Before the Industrial Revolution, Mum might well have been out in the fields planting or harvesting the crops, weaving cloth with other women in the household, or in the marketplace trading the cloth for other goods needed by the household. The care of children was shared between a number of adults, and children, too, were involved in the everyday activities of the household from a very early age.

Although households or 'families' were usually clustered around a married couple, marriage itself had different meanings and social functions to those it has today. For the upper classes, marriage was about creating alliances and preserving and expanding their wealth and property.

For the lower classes it was a matter of economic survival and, for this reason, most men and women from the poorer sections of society did not marry until their mid-to-late twenties, for the simple reason that they could not afford to. The whole notion that marriage exists for the emotional fulfilment of a man and a woman would have seemed eccentric and peculiar to the Gartrells, our late seventeenth-century family. This idea—along with the belief that the family and 'family values' are somehow the moral cement that hold society together—only really began to take hold in people's minds around the end of the eighteenth century, at the height of the Industrial Revolution.

The advent of the Industrial Revolution transformed the whole economic structure of European society, and, with it, the structure of the family, too. There was a huge movement of people from the country to the cities. These new urban populations left behind the households where work took place in and around the home. Now work was in the factories—the 'dark Satanic mills' of Blake's famous poem. The workers left home early in the morning and returned home at night. Factories moved production out of the home and entrenched the separation of working and domestic life. They shifted the responsibility for the care of small children more and more on to the mother. Whereas previously the members of the extended household might all have kept an eye on children as they went about their daily tasks, they were now likely to be several miles away, sweating at a loom or lathe. More and more, the extended households of rural life simply dissolved in the cities, leaving behind the nucleus around which they'd been built: husband and wife. The 'nuclear family' was born.[3]

As part of this process, women began to lose their involvement in the economic activities of households, and a rigid division in the roles of men and women set in. Increasingly, both working-class and middle-class men began to see themselves as belonging to the world outside the home, the world of labour and commerce, energy and action. Women, especially in the middle classes, were identified more and more with the world 'inside', the domestic sphere, and were assigned the responsibility for maintaining and nurturing not only the material comforts of the home, but its emotional and spiritual dimensions. In other words, women became the custodians of feelings, to whom men looked for comfort and refuge from the outer world. What we might call a division of emotional labour within the family set in—one reflecting the broader division of labour according to gender within society.

In the process, the whole meaning of marriage and the family within society also began to change. New ideas about romantic love and its importance within marriage became popular—and the principal way in which these ideas spread through society was through the reading of novels.

THE INVENTION OF ROMANCE

It might come as a surprise to many modern readers to know that reading novels was once considered a threat to public order and good morals. This was the case in Germany in the latter part of the eighteenth century, where churchmen and scholars of a reactionary turn of mind issued stern tracts warning that novel reading—especially by servants—would lead to unrest among the lower orders, loss of respect for the Church and immorality. The reason for this outbreak of moral panic was the fact that unprecedented numbers of people were actually learning to read. And what were they choosing to read? Not the Scriptures or commentaries and sermons written by the clergy. They were reading novels—a type of literature that had only really developed and become popular in the preceding 30 or 40 years.

In one way those eighteenth-century prophets of doom were right: novels did help to change the world. Many of the novels devoured by the new generations of readers depicted a new kind of relationship between men and women, and what we might call a new culture of the feelings. Feelings themselves, the spontaneous outpouring of pure emotion, became a central subject for the new novels, and romantic love between a man and woman was portrayed as the most exalted feeling of all. Today's Sensitive New Age Guy has his antecedents in the literature of the late eighteenth century. No novel was more famous in Germany at this time than *The Sufferings of Young Werther*, published by Johann Wolfgang Goethe in 1774, when he was just 25. The hero of Goethe's novel is so overcome by the sheer hopelessness of his deeply poetic but unconsummated passion for Charlotte, the wife of his friend and employer Albert, that he shoots himself at the end of the book. Werther was the Kurt Cobain of the 1770s—numbers of young men in France and Germany are reported to have ended their own lives in the same manner after reading the novel.

Living as we do in a late twentieth-century culture so deeply imbued with fantasy images of romance and the emotional fulfilment we're told we can find being part of a loving couple, it's hard for us to grasp just how shocking and subversive these images were when they first appeared. In pre-industrial Europe, marriages were essentially made for economic reasons. This was true at all levels of society, from the aristocracy to the peasantry. Passionate love was not considered to be a necessary ingredient in a marriage. One of Chaucer's characters in *The Canterbury Tales* declares that there are six things a wife wants in a husband: that he be rich, generous, wise, hardy, obedient and 'fressh abedde'.[4] The list of requirements does not include romance or ardour.

Indeed, sexual passion was often thought to be incompatible with marriage. Among the European aristocracy, extramarital liaisons were the norm rather than the exception. French kings built palaces to house their mistresses, who were often women of considerable social standing and influence. The principal purpose of marriage was to legitimize children, and to ensure the survival of dynasties and the inheritance of property, but the real emotional attachments of both men and women were not, on the whole, to their spouses. The dilemma of Werther would not have made sense to most members of the aristocracy. Why did Werther not seduce Charlotte and have done with it, they would have asked themselves.

The answer to this question lies in the rise of a specifically middle-class ideal of romantic love. Novels played a crucial role in depicting and dramatising this ideal of romantic love for a mass audience—predominantly, the emerging middle classes. They depicted love between a man and a woman as a union of souls, in which each 'completed' the other. And, unlike the poetry and drama of previous centuries, the novels of the eighteenth century showed marriage as the natural and proper domain in which such love might flourish. One important feature of this ideal of romantic love was a tendency to separate sex from love, to regard romantic love as an expression of the finer feelings, unsullied by the base desires of the flesh. This is the kind of love we encounter in Jane Austen's novels, though on the whole Austen's heroines have the good sense to fall in love with men of means and family. It is the kind of love that survives to this day in the novels of Barbara Cartland.

Gradually, a new idea of what marriage was about took hold. Instead of being collaborators in the everyday work of a household, husband and wife became what the British sociologist Anthony Giddens calls 'collaborators in a joint emotional enterprise'.[5] Giddens sees the emergence of the ideal of romantic love as a decisive break with the past, opening up a new range of emotional possibilities in relationships between men and women. Some of these possibilities had a liberating potential, especially for women. The heroines of many of the archetypal romantic novels are independent women, who, through their own strength of character, bring about a transformation in the man they love, initiating him into a culture of feeling in which they are the more experienced. They 'actively produce' love in their future mates.[6] But as Giddens points out, whatever the ideal of romantic love might promise in the way of emotional equality—or 'intimate democracy' as he puts it—the reality of middle-class marriage turned out to be very different. The romantic novel charted the often turbulent course by which a man and woman might arrive in the safe harbour of marriage, but it gave very little practical instruction on what was supposed to happen afterwards.

In practice, the work of running marriage as a joint emotional enterprise soon became divided along gender lines. Women became responsible for managing the emotional side of it, while men looked after the material side. 'The fostering of love' became predominantly the task of women.[7] While this division of labour produced some very happy marriages, more often than not it led to an increasing separation between the worlds men and women inhabited and an increasing emotional distance between them as partners, which was taken for granted as the natural state of things in a long-lasting relationship. Part of the price paid by women for this separation was the confinement of their sexuality within the strict boundaries of marriage, while men slaked their 'base desires' with prostitutes and loose women. As Giddens puts it, 'this at the same time allowed men to maintain their distance from the burgeoning realm of intimacy and kept the state of being married as a primary aim of women'.[8]

This is a sketch in very broad brush-strokes of how the ideals of romantic love and middle-class marriage came into being. Incomplete though it may be, it shows that our ideas and assumptions about relationships between men and women, and what they are supposed to mean to us, change over time. The 'culture of the feelings' in which we live is just as mutable as any other aspect of culture. These changes in the culture of the feelings during the late eighteenth and early nineteenth centuries coincided with, and were shaped by, deep and decisive changes in the economic basis of society. We are now on the threshold of another decisive break, both in the nature of the economy and the culture of the emotions. Many of the Western societies that pioneered the Industrial Revolution are now becoming post-industrial economies. In such societies, including our own, the force of the economic changes associated with this shift are also rendering the whole economic basis of middle-class marriage obsolete. At the same time, and partly in response to this process, the emotional meanings of marriage are being reshaped; and it is women who are taking the initiative in mapping out whatever the new emotional territory of marriage might be. Men, we might say, are still trying to navigate according to the old map, or are having trouble reading the new one. To see how and why this is happening, let's step into the time machine once again and move a good deal closer to the present.

ON THE JOB

Our time machine has arrived in the year 1961. However, something seems to have gone wrong with its navigational system and instead of landing on terra firma we are in orbit around Earth. Suddenly, a cone-shaped capsule with a red hammer and sickle on its side swims into view. The Russians have put the first man in space. Yuri Gagarin is looking down from his tiny craft at the blue orb of Earth floating in interstellar night. He sees the whole planet turn beneath him. America follows the vast reaches of the Union of Soviet Socialist Republics and Europe into the dawn. The world is locked in Cold War and Gagarin's flight is a propaganda victory. Suspended in the firmament, the first man ever to gaze down on the whole of his species toiling and dreaming below, Major Gagarin feels he could survey the vast expanse of human history, perhaps even peer into the future. He wonders how the world will have changed by the end of the second millennium. Will it be a smoking ash-heap, decimated by nuclear war? Or a prosperous paradise of harmony and enlightenment?

Well, the answer, of course, is neither. But suppose the first cosmonaut had had a telescope that would enable him to look down into the homes of individual people, into the factories and offices where they worked—and then look 30 years into the future and see the same things again. From his high eyrie, a momentary master of space and time, he might have made out the features of one of the less spectacular but most significant transformations of our century.

First of all, what does he see, in his own time? Imagine that as Gagarin decides to train his telescope on Earth, Australia is passing beneath him. What is the scene inside the average suburban Australian home in 1961? Mum with a kid on her lap, a roast in the oven and Johnny O'Keefe on the radio? And inside the factories, lines of men with crew cuts and blue overalls, labouring at the machines, waiting for the whistle that will release them for the journey home to wives and children, or to the front bar of the pub and the easy fellowship of other men?

That's pretty much the picture, though not the whole picture. According to the census of 1961, women made up a quarter of the Australian workforce. However, of the total number of women between the ages of 25 and 45—the prime child-bearing years—only around one in five were working. Often they had no choice in the matter. Women who had permanent jobs as teachers or public servants were obliged to resign from them when they got married. For those women who were in work, there were constant reminders that their work wasn't valued as highly as men's. A woman working alongside a man in a factory, bank or office, doing identical work was still paid a lower wage.[9]

But if Yuri Gagarin's telescope had let him see into the same household sometime in the mid-1990s, the chances are Mum would be at work, the kids would be at child-care, and dinner would be sitting in the fridge, waiting to go into the microwave after Mum gets home. Thirty years on, women now make up 43 per cent of the Australian workforce and in those prime child-bearing years, an average of two in three women are working. In fact, the percentage of women working in this age bracket is *higher* than the overall percentage of women working across all age groups. Moreover, the change in what women actually *do* is reflected in their attitudes. In 1991 only about 30 per cent of women still thought that motherhood was their most important role in life, compared with nearly 80 per cent in 1961. Perhaps most significantly of all, nearly 60 per cent of married-couple families in Australia with dependants have both partners in the workforce. The two-income family is now the norm in middle Australia.[10]

What this means in practical terms is that the industrial nuclear family is in a lot of trouble. The division of labour that sustained it for 200 years—husband as breadwinner, wife as homemaker—ceases to make much sense when wives are out there winning the bread, too. In fact, being an industrial nuclear family may be a positive disadvantage in today's economic circumstances. According to an Australian Bureau of Statistics survey released in 1995, traditional families in which the man is the sole breadwinner are particularly susceptible to 'income downshifts'—a statistician's polite way of saying they are likely to lose out when times are hard. The same survey spells out a grim message for traditional families: they are at greater risk than two-income families of 'struggling on low incomes or becoming heavily reliant on government support'.[11]

This is a crucially important point to grasp if we want to understand what is happening to men in Australia in the 1990s. The breadwinner role is becoming increasingly untenable. Its rationale within the nuclear family has disappeared as women become co-contributors to the family income, and it is under pressure from economic changes that have made the struggle for a reasonable standard of living—enough income to raise children and pay off a mortgage—much tougher than it was 30 years ago. One of the themes that will emerge in the course of this book is that many Australian men are trapped in a kind of time warp. They are continuing to behave as though the breadwinner role was still a viable option, a firm foundation on which to build their masculine identity, in a time when it is already largely obsolete—and this tends to bring them into conflict with their partners and themselves.

Other men, however, are adapting to these changing circumstances and coping well. According to Phil Cleary, former champion footballer and, until the last election, federal member of parliament for the electorate of Wills in Melbourne's working-class northern suburbs, there has been a process of pragmatic adjustment. Cleary's constituency—once home to a thriving light industrial sector, especially in textiles, clothing and footwear—was hit particularly hard by the economic restructuring of the 1980s. Simple economic necessity has meant that in the 1990s, the ordinary families of Wills can no longer survive on a single income. According to Cleary, men are outgrowing the breadwinner role because they have to. 'The economic imperative will change the culture,' he says.

> If more families need both partners working, they'll go ahead and do that . . . if you're in that situation, why would you care if your wife earns more? There was a time before when men could actually be the one income earner—if you said to the man then, your wife or your mother will go out to work, they'd have rejected that. But now, where both partners need to work, who can reject that?'

Unfortunately, for many former breadwinners in Wills—and similar suburbs around Australia—adapting to life in a two-income family is not an option because they are out of work. Intractable long-term unemployment is now a fact of life in much of what used to be Australia's industrial heartlands. However, there's a hidden dimension to this unemployment that has not been widely discussed in the media or other public forums. Men, in particular working-class men, have been particularly hard hit by it. Male-dominated industries suffered heavy job losses in the last two recessions. According to Bob Gregory, a prominent Australian economist, over the last 20 years, one in four jobs in traditional blue-collar areas such as mining, heavy industry, construction and agriculture have disappeared. These are areas where men have made up the overwhelming majority of the workforce. Moreover, once the jobs go, they generally go for good. The news for women, however, has not been so bad. There's a 'gender asymmetry' in the way successive cycles of recession and recovery affect the sexes. Gregory's work shows that men have tended to lose jobs on the economic downswing, while women have gained them on the upswing. In overall terms, over a decade of rapid restructuring, rationalization and globalization, men have been the losers and women have been the winners.[12] According to the Australian Bureau of Statistics (ABS), this trend is likely to continue: men's participation in the workforce will continue to decline, while women's will increase.

If we look at some of the other trends in the economy over the last ten years, it becomes easier to see why this should be so. It is now well known that the only sector of the economy where there has been strong and consistent growth is in services—in areas such as banking, tourism, hospitality and the new information technology industries. In the financial year 1993/94, for example, 75 per cent of the new jobs created were in the services sector, which is a major employer of women. The services sector now accounts for nearly three-quarters of total employment in Australia. Seen in conjunction with the other major trend in the job market—the shift towards part-time work—the growing importance of services in the economy signals a change in the overall gender balance of employment. Half of all the new jobs created in the last ten years in Australia are part-time jobs, and three-quarters of those new part-time jobs are held by women. Forty per cent of women now in work are working part-time, compared with only 10 per cent of men. Interestingly, too, over the last ten years women have proved to be more successful than men at starting small businesses and turning them into ongoing concerns which turn a profit.[13] In other words, women seem to have been better able than men to capitalize on the shift from an industrial to a post-industrial, service-based economy.

These trends are by no means confined to Australia. They have emerged in a number of countries with developed industrial economies, which have undergone similar processes of restructuring in the 1980s. According to the influential news magazine the *Economist*, between 1980 and 1992, women accounted for 60 per cent of the increase in the United States workforce while in the European economies, the figure was even higher.[14] The American Bureau of Labor forecasts that the fastest-growing new areas of employment in the United States over the next five years will be residential care, computer and data processing, health services and child-care—all areas where women occupy over two-thirds of existing jobs. Across the whole OECD, unskilled work—traditionally the province of working-class men—has declined to the point where Spain is now the only OECD country in which blue-collar jobs outnumber white-collar ones. Overall, concludes the *Economist*, 'the labour market is increasingly friendly to women', while 'there are growing numbers of men outside the labour market in a way that women are accustomed to but men are not'.

There are some details missing from this broad canvas, however, and they are related to class. Not all women have benefited from the expansion of jobs during the 1980s. In Australia, it still remains the case that, while women overall tend to have lower unemployment rates than men, women whose husbands are out of work have higher unemployment rates than the wives of men in work. This strongly suggests that class—or what is now referred to as 'socio-economic status'—is, in some cases, more likely to affect your chances of being employed than gender. In other words, if you are working class or lower middle class, you are much more likely to be unemployed than if you're middle class, regardless of whether you're male or female.

This is a point stressed forcefully, though with a slightly different slant, by Paul Matters, secretary of the South Coast Labor Council in Wollongong. Paul began his working life as a locomotive driver at BHP, a job he did for ten years before his marriage broke up and he was left to care for his two small children. Later he worked as a labourer and now heads the Labor Council, the largest regional trade union body in Australia. Paul believes that the combined effect of structural change in the economy and equal opportunity policies in the workplace has been to create 'gender mobility' rather than gender equity. By this he means that opportunities have opened up for some women—predominantly middle-class women—to move upwards through the existing structures of employment and institutional power, without actually changing those structures or bringing about a more equitable distribution of work, wealth and power between men and women. Moreover, in industrial cities such as Wollongong, few new jobs have been created for women to replace those lost in areas of traditional male employment. In fact, he argues, the economic changes of the 1980s and 1990s have tended to promote downward mobility for men, while many of the opportunities that have opened up for working-class and lower-income women are themselves low-wage, low-status jobs which offer little prospect of career advancement or job security. This is a trend that is common to most developed economies comparable to Australia's: as one study puts it, women continue to be 'concentrated overwhelmingly in a very narrow range of relatively poorly-paid occupations, such as clerical and sales'. Expanded employment opportunities for women do not mean that their access to power, status and influence in the 'commanding heights' of the economy have increased. They are, however, having an effect on the micropolitics of the family and domestic life.[15]

At the same time, the structural changes in the economy that I've outlined affect men in ways which go beyond the workplace. There are many cities and regions in Australia, such as Wollongong and the northern suburbs of Melbourne, where the factories, shipyards and smelters have closed down and are unlikely to reopen. Yet we hear very little about the men who live in these places and the impact that a future of probable permanent unemployment has on their lives. When men in these communities become unemployed, they do not simply lose their jobs. Not only they do lose their role as breadwinner in the family, but also their connection with a whole network of relationships based around work. Often, unions are an important source of social as well as industrial solidarity in places such as Wollongong. However, according to Paul Matters, unions in Australia have tended to lose interest in their members once members lose their jobs. One interesting exception is the Building Workers Industrial Union in Victoria, which appointed Anna Hetzel, a Uniting Church minister, to be chaplain to the building industry and minister especially to the needs of unemployed building workers and their families. Hetzel reports that the men who cope best with unemployment are those who get involved in looking after children and running the household. For these men, she says, the 'role reversal' involved is not an easy one, but it goes a long way towards restoring the self-esteem and sense of purpose they lost when they lost their jobs. Whether this is a more widespread trend among unemployed men is very difficult to know. Until now, statisticians have not been very interested in the private lives of the unemployed.[16]

Where new jobs have been created in service industries, men have not shown a great deal of alacrity in taking them up. The Australian workforce is still highly segregated into male-dominated and female-dominated occupations. While women have moved into many jobs and vocations, such as the armed forces, which were previously the sole preserve of men, there has been much less movement in the opposite direction. Overseas studies suggest that men are especially reluctant to take on jobs in areas dominated by women. Part of the explanation for this may be that jobs in these areas continue to be lower paid and less secure than men's jobs. Yet there's been little increase in the percentages of men joining professions that are relatively well paid and offer reasonable career prospects—such as nursing. A European Union study of male and female working patterns in its 12 member countries drew the conclusion that blue-collar men were 'willing to undertake low-paid and low-skilled jobs, provided they are not feminised'.[17]

It would be easy for us to lose our way here in a forest of trends and statistics. But if we stand back for a moment or imagine ourselves looking down from Gagarin's space capsule, or today's Russian–American joint venture—the space shuttle—the broad picture that emerges is clear. Economic restructuring has created opportunities for women in the workforce, and closed off some choices for men. Just as the logic of capitalist production in the nineteenth century—aided and abetted by governments and, incidentally, the trade union movement—pushed women out of the workforce, it is now sucking them back in. Moreover, late twentieth-century capitalism prefers a workforce that is 'flexible', highly casualized and has good 'interpersonal skills'. Women, who have been accustomed to moving in and out of the workforce and working part-time as they juggled employment and child-rearing, are in many ways better adapted to the needs of today's labour market than men.

Meanwhile, men, especially low-skilled, blue-collar men from traditional working-class backgrounds, are finding themselves left further and further behind. In addition, they are seeing their role as breadwinner in the family becoming increasingly irrelevant. There's little evidence that men in this category regard themselves as being in direct competition with women for jobs, or that they overtly blame women for their own dim prospects in the labour market. However, the rhetoric of groups like the Promise Keepers in the United States, which is all about strong family values and restoring men to their rightful place of authority within the family, carries an implicit message that women's proper place is in the home and not the workplace. It is no accident that the primary social base of the Promise Keepers is among white men who belong to America's working poor or who are out of a job.

The transformation in men's and women's places in the economy since Gagarin made his pioneering space flight is a profound one. Yet the picture I've painted of this transformation still lacks two important details. One pertains to what we might call the hidden history of women's participation in the world of work. Since the Industrial Revolution, working-class women have moved in and out of the world of work at different stages of their lives, depending on their own economic needs (and those of their families) and the demand for their labour in the economy, which typically increased in times of war. Until this century, a major form of employment for working-class women was domestic service in the homes of the middle class. They also worked outdoors as agricultural labourers—think of Tess in Thomas Hardy's novel *Tess of the D'Urbervilles*—and in factories, though during the nineteenth century the trades unions in Britain campaigned to have women excluded from many forms of factory work. From a strategic point of view, this was perhaps understandable, since women were paid less than men and the cost of their labour thus undercut male wages. But there was a strong element of gender warfare at work here too, as men strove to assert their dominance in the factory and the working-class culture associated with the trades union movement.[18] Similar strategies were employed by the trades union movement in Australia.

In nineteenth-century Australia, too, working-class women worked for their livelihood. According to the census of 1871, women made up 28.2 per cent of the workforce in Sydney (a slightly higher figure than the 25 per cent of the labour force they comprised throughout Australia in 1961!). The vast majority of these women were single, and worked either in domestic service or industry. However, as Michael Gilding shows in his book *The Making and Breaking of the Australian Family*, there was a substantial 'informal economy' in which married women—and in particular, working-class married women—continued to work inside and outside the home in late nineteenth-century Australia in a variety of contexts. Despite this, most married women continued to be economically dependent on their husbands—not least because of the large number of children common in families at the time.[19]

The point here is that work alone is not a necessary and sufficient condition for women's emancipation. Indeed, it seems that for some women stuck in low-paid, arduous jobs, it was work itself from which they hoped to be emancipated. Writing in Britain in 1886, an investigator from the Select Commission on the Shop Hours Regulation Bill noted that 'the majority of shop assistants look upon marriage as their one hope of release, and would, as one girl expressed it, "marry anyone to get out of the drapery business"'.[20] A whole range of factors have come together to make women less financially dependent on men, both in and out of marriage: smaller families with fewer children, family allowances and other social payments to single, separated or divorced women with dependent children; the requirement that men pay maintenance or child support to separated wives; and the provision of child-care, both state-funded and private. Changes in social attitudes have, in many ways, been just as important. Work is no longer something that women do to bide time until they get married, and once they do marry, or enter a long-term relationship, their participation in the workforce is no longer regarded as simply 'helping out'—topping up the family income provided primarily by their mate. Moreover, the whole structure of modern capitalism has shifted fundamentally in such a way that women's work is now integral to capitalism's day-to-day functioning. It is almost impossible to imagine women being pushed out of the workforce in the way they were after both world wars.

It seems clear that men will have to make major changes to their ideas about their role in the family and their place in the world in order to adjust to these enormous changes in the lives of women. Yet the evidence that they are doing so is mixed, and, as I've hinted above, some Australian men seem trapped in the time warp, still living and behaving as though it were 1961 and not the late 1990s. Nowhere do the old attitudes and the old division of labour between breadwinner and homemaker seem to persist so strongly as in the one area of work we haven't touched on yet: housework. Let's take a closer look at what is happening in the kitchens, laundries and playpens of Australian homes.

A MAN AND HIS WHITE GOODS

In an essay written in the early years of this century the Austrian writer Hugo von Hofmannsthal described art as a kind of seismograph of social change. According to Hofmannsthal, the artist's sensibilities are so finely tuned that they are able to detect, often unconsciously, the stirrings of great social transformations that are only just beginning, much as a seismograph registers faint tremors transmitted through the Earth's crust from many thousands of miles away.

If Hofmannsthal were writing today, it's more than likely he would fix on advertising executives rather than artists as the contemporary seismographs of social change. Today's admen and adwomen assign each potential consumer to one of a set of categories based on age, income, occupation and outlook. Just as they presented us in the 1980s with images of the independent, resolute career woman, choosing her car or bank or superannuation fund without referring to a man, so in the 1990s they have helped to breathe life into the New Man. Television advertisements for Westinghouse and Panasonic being screened as I write show men using a variety of white goods from fridges to washing machines. The adverts stress the user-friendliness of the appliances for those unfamiliar with their operation—as in the microwave oven that has 100 recipes stored in its memory and instructs two men how to make a casserole by showing each stage of the recipe on a liquid-crystal display. The message is clear: men may be a bit slow, but they are getting into the laundry and the kitchen and getting their hands dirty.

Unfortunately, these images of 'blokus domesticus'[21] seem to bear little relation to social reality in Australia. The most recent data, from a survey completed by Michael Bittman in 1992, show that on average women spend more than seven times as long as men every week doing laundry, ironing and clothes care, between four and five times as long cleaning, three and a half times as long looking after children, and about three times as long cooking. By contrast, men spend four times as long as women on home and car maintenance. Shopping, gardening and playing with children are the tasks most evenly balanced between men and women. Overall, the average amount of time spent on housework by men has increased by only one hour a week since the mid-1970s. Where the amounts of time spent by men and women on unpaid domestic work appear to have converged over this 20-year period, it's primarily because women are spending less time on 'home duties', not because men are doing more.[22]

Bittman's work also shows that the 'inside/outside' distinction is still firmly entrenched in the gender division of work around the house. Men still do the majority of 'outside' work, such as home maintenance, looking after the car, cleaning the pool and mowing the lawns. It would be perverse to suggest that there is anything intrinsically wrong with this arrangement. Many women may have no desire to spend their weekends underneath a dripping sump or pushing a lawnmower around. However, the fact remains that the total time spent by men doing these 'outside' tasks is still considerably less than the total time women spend on domestic work 'inside'.

According to Michael Bittman, 'blokus domesticus' is a species suffering from arrested development, the product of a stalled revolution in the domestic sphere. The phrase 'stalled revolution' was first used by the American writer Arlie Hochschild in her book *The Second Shift*, but Bittman believes it applies equally well in the Australian context. Focusing on the kitchen, he points out that the average time men aged 25–59 spent preparing food or cleaning up afterwards rose by more than an hour from 1974 to 1987, but has remained on a plateau ever since—a development he characterizes as going from 'slow motion' to 'no motion'.

Perhaps the most telling symptom of the 'stalled revolution' is the finding that there has been little significant change across generations. Young men do about the same amounts of housework now as their fathers did when they were young, although there has been a very modest increase in the time they spend cleaning. However, despite the overall increase in cooking time, 'the "stalled revolution" is nowhere more evident than in the failure of younger men, raised in post-feminist households, to increase their contribution to cooking'. In short, Bittman concludes, 'no generation of "new men" is about to come down the pipeline'.[23]

This would seem to be further evidence that men are behaving as though the breadwinner/homemaker distinction were still firmly in place, long after it has ceased to be relevant in the majority of Australian families. However, before we consign 'blokus domesticus' to purgatory or send him off to the re-education camp, it's worth recalling one more important statistic. Overall, men still spend an average of almost exactly twice as many hours in paid employment as women. On top of this, more and more men are working longer and longer hours. Over the last 15 years, the proportion of men in Australia working very long hours—officially defined as more than 49 hours per week—has grown in every occupational group, and across all groups by around 10 per cent. We tend to think of managers and high-earning professionals along with computer nerds as spending long hours in the office, but, in fact, other groups such as plant operators, sales- and tradespeople, and shift workers also work very long hours. This is the one area in which men's and women's patterns of working life are *not* becoming more similar. Not only is the overall proportion of men working long hours roughly double that of women, but the percentage of men in this category has grown at a faster rate than women.

This is a very sobering statistic, if only because the labour movement fought such a long struggle to reduce the length of the working week. The trend towards increasingly long working hours for men can be explained partly by economic necessity. Studies of wage and salary earners in Britain, for example, have shown that men's working hours typically tend to *increase* when they have children, often because of a need for more family income.[24] This, however, is only part of the picture.

Longer working hours are themselves a symptom of a deep structural change in the economy and the nature of work itself. Increasingly, economies such as ours, which have undergone a rapid process of modernization and globalization, require a new kind of workforce. This new workforce operates according to what's known as the core/periphery model. In this model, the core of the workforce is highly skilled, flexible, adaptable to constant change and highly mobile. Workers in this category will tend to work very long hours and be highly paid. The peripheral workforce—by far the larger overall percentage of workers—will tend to be low skilled and low paid, and they will have little, if any, job security. Typically, they will either work part-time, or experience alternating periods of work and unemployment. Overall, the picture will be like this: a relatively small elite group working very hard and enjoying a very high standard of living, and a much larger group of 'drones' shunted in and out of the workforce as required, working less than the current 38-hour week and subsisting not far above the poverty line. According to the Australian Bureau of Statistics' latest survey of the Australian labour market, the beginnings of this trend are already emerging here.

These kinds of economic developments have very serious implications for men's efforts to achieve a greater balance between their family lives and their work. The two main factors that affect men's participation in housework are the number of hours they spend in paid work and the presence of pre-school children. This suggests very strongly that men will only start to do more around the house when they begin reducing the hours they spend at work. At present, the trend is in the opposite direction. The only lever that is likely to bring about a shift and re-start the 'stalled revolution' is a greater role for men in bringing up their children. In Chapter 9, I'll look in much more detail at the changing nature of men's involvement with their children, and especially at Australian men's efforts to experiment with a more democratic approach to parenting, where the work of child-rearing is shared more equally between father and mother. For now, it seems to me that if we want to understand men's difficulties in moving out of the breadwinner role, we need to be aware of the economic pressures that have been brought to bear on them by the changes of the last decade or so. These economic changes also have a bearing on the vexed question of housework.

Of course, work—and long working hours—have not stopped women from doing housework and looking after children when paid work was finished for the day. Women's 'double burden' became a catchcry of feminists during the 1970s. The double burden wasn't restricted to the capitalist economies of the developed West. In socialist countries such as East Germany, where the vast majority of women worked whether they had children or not, child-care was free and practically universal. Both men and women worked an average nine-hour day, yet equality in the workplace did not lead to equality in the home. As East German feminists pointed out, women in the 'workers' and peasants' paradise' were working full-time, *and* doing the lion's share of the housework and looking after children when work was over.[25]

In Australia, the trend has been for women to do less housework as they spend more time in paid work, without men taking on more housework—except in the area of child-care. It's quite clear that women are adapting to increased participation in the workforce by reducing the amount of time they spend on unpaid domestic labour. Yet many of them are still carrying a very substantial double burden of paid work *and* unpaid domestic labour. As the most recent ABS survey shows, there's very little evidence that men start doing more housework when their wives start working longer hours in paid employment and doing less housework. Indeed, when Mum goes out to work, the overall amount of housework done by other members of the household tends to *decrease*.

Why should this be important? Do women really care how much housework men do? The commonsense answer to this question would seem to be a resounding yes. The British feminist Beatrix Campbell puts it this way: what women want above all else from men is co-operation, a willingness to share responsibility for running a household and a relationship as a joint enterprise.[26] Co-operation seems to me an eminently practical definition of the changes women would like to see men make in the domestic sphere. Often, however, women are only too happy to collude in male helplessness in the domestic sphere, or to assume that men don't know what they are doing when they turn on a vacuum cleaner or load the washing machine. Some writers have argued that this arises out of women's desire to hang on to power or authority in the one area where, traditionally, they have been able to wield it in the confines of the nuclear family. I think, however, that Lynne Segal is closer to the mark when she suggests that it is, in fact, 'women's comparative powerlessness, both inside and outside the home, which induces this desire to feel uniquely needed, in some way—if only to scrub the toilet basin'.[27] Whatever women's reasons for being reluctant to give up control over the management and mechanics of housework, men will not become either proficient at it or accustomed to doing it unless they can learn by their mistakes—something women are sometimes loath to let them do.

Beyond this immediate level of domestic negotiation, we need to look more closely at the larger obstacles that stand in the way of men changing their attitudes and expectations. One obstacle is plainly the hours of work themselves, especially when they begin to nudge the 50-hours-a-week level. Men who are working from nine in the morning until seven at night and then travelling home are simply not physically present in the home for long enough to make a substantial contribution to looking after children, cooking or housework, except on the weekend. Yet many men—such as taxi drivers—work much longer hours than this. The hard economic facts of life for low- and middle-income earners in Australia may often mean that working hours of this order are a matter of necessity rather than choice.

One further theme, which I stress throughout this book, is the very close relationship between the way work is organized and the way men and women live their lives. We cannot hope to give men a more active and equal role in the family, to elicit more 'co-operation' from them, unless we are prepared to tackle head-on the structure and distribution of paid work in our society. Indeed, we cannot hope to change masculinity itself unless we address these larger issues. The best possible way to ensure that boys grow up knowing how to cook, vacuum and wash their clothes, and accept that these activities are part of their responsibilities as adult human beings, is for them to see their fathers cooking, vacuuming and washing clothes on a regular basis. This cannot happen if men are spending 60 hours a week at work. Moreover, these kinds of working arrangements will not change unless men themselves are prepared to agitate for something different. Again, I'll have more to say on this subject later. It seems to me that if women want men to co-operate more in doing their fair share of housework, the issues of working hours and the need for 'family-friendly' workplaces are the place to start.

It is hard to imagine a revolutionary movement with the slogan 'Workers of the world unite! Off with your chains and on with your aprons!' sending thousands of men running to the barricades. The breadwinner role may be obsolete—but replacing it with a new role for men involves nothing less than transforming the structures of post-industrial capitalism itself. Unfortunately, the social groups that have been most effective in the past in altering the way in which capitalism works and helping to shape the welfare state—the trades unions—are in a state of decline and disarray. It is hard to imagine men mobilizing within trades unions for better child-care and shorter working hours so that they can spend more time with children. Nevertheless, trades unions have mobilized and run industrial campaigns in support of shorter working hours, paternity leave and allowances for other 'family' issues in the past.

There are very good reasons why young men, in particular, should become active on these issues now. In a recent survey which asked young Australian women aged 18 to 22 to imagine their lives at the age of 35, over 60 per cent of the respondents saw themselves working full-time *and* married with one or two children. Clearly, these women see a family as no obstacle to their careers. They see themselves as responsible for winning the daily bread. Yet there is something missing from the picture of a future life they envisage for themselves, and that is their husbands. In order for the current generation of young women to fulfil their aspirations of full-time work and children, they will need to find partners who will be prepared to share equally the responsibility of raising children. In addition, their partners will more than likely have to make sacrifices in their own careers (if they are middle class and lucky enough to have careers), and be prepared to work shorter hours or take some time off on paternity leave. Otherwise, the equation simply won't add up. The pressure is on today's generation of young males to meet the expectations of their female contemporaries. If they don't, the women in their lives are likely to become more and more disenchanted. These women are likely to question just what it is they are getting out of marriage—and what they gain from long-term relationships with men.

THE END OF THE GENDER CONTRACT

Why men have more to lose than women from the end of the nuclear family

> At last I am free
> I can hardly see in front of me
> I can hardly see in front of me
> And now love please hold me
> Come closer my dear
> It feels so good
> Just having you near
> But who am I fooling
> When I know it's not real?
> I can't hide
> All this hurt and pain I feel.
> (. . .)

Robert Wyatt recorded this song—originally by the American funk outfit Chic—over a decade ago. Wyatt was a member of the avant-garde rock band Soft Machine in the 1960s, until a car accident confined him to a wheelchair for the rest of his life. His version of *Now That I Am Free*, sung in a haunting, plaintive falsetto, is pierced through with an almost unbearable vulnerability, as though he can't quite believe the depth and intensity of the 'hurt and pain' he's feeling. From any other singer, the song and its lyrics would sound maudlin, full of the clichés of Tin Pan Alley. Coming from Wyatt, it has the quality of a kind of revelation, a dreadful awakening to loss and abandonment.

In many ways, *Now That I Am Free* could be an anthem of sorts for the large number of Australian men who go through divorce or separation every year and, increasingly, end up in counselling, a men's group or therapy to try cope with it. The stories of their grief tend not to make it into the pages of our newspapers or onto our television screens except, unfortunately, for the occasions when men resort to—sometimes deadly—violence against the women who have left them.

Public responses to such events—responses of rage and horror—do not necessarily provide clarity in understanding where such violence comes from. It's often argued that this violence springs from men's assumption of a right to dominate the women they form an attachment to, and that violence is simply a way of reasserting control when a woman has taken it away from them by leaving. (This is a question I'll explore in more detail in Chapter 4.) However, this is not the whole story—or else it would not sometimes happen that men turn the gun they've used to kill their former mate on themselves. In these cases, control is both achieved and lost forever in one Pyrrhic moment. For these men, the way they choose to extinguish the pain of abandonment is to extinguish the life of the woman they love and then extinguish themselves.

This should in no way be understood as an attempt to excuse the use of violence. Rather, I wish to suggest that the source of such criminal actions can, *in some cases*, be understood (but not exonerated) as an extreme response to the feelings of loss and vulnerability experienced by many men when they are left by their wife or partner. Many men report feeling 'devastated' when a relationship ends, and they find themselves suddenly exposed to a level of emotional suffering they've never before had to deal with.

Why should we think there is anything significant or new about this? After all, we have centuries of poetry and song in which men lament lost love. Why should we imagine that men are suffering any more today than they did in the time of Shakespeare or Petrarch?

The answer to this, in late twentieth-century Australia, can be partly explained statistically. According to Peter Jordan, author of two major studies of divorce in Austalia, it's predominantly women who are doing the leaving and men who are getting left. Between 60 and 65 per cent, or roughly two in three, of marital separations are initiated by women. Only around 20 per cent of men actually take the first step in ending a marriage. Consistently, a clear majority of men say that they did not want their marriages to end and that they sought a reconciliation with their wives. Around 40 per cent of the men Jordan surveyed felt that they would never get over the divorce. In many cases, the men were shocked and disbelieving when their former partners had told them they wanted to end the marriage.[28]

How do we account for this striking disparity—that women are much more likely to end relationships, while men apparently have a much greater stake in preserving them? According to Peter Jordan—and his findings are borne out by other studies of divorce and separation—the principal reason has to do with differing expectations about what relationships are supposed to involve and, in particular, a kind of imbalance in the importance men and women give to the emotional dimension of their lives together. Consistently, he writes, wives who've initiated a divorce state that 'their needs and emotions are not being fulfilled within the relationship', and that men consistently ignore or trivialize their partner's attempts to draw attention to problems in the relationship.[29] Jordan sees this as evidence that men are inclined to hand over to women the responsibility for their shared emotional lives at an early stage in relationships, and then expect not to have to contribute to their continuing maintenance. Often, when questioned, the men he surveyed would fall back on quite traditional views about a woman's place and their own role as provider.

Jordan's work on divorce is not purely statistical. It is informed by his own experience as a counsellor with the Family Court, where he's worked extensively with separated and divorced men. Interestingly, he observes that the Family Court is now used largely by families from working-class and lower-income backgrounds; the middle classes, he says, tend to settle out of court. This may go some way towards explaining the persistence of very traditional views about men's and women's roles in the family among the men he counselled. Yet, in his view, there's a certain tragic element to these men's belief that they have done the right thing as husbands and lovers—a sentiment he captures in a poem based on his counselling experiences. The poem, entitled 'Even Bastards Care', speaks with the voice of a man who's tried to do what he thought was expected of him:

I yelled at my children
Then went to work
I gave her a home
I did the right thing
That's how I cared.
She asked for my time
I had my own interests
I paid all the bills
I did the right thing
That's how I cared.

The narrator of the poem is dumbfounded and shattered when his wife walks out on him, as the full magnitude of what he has lost dawns on him:

Feelings flood through me
Hurt and despair
Why didn't I listen
What care meant to her
But who would believe
Even 'Bastards' care.[30]

Some readers may find it difficult to believe that the kinds of attitudes to marriage and relationships encapsulated in these lines are still common among Australian men. Many of the men I've interviewed in the course of writing this book attested to having grown up with views and assumptions such as these, and to having carried them into their marriages—though many of them had been forced to change their attitudes as a result of a crisis in the marriage. Despite the very rapid pace of change in the lives of women over the last 30 years, it should hardly surprise us that the attitudes that shaped and sustained the nuclear family for 200 years should continue to exert a powerful influence, even while the economic infrastructure that gave rise to the industrial nuclear family is being demolished. The general consensus among researchers in the area of 'family studies' is that men are still much more influenced by these traditional attitudes than women, and that they have more of an emotional investment in marriage. They appear not to cope as well as women with the emotional stress and strain of divorce. Forty per cent of the men questioned in Peter Jordan's latest survey said they thought they would never get over their divorce. Men are more likely than women to remarry or 're-partner'. The odds of a divorced man re-partnering (through marriage or a de facto relationship) are about three times as high as the odds for a divorced woman. There may be a number of explanations for this: men are less likely than women to have children living with them—and are thus able to 'get out more'—and, in general, men end up financially better off than women after divorce, which may make it easier for them to find a partner. However, there is also evidence that some women simply find the independence of a single life enjoyable and have no particular desire to find a new mate.[31] The same does not seem to be true of men, or at least not to such an extent.

One common way of explaining men's greater desire to hang on to their marriages, and their greater difficulty in coping with separation, is to see it as a reaction to loss of control over their former partners and children.[32] While this may be true in some cases, built into this explanation is the assumption that men are naturally controlling, or that what they are grieving for is necessarily their sense of control, rather than the intimacy they enjoyed with their former partners. Denying the legitimacy of men's feelings in this way will not make it any easier to achieve better relations between men and women after divorce, and it is patronizing and humiliating to men. The painful paradox about men and marriage is that they often don't realize the extent of their emotional investment until they lose their marriage. As the title of a famous country ballad goes, 'You don't miss your water/Till the well runs dry'. Men may still be prisoners of an anachronistic understanding of their place in the world—but they are offered very little constructive support in trying to fashion a new role for themselves. Men are more likely to be admonished for their attitudes than encouraged to take on a greater responsibility for their emotional lives or find other ways of 'caring' than paying the bills and shouting at the children.

In this sense, men would appear to be the losers in the breakdown of what George Klein calls the 'gender contract'. Klein—a counsellor, therapist and behavioural scientist who has worked with men in New South Wales for over a decade—believes that an implicit contract between men and women has sustained the nuclear family.[33] The terms of the contract were relatively simple: women took over the responsibility for the emotional and physical care of their mate while men took on the material aspects of care—the provision of money, shelter, food, clothing and increasing quantities of consumer goods. In so doing, they became 'de-skilled' in dealing with their emotional experience. What's particularly illuminating about Klein's notion of the gender contract is its suggestion that men, too, had to give something up on entering into the gender contract: direct access to their own emotions. Women became the interpreters, and in so doing they acquired power over the emotional sphere, the domain of intimacy, referred to by E.M. Forster in *Howards End* as the world of 'telegrams and anger'.

In the past, the outer form of the gender contract had been preserved by women's economic dependence on men, and the difficulty in obtaining a divorce. Now that these obstacles have been removed, women seem much less inclined than in the past to preserve the form without the emotional content. They are much more likely now than they were 20 years ago to tear up the gender contract unilaterally. Another way of understanding this divergence is to consider that women are increasingly reluctant to ignore the gap between social fantasies of what the nuclear family is and their own experience of it. Men, on the other hand, seem able to live with that gap, but respond with shock and incomprehension when it's exposed to them by a woman walking out the door. Klein argues that women are more likely to do this in their late 30s or early 40s, when they have achieved a measure of emotional stability and independence as individuals, which many men seem to lack. Thus, men going through divorce or separation can find themselves suddenly strangers not only to their former partners, but to themselves as well, overwhelmed by emotions they didn't know they had. As we'll see, these men often feel isolated from other men, unable to turn to them for support and empathy.

The breakdown of the gender contract is not necessarily a destructive process, for women or men. Anthony Giddens sees it as the necessary precondition for creating what he calls the 'pure relationship'.[34] Purity, he's quick to point out, has nothing to do with sex in this context. By 'pure' he means a relationship that is entered into entirely for its own sake, not on the basis of any contract, but in such a way that two people become part of each other's journey or 'project' of self-realization. It is also a relationship that lasts only as long as 'it is thought by both parties to deliver enough satisfactions for both parties to stay within it'.[35] What this means in practical terms is that the pure relationship is provisory, always open to question: it is the journey that is important, not the destination, and we may choose a succession of travelling companions along the way.

Whether or not heterosexual men and women are really choosing to live their emotional lives as though they aspire to a 'pure relationship' is difficult to say. The evidence seems to be that they are inclined to try a more conventional marriage first, though they may often abandon it after only a few years. The pure relationship is probably more highly developed among gay men and lesbians than it is within the straight population. What does seem convincing, though, is Giddens' observation that women are the pioneers of the pure relationship, the 'emotional revolutionaries of modernity'. The more they move towards the pure relationship, 'the more male emotional dependence becomes unbearable'.

It seems to me that we need to see the breakdown of the gender contract and the kinds of economic and social change I've described earlier in this chapter as parallel processes, occurring side by side and influencing each other, while having their own particular momentum and timetable. Only by seeing the interaction between these processes can we really understand what is happening to men, and why it is that many of them experience such a strong sense of powerlessness while still seeming to hold much of the power. In particular, we may begin to comprehend that it is not men's lack of emotion, but rather the lack of an emotional vocabulary, a way of making sense of their own and others' emotions, that makes it so difficult for them to respond to what it is that women seem to want and expect from their relationships with men. In this situation, women are often set up once again as the interpreters and possessors of 'expert knowledge' in relation to the emotions—a role that may not be helpful either to men or to women.

For many men faced with such a welter of new challenges and demands, the simplest response is avoidance. In Chapter 4, I'll explore the experiences of men who've been forced to confront their attitudes to themselves, their wives and partners, and often the core of their masculinity itself as part of the process of trying to give up violence in their intimate relationships.

4

Reports from the frontline—men, women and violence

> I'd never heard of a men's group. I found out about this place through courts. Me and my partner . . . we were going together a few months—she fell pregnant and I wasn't ready for her changing moods. I had my own way, I was the man of the house, and all of a sudden she had these mood swings and wanted to do things her way and I couldn't handle it. She was six months pregnant, I came home from work at lunchtime, we had a huge argument, she laid a few punches, I give her a bit of a right hook and gave her a humungous shiner. I shit meself on the spot and thought 'What have I done?'
>
> Dave, Doveton Men's Group

Dave is telling his tale to the men's group at Doveton—the same one in which we met Ron, at the beginning of this book. Dave is in his mid-20s and works as a mechanic in a large auto repair shop.[1] Like Ron, he's been attending the Men's Violence Support Group every Monday night for a couple of years. He narrowly missed out on going to gaol.

> I gone back to work and an hour later the jacks have turned up—you know, the cops—and said, you know what we're here for. I went to court, they put me in the cells for a day, he wanted to give me 12 months and I turned white, felt like me feet had dropped off, didn't know what to do or say.
>
> I reappeared in the arvo, I was lucky my solicitor knew about this place and he put me onto it.

Instead of spending 12 months in gaol, Dave was put on a two-year good behaviour bond—a condition of which was that he attend the group at Doveton. In some ways, the atmosphere in the support group is a little like an AA meeting. It's a way for these men to support and encourage each other in their mutual resolve to give up violence. Also like AA, there's an almost religious undertone to some of the men's stories, a note of the confessional mingling with a sense of revelation as they describe the painful process of self-discovery they've been through:

> I didn't even know I had an anger problem. I just thought it was other people being nasty to me. I've been here nearly two years, and I'm just getting the tip of the iceberg, I'm starting to learn so much about myself that I never knew was inside me.

Dave is still living with his partner, and he says there's been a marked improvement in their relationship since he's been coming to the group. As a young father in his 20s, he's relatively unusual among the members of this and similar groups. Most of the men who attend courses or join groups to deal with their violence tend to be in their 30s or 40s (though the oldest member of the Doveton group is 65), and often they have a long history of violence and abuse. What is typical about Dave's story is the violence in his own family when he was growing up.

> I grew up with my Dad bashing my Mum every night, with alcoholism—I always thought till I was about 18–19, I thought that was cool. I've got a real clear memory, like yesterday, of my Dad smashing my Mum's head against the front tap. Now I know it was wrong for him, and to be on top, have your own way, especially with your partner, it's just not right. You've got to communicate, even things out.

'Even things out' is precisely what men's violence groups aim to do. They focus on getting the men who join them to accept a more equal relationship with their partners. The road to this acceptance is a long and difficult one. It involves the men who take it being prepared to give up the power they've exercised through violence. At the same time, they are forced to examine their own attitudes to women and to themselves as men. Many, like Dave, have 'had their own way' or feel they are entitled to have it. Yet many, again like Dave, have been on the receiving end of violence themselves. They are part of a cycle of violence and abuse that is passed on from generation to generation. Again and again the men in the Doveton group, and others I visited, told stories of how their fathers had routinely beaten them, their mothers and their siblings. Often, the fathers themselves had been beaten or witnessed violence as children. For these men, violence became the norm, an acceptable and conventional method of resolving conflict or gaining and maintaining the upper hand in their relationships.

As in most self-help groups, the process of breaking out of this cycle begins by admitting that you have a problem. At the beginning of the hot January evening I spent at Doveton, the group formed a circle and each man took it in turn to do a 'check-in'. 'I'm Ron and I've got an anger problem', 'I'm Dave and I've got an anger problem and an attitude problem'. The voices followed each other like an incantation. Then the men described what had happened to them over the previous week, how they'd been feeling and whether there had been any occasions where they'd been on the point of lashing out. A few of them related anecdotes about situations where they might previously have become abusive or violent—for example, an argument over unpaid bills—which they'd managed to negotiate successfully without aggression.

About halfway through the check-in, a big, broad man in jeans and a tank-top with a biker's beard and tattoos down his arms began describing how he'd spoken to his wife on the phone a couple of nights before. She'd left him after a history of violence in their relationship. Now he wants her to come back. Halfway through his story, he broke down in tears. One of the other men took him in his arms and hugged him. The group murmured words of comfort and condolence.

Scenes like this one make it difficult not to feel that there is something unusual happening here, something out of the ordinary pattern of suburban Australian masculinity. For some of the men in the Doveton group, the emotional territory they visit on these Monday nights is so far from their everyday experience of what it is to be a man that they feel they're standing at the threshold of a revolution. Yet there's a paradox about groups such as this one. Hearing the men tell their stories, I felt a wave of sympathy for their honesty and courage before the others in the group, the way they were prepared to make themselves vulnerable and show emotion openly in a way they'd never dream of at the pub, or in any of the other settings where men get together. But, I had to keep telling myself, these very men have beaten their wives and children, often repeatedly, and in some cases forced their families to live under a reign of terror in their own homes.

This paradox has shaped much of the public controversy about the work done by men's violence groups, which have taken a long time to be accepted as a legitimate response to domestic violence. Interestingly, some of the strongest support for the groups (as well as the fiercest opposition) has come from women. Alison Newton, who's worked with women and children victims of domestic violence in a poor suburb of Adelaide for 15 years, describes the men who join such groups as 'trailblazers', leading the way for other men to renounce violence and find new ways of negotiating their relationships with women. Courses and groups similar to the one at Doveton have existed in Melbourne and Adelaide since the early 1980s (there are now around 30 operating in metropolitan Melbourne alone), and they are now well established in most States, with the exception of New South Wales.

Nearly all the men who attend these groups are there because of a crisis in their relationships brought on by violence. Some of them, like Dave, are there because the law has put them there, usually as a mandatory alternative to prison. Others join because their wives or partners have left them, or threatened to leave unless they do something about their violence. They come from a broad range of class backgrounds and occupations: in the groups I visited there were teachers, plumbers, machine operators, engineers, small businessmen, social workers and train drivers.

My own view is that these groups represent the unseen and unacknowledged face of the men's movement, a face much less visible in the media than the Sensitive New Age Guy or the Born-Again Blokes, but much more significant as a symptom of real change among Australian men. This might seem a bold claim to make, especially since the great majority of Australian men are not violent in their intimate relationships. Surely, it could be argued, the experience of men who pass through the groups is so extreme, their behaviour so atypical it does not have much relevance to men in normal, non-violent relationships?

I don't for a moment want to suggest that a propensity to violence is lurking in the breasts of all Australian males. However, much of the work of the anti-violence groups involves changing attitudes as much as behaviour and, in particular, attitudes to power: who should exercise it and how it should be exercised. It seems to me that what goes on in the groups gives us valuable insights that go beyond the immediate context of dealing with violence and tell us something about the way men in our broader society see themselves and their place in the world. As well as the all-too-tangible common story of abuse, injury, manipulation and cruelty these men tell, there is a hidden story of isolation, loneliness, fear of intimacy and fear of abandonment, which runs through their lives; a story that resonates in the lives of many other men who have never struck a blow in anger.

THE MASK IN THE MIRROR

> There was one particular night—the first couple of weeks I didn't want to be at the course, I was only there because I had to be. One night we did this exercise where we had a mask, we had to close our eyes, look at ourselves in the mirror and see what we looked like—and that scared the hell out of me. After that I realised I did have a problem, and I had to work on it, and I became more involved in the group, like I should have been from the start. It was shock treatment—it was me looking at the mask and realising my wife and my children see me like that, that's enough to scare the hell out of anybody.
>
> Trevor, Box Hill Men's Violence Group

Men's violence groups do not aim to provide therapy for the men who join them. The men and women who run them make it very clear that 'violence is the issue'. Men come to the groups to learn how to stop using violence, not to embark on a voyage of self-discovery (though this often seems to happen as a side-effect). Again and again group leaders stress the point that the safety of women and children is their primary concern. Nothing that happens in the group should have the potential to make the lives of the men's families more dangerous. Most of the groups are highly structured and follow strict guidelines: men must take responsibility for themselves and their actions rather than blaming their partners ('She drove me to it'); they must be prepared to talk about their actions and beliefs, and be challenged by the group's leaders and other participants; and they must recognize that they cannot hope to change their partner's behaviour through attending the group, only their own.

Often, the first step is getting men to acknowledge that they are violent—or 'abusive', the common term used in the groups to take in both physical violence and psychological abuse.

> We've been married 25 years. From what I've learnt I could say now that I was abusive from before I was married. Sharon was two to three months pregnant when

> we were married . . . I think maybe I had some resentment about that.
>
> I never knew I was abusive. I thought I was a pretty loving sort of a husband. I thought, 'I'm alright, I never never hit her, I look after her, buy her clothes, make sure she's enjoying sex.'
>
> In the first session, I thought what am I here for . . . then I found out that mental abuse is considered by the women to be the worst of all, so I'm the worst of all.

Colin is an interstate locomotive driver. He's a lean, wiry man in his mid-40s. Every Thursday night he drives 300 kilometres from his home in Junee, in rural New South Wales, to attend a men's violence group in Campbelltown, in Sydney's outer south-west. There are very few such groups in New South Wales, and none in the country. Colin joined the Campbelltown group when his wife left him after 26 years of marriage. He told me that he was 'devastated' when she left. Like Dave, he didn't know that he was being abusive and thought of himself as a 'loving husband'. By his own account, he never hit his wife. Instead he maintained a reign of psychological terror, undermining his wife's self-confidence and convincing her that she was inadequate.

> I belittled her at times—I didn't even remember—I belittled her in the street—she didn't want to be hurt any more, she tried everything but nothing would ever be right, nothing was ever good enough.
>
> Even the sex—even if we were having it three times a day I'd question her afterwards to make sure she was enjoying it, and I have a way of questioning which becomes an inquisition—there's everything but thumbscrews. Then at the end of it we'd have sex to make up.

The crucial basis for the work that men's violence groups do is an assumption that all abuse, whether physical or mental, centres around power and control. In Colin's marriage, his need to be in control extended to all areas of his and his wife's life together, especially their sex life:

> I figured if I couldn't average sex once a day minimum I was being short-changed, missing out. It was like a constant form of torture—I was brainwashing her all the time to convince her that we should be having sex once a day minimum. That was our average, that was what I was aiming for.
>
> With my shift-work I'm away 24–36 hours at a time, so I had to catch up to keep up the average—morning, noon and night.
>
> I wanted to, I still want to—but now I'm trying to back off, teach myself that less often is better . . . even mental abuse is violence, you've got to approach it in a non-violent way, and only with respect. It's hard though, I'm trying to forget the average, but it keeps coming back to my mind.

Colin's preoccupation with 'the average' might seem compulsive, almost pathological, but his need to enforce it, over and above any feelings his wife might have, reflects deeply ingrained attitudes about his role as a man and what that means in marriage.

> I expected when I first got married that I would be the breadwinner and the provider, that I would be the head of the household. Not much has changed, all the way through the marriage, I still believed all of that, that I was the protector and she would be the homemaker, the babysitter, the housecleaner, all the things a wife was expected to be. I expected her to do her duty in all things from housework to sex, that was her role.

What Colin's story makes plain is that his behaviour springs not from some dark well of pathological desires or sadism, but from perfectly commonplace assumptions about men's and women's roles, which have dominated what we might call the 'ideology of the family' for much of the last 200 years. It's precisely these assumptions that men's violence groups set out to expose and break down. The underlying aim of the groups is not simply to stop violence, but to effect a shift in the power balance within a relationship. They confront men with the recognition that giving up abuse means relinquishing power. We might characterize this shift by saying that it involves a man giving up the role of an absolute monarch or totalitarian despot, along with the means of subjugation employed in despotic regimes—compulsion, terror, inquisition and physical force—and becoming a citizen in a democracy, in which members have equal rights and equal responsibilities.

For many of the men, this shift means changing emotional habits and underlying attitudes, which have become entrenched over years—sometimes over a whole lifetime. Often, it's not only the man who has to make the step of admitting to himself that his relationship with his wife or partner is an abusive one. Women, too, may deny to family and friends—and to themselves—that there is anything 'wrong' with the relationship. Tim, another member of the Campbelltown men's violence group, told this story about how he had come to join the group. He's a plumber from Newcastle, who is in his early 30s, married with four children.

> Alison was leaving me. Some friends in Queensland sent us down a book . . . she said 'It sounds like this is domestic violence,' and it was—it was obvious, because there was physical abuse involved in our relationship. We'd been married for 11 years. There'd always been conflict, even when we were going out.
>
> She always said to me, 'You can't keep doing this.' She was building up to saying 'I've got the guts to leave you now, mate,' but she'd never quite get there.
>
> Then all of our children went to school and she was by herself and she started to reassess her life and she didn't like the way it was and so she said 'What am I doing here? I don't like this relationship, and I'm going to change it.'
>
> She didn't feel she had the same rights as me—I made it hard for her to do the things she wanted to do.

Like Colin, Tim says he didn't know he was an abusive husband and, also like Colin, he'd assumed that as head of the household, working ten hours a day to provide for a young family, he was entitled to make the decisions. For Tim, this was simply how it had been in his own family when he was growing up. His father, he says, was never physically violent, but controlled everything his mother and he and his brother did, often breaking things that belonged to them to punish them. When Tim's wife told him she was thinking of leaving, he agreed to have some counselling but found it didn't help. Since joining the Campbelltown group, however, he says that both he and she have noticed changes in their relationship.

> I know Alison more, have more of an understanding of how she feels—also I have more of an understanding of my feelings. Instead of being just angry and frustrated—I ask *Why* am I angry and frustrated?—instead of dismissing her feelings.
>
> She says I'm able to share my feelings more with her—instead of just clamming up or ranting and raving—it's more, 'This is what I'm feeling and why', then she can understand me a bit better, know where I'm coming from instead of just saying 'You're a turd, you're angry,' she's become more understanding of me—she'll ask why.

Interestingly, Tim also feels that this shift in their relationship has taken some of the burden off him as the provider.

> I've realized, OK this is a partnership, it's not all on my shoulders if things stuff up. Before if anything went wrong, if we went bankrupt or we lost the house or whatever, I would feel responsible, but these days it's more equal, we're both responsible.

Listening to Tim's story, and feeling his own sense of the possibilities and perspectives he'd never imagined before opening up in his life, it's all too easy to feel that this group offers some kind of miracle cure for marital problems. But stories like his and Colin's carry a dual and divided message: on the one hand, they show how much some men do want to change and, on the other, how much there still is to change at a social level before equality between men and women becomes the assumed starting point in their intimate relationships with one another.

In fact, the success of the groups is achieved through a long and difficult process of shifting attitudes over time, often in the face of strong resistance from the men in groups, who tend to believe that the blame for their behaviour lies with their partners and not with themselves. Once they begin to acknowledge their own responsibility for violence, they are asked to examine more closely the range of behaviour that can constitute abuse. Physical abuse is defined as any act of physical violence or aggression, from pushing, slapping, hitting or kicking through to assault with a weapon, rape or murder. Sheer superiority of physical strength can also create a climate of fear in which actual violence becomes unnecessary. Here's how Ron from the Doveton group described his relationship with his ex-wife:

> When I got angry, because I'm a large fellow, I'm six foot four, 22 stone, just getting angry and being as big as I am, just raising my voice would give most men cause to fear me. My ex-wife was five foot six—that gives you some idea of the fear that I could cause.
>
> I was always verbally abusing her, putting her down, telling her she couldn't do anything right, or saying to her 'you're making me feel like I'm nothing,' when in fact she was doing everything to please me, and I was throwing it back in her face.
>
> Every time we had an argument, I'd throw a tantrum—when you're as big as I am, you don't have to hit, you don't have to throw a plate, you don't have to put your fist through the wall, the effect is exactly the same.

More nebulous, but often more insidious, are the forms of emotional or psychological abuse: repeated questioning of the other person's ability to perform simple tasks, public humiliation, belittling or demeaning comments—in other words, any kind of behaviour calculated to undermine a partner's self-confidence and self-esteem. According to Dallas Colley, who's worked with both victims and perpetrators of domestic violence in South Australia for over 15 years, many women she has worked with say they find this kind of sustained psychological attack more damaging and harder to deal with than actual physical violence. 'I wish he'd just hit me and get it over with' is a sentiment often reported by women living in long-term abusive relationships.

These forms of psychological abuse are usually connected with an overpowering need to control. For example, a man might calculate the exact time he believes his wife should need to do the shopping or to go to the laundromat, and punish her if she exceeds this time. His desire to control may extend to the amount of money his wife spends, the friends she associates with and even the way she cooks his food. Any deviation from what he sees as appropriate behaviour is regarded as a direct challenge to his authority as a man. Rick, a guillotine operator, joined the Doveton support group at the insistence of his wife, after he'd threatened her with a crowbar. This physical threat was preceded by a long history of psychological abuse.

> I used to come home every night and, for no reason, that'd be it, I'd be pissed off straight away. I'd be happy at work and then just abuse the wife for no reason, just because something didn't go my way or I didn't get what I wanted. All of a sudden my wife decided she was going to have an opinion and I didn't like that—after all these years when I made all the decisions she was wanting to make her own decisions, spending money without consulting me, going out without consulting me, getting the phone bill over the top. All of a sudden that power was taken away from me and I didn't like that.

All of these examples make it clear that violence and psychological abuse are closely linked to the distribution of power in a relationship—power that is usually skewed in favour of the man. But what is also common to the stories of many of the men I've quoted is a pattern of emotional isolation. Typically, they reported that they had no close friends and that their only close relationship was with their wives. Many spoke of not trusting other men and not having anyone to talk to about their problems or emotional difficulties other than their wives. It's only when we start to fill in this side of the picture that the sometimes extraordinary lengths men go to to control their partners' lives begin to make sense. The face behind the 'mask in the mirror' is not necessarily an impassive visage motivated by calculation or cruelty. Often the mask conceals barely governed feelings of panic and terror at the thought that they might lose this, the one source of intimacy and emotional succour in their lives.

From their own accounts, it would seem that many of the men who attend men's violence groups experience quite dramatic changes in their own lives and the way they see themselves as men, changes that most of them feel are positive and liberating. For many of them, these changes flow from breaking out of their own isolation, having the opportunity for the first time to speak openly with other men about their personal lives, and feeling that they are no longer alone or unique in their abusive behaviour. We should remember, however, that the primary purpose of the groups is to stop violence against women and children and their success in doing this is the main criterion by which they should be judged. For most of the ten years that such groups have been in operation in Australia, there's been intense controversy about how effective they are in stopping domestic violence. Many of the sceptics also ask whether we should deal with domestic violence any differently from other kinds of violence, which are, after all, criminal acts and punishable as such.

THE PROS AND CONS OF 'PERPETRATORS' PROGRAMS'

> I came into doing this work quite by accident in 1982. After some persuasion I agreed to co-lead a men's group, and at the back of my mind I thought, 'I'll do it once

> to prove it doesn't work'. Now, some 40 or 50 groups later, I'm still doing it.
>
> Previously I worked with women—so I had a huge bias towards women and had heard a lot of women's stories about abuse by men. Here I was, as a woman and a feminist, almost going over to the enemy camp—and what I saw in that first group was men making serious attempts to not abuse their women partners.
>
> Dallas Colley, Domestic Violence Resource Unit, Adelaide

At first glance, it's hard to see how anyone could object to the idea of a social strategy that tries to stop men battering their wives. Commonsense suggests that if we really want to do something about domestic violence, we need to deal not only with the symptoms—the very real situation of the women and children who suffer injury, torment and, in some cases, death at the hands of the men who purport to love them—but also with the cause, namely, the men themselves. However, the very existence of groups for violent men, the question of who funds them and their relationship with the criminal justice system have all been hotly debated. In order to understand why this should be so, it's useful to look into the history of men's violence groups in Australia.

Much of the early work in Australia drew its inspiration and methods from the 'Duluth model' a highly structured program pioneered by the Domestic Violence Intervention Project in the American city of Duluth, Minnesota. The Duluth model has become the benchmark for working with violent men around the world. It places an absolute premium on the safety of the women and children who've been the victims of domestic violence. Its other basic premise is that men's violence groups—known variously in the United States as 'perpetrators' programs' and 'batterer intervention programs'—should operate in conjunction with the criminal justice system. The developers of the Duluth model believe this sends a very clear message to the men who join the groups that if they continue to use violence, they'll face the full force of the law. In other words, violence will not be tolerated, whether it occurs behind the living-room curtains or in a public place in the full view of witnesses. Only in this way, it's argued, can men be made to take what happens in the group seriously: '. . . the important lesson to be learnt is that only because legal sanctions precede, and remain in place during participation in the program, do the groups have some impact'.[2]

Although the Duluth model has been very influential in Australia, groups for men who use violence have evolved differently here and have not necessarily been closely linked to the criminal justice system. The basic principles of the Duluth model have been augmented and complemented by the work of Alan Jenkins, who developed a set of guidelines for counselling abusive men in Adelaide during the 1980s. Jenkins' book, *Invitations to Responsibility*, has become something of a Bible for those involved in running perpetrators' programs and is often recommended to the men who attend such programs.

Jenkins' approach rests on the recognition of a division of emotional labour in society paralleling the division of material labour—a notion that, as we've seen, can be traced back to the birth of the modern middle-class family in the late eighteenth century. Men, he says, have been used to exercising responsibility in business, on the factory floor, in government and in any number of public roles—but they have handed over the maintenance of their emotional lives to women. In so doing, they have absolved themselves of responsibility for their emotions and actions in the private sphere of the family.[3]

Jenkins encourages the men he works with—often on an individual basis as well as in groups—to take back this responsibility by considering what kind of relationship they want with their partners. Most violent men, he says, will admit that they don't like what they do, but haven't considered that there might be alternatives to violence. Most will say that they would prefer a relationship based on respect and affection rather than fear, but see the problems in their relationship stemming from their partner's behaviour and not their own. By inviting men to see that they can take responsibility for the nature of their relationships, and in so doing improve the quality of their relationships, Jenkins believes they can be induced to make long-term, lasting changes in an environment that, as he says, is both respectful and challenging, rather than confrontational.[4]

This approach is not without its critics, who believe that it shifts the emphasis away from preventing violence and other forms of abuse. In inviting the man to come out from behind the mask, Jenkins' critics argue that we as a society run the risk of allowing perpetrators' programs to become therapy sessions for men, rather than a practical means of ensuring the safety of women and children. I'll have more to say on this issue a little later.

Most groups in Australia employ a mix of elements from the Duluth model and Jenkins' approach. Perhaps the most trenchant objection to the groups, however, is one of basic philosophy rather than style. It springs from a belief that the groups represent a soft option for violent men, while sending a message to the rest of society that violence against women and children is not taken as seriously as other forms of violence.

The argument runs like this: If I walk up to a stranger in the supermarket, the street or the cinema and punch or kick her (or him), there is a strong chance that I will be charged with assault, and the possibility that I will receive a prison sentence if that assault caused bodily harm. However, if I assault my wife or partner in the privacy of my own home, my solicitor might argue in court that instead of going to prison I should attend a perpetrators' program, where I will make a sincere effort to end my violent behaviour. Opponents of such programs argue that this approach simply reinforces an existing double standard where violence in the home and, more explicitly, violence against women and children is seen as less serious than other forms of violence, and is not treated with the same severity by the law.

There is considerable force in this reasoning, not least because of what we might term the creeping legitimization of violence in the broader society. It is not at all uncommon now to read reports of youthful celebrities in the United States who go on the rampage at parties, commit acts of violence, and are subsequently given suspended sentences by the courts and ordered to attend an 'anger management' program. This measure is by no means confined to men: Courtney Love, the tough-talking, hard-living singer and leader of the band Hole, was sent on such a program by a court after assaulting a fellow female musician backstage at a pop festival.

Certainly there are strong civil libertarian arguments for alternatives to incarceration, but there's also danger in a trend that would see more and more violent offenders prescribed a course in anger management. The danger is that we pathologize 'anti-social' behaviour by regarding it as a symptom of illness, rather than a failure to behave ethically towards other human beings. The more we regard displays of aggression as pathological, the less scope there is for emphasis on individual responsibility in the use of aggression.

The notion that men hit or lash out because they're unable to 'manage' their anger implies that they are not in control, that they are the victims of their own emotions. However, this is a notion that proponents of strategies for dealing with violence such as the Duluth model have worked very hard to refute. They see violence not as a loss of control, but as a means of asserting and maintaining control over others. Harvey Tuck, who works with violent offenders in the Victorian prison system, describes the distinction in this way:

> When you ask men, 'are you violent?', the man's excuse—the one he gives to his wife—is, 'I'm sorry darling I lost control'. He wakes up in the morning, he can look at himself in the mirror and say, 'I'm not a

> violent man, I lost control'. It's comfortable for him—but for everyone else it makes it worse. If you believe that the man in your life loses control, you are never safe, because he can lose control at any moment, you are constantly in a state of fear. If that fear controls you, that man never has to be violent ever again.
>
> So people learn to be careful and cautious, and that's one of the issues in addressing male responsibility—it's not that you lost control, but you wanted control, you took control, you used violence to establish control, and you had a choice every step along the line. When you push that line with men, they say yeah, actually that's true.

If, as a society, we treat violence as the product of an individual's dysfunctional emotional adjustment, and respond to it with an approach that is essentially therapeutic, there is some danger that we will institutionalize a defence of 'diminished responsibility'. This is why many people who work directly with the victims of domestic violence, whether in women's refuges, the court system or the police force, argue that men's violence groups should operate in tandem with the criminal justice system, and should not be allowed to cushion the full force of the law. Family Court Judge Sally Brown, who became interested in the pros and cons of groups for violent men while a Justice of the Magistrates' Court, says the proper place for the groups may be in prisons while the men are actually serving a sentence.

> I don't think the violence itself can be negotiable. If there has been extreme violence—and I mean incidents of broken jaws, lacerations, kettles of boiling water poured over people—I don't think it's consistent with the principles of the criminal justice system to say if you'd done that to a stranger you would get a gaol sentence, but because you've done that to your partner you can go off and get a bit of counselling. Somehow or other we have to strike a balance between the needs of the victims, a desire to change the behaviour of the perpetrators and a desire not to treat the perpetrators of domestic violence more leniently than other violent people.

There are, however, a number of problems associated with this approach. One is that not all violent or abusive relationships involve violence of the order described by Justice Brown. As we've heard, some involve no actual physical violence at all, yet women may find psychological and emotional abuse just as debilitating and destructive as being hit.

A more complex problem is presented by the fact that many women who have been involved in a violent relationship may not wish the man to be sent to prison, or even necessarily to be charged with a criminal offence. Nor may they wish to end the relationship altogether, though they may instigate a separation, hoping that this will shock the man into doing something about his behaviour. At the other end of the spectrum, many women may be too fearful of recrimination to call the police or lay a charge against a violent husband.

This has led some Australian states to pass legislation that shifts the onus for laying charges or applying for an apprehended violence order (AVO) from the victim to the police. The apprehended violence order, also known as a restraining order, is not a criminal charge, but sets out a series of restrictions on the man's behaviour, which are intended to ensure the safety of his partner and children. If the man breaks any of these restrictions, a criminal charge may be laid against him. In some jurisdictions in Australia, police now take a much more proactive approach in applying for such orders. Overall in New South Wales, 48 per cent of applications for apprehended violence orders are taken out by police. In the area covered by Burwood Local Court, an area where an integrated policy of close co-operation between police and the chamber magistrate, streamlining of the application process, and support and counselling for victims has been introduced, police make 89 per cent of applications for AVOs.

There are powerful arguments in support of this approach, perhaps the most important of which is that it sends a clear public signal that the justice system and society as a whole take domestic violence as seriously as other forms of violence. It may also instil a greater confidence in women that their cries for help will be heard and responded to. Bill Wheeler, the Clerk of Burwood Local Court, told me that the number of women withdrawing apprehended violence orders has declined steadily since the court introduced its integrated policy.

In some contexts, however, this approach may be inappropriate or even counterproductive. In some Aboriginal communities, there is often a strong aversion on the part of women to involving the police and the courts in cases of domestic violence. In particular, any action that might lead to an Aboriginal person being taken into custody and held in police cells may well be seen, for reasons that are all too clear, as something to be avoided at all costs. Under certain circumstances, responses to domestic violence that are predicated on police involvement with or without the express consent of the victim may actually discourage women from seeking help and reinforce their isolation.

Without in any way wanting to minimize the seriousness of domestic violence, there would seem to be a strong case for arguing that in important ways it *is* different from other forms of violence. If, as a victim, the person who has assaulted me is someone to whom I have a strong emotional attachment, and who professes to be equally attached to me, I may not wish to see that person punished, but rather assisted to change their behaviour. It's in cases such as these that groups for men who use violence can be seen to fill a social need.

Furthermore, the evidence from a number of recent studies conducted in Australia and overseas indicates that men's violence groups are most effective when the participants take part on their own initiative and of their own volition, rather than as a result of a court order.[5]

Although their relationship with the justice system continues to be a matter of controversy, the reality is that such groups are now well established in most states, with the exception of New South Wales. In Victoria, they now receive considerable funding from the state government. A co-ordinating body, the Victorian Network for the Prevention of Male Family Violence, has produced a manual setting out standards of practice for group leaders and facilitators and works closely with a number of women's organizations that represent the interests of the victims of violence. In other words, the groups are a fact of life. The question remains, however, as to whether or not they actually work. Do the women whose partners attend them notice a change in the man's attitude to them, and is there a cessation of violence?

Here, too, opinion is sharply divided. Jenny Nunn, a Domestic Violence Outreach Worker attached to a women's housing service in the outer south-western suburbs of Melbourne, told me that she'd stopped giving out information about men's groups in the area to women who wanted their violent partners to attend one. Her reason for doing so was the feedback she was getting from women whose partners had already been through a perpetrator's program. Consistently, she said, the women reported that while actual physical violence might have lessened or stopped, emotional or psychological abuse had actually increased while the men were attending a group.

This is a widespread criticism of the groups, but it tends to be based largely on anecdotal evidence. Sceptics and critics also cite recidivism among the men who attend the groups, lack of proper monitoring, and the danger that abusive men will learn new techniques of control and intimidation from each other as reasons why the groups should not be seen as a panacea for dealing with domestic violence. A further concern is that women may be lulled into a false sense of security by the fact that their partner is attending a group, and actually expose themselves to further violence by staying with him rather than choosing to leave.

However, advocates of the groups—among them many

women who, like Jenny Nunn, work with victims of violence—say that women *do* report positive effects from the groups, and that the very existence of such groups is helping to change community attitudes to men's violence. According to Alison Newton, who dubbed the men attending the groups 'trailblazers' when she began her career as a social worker in Adelaide's poor western suburbs 15 years ago, it was extremely rare for men to seek help for abusive behaviour on their own initiative. Now, she says, it's not rare at all, and she believes that if governments put sufficient resources into funding the groups 'we will see a lot of changes'.

Alison Newton's view has received considerable support from other practitioners working with violent men, and from overseas studies of the effectiveness of men's violence groups or 'perpetrators programs'.[6] The first Australian study, conducted by Dr Ruth Frances—a researcher in the Department of Criminology at the University of Melbourne—also gives the groups a positive report card.[7] Her study set out to evaluate the effectiveness of eight groups in suburban Melbourne over a three-year period, and specifically addressed issues such as the safety of victims, success in reducing levels of physical and psychological abuse, and positive effects reported by partners. Frances is at pains to stress that her findings do not amount to a scientifically verifiable assessment of the groups. As she points out, for ethical reasons a researcher could not set out to make such an assessment, since strictly scientific procedures would require the use of a control group with a 'no-intervention' policy, even if the researcher felt that any of the women in the control group were at risk from their partner's violence.

However, on the basis of interviews with 46 women whose partners were attending groups, Frances concludes that they do generate considerable benefits. The majority of women reported an improvement in their partner's behaviour and said the groups had been very effective in lessening violence. When asked to give concrete examples of how the man's participation had made a difference to their relationships, women gave responses such as: 'He stops and thinks before he flies off the handle,' 'He's calmer and more rational,' 'He talks more about his feelings,' 'He spends more time with the kids.' At the same time, Frances found that the women had a very realistic appraisal of the risks associated with staying with a violent partner and did not believe that those risks had disappeared simply because he was attending a group. Interestingly, many women also reported that their partners had sought help for their violence of their own volition, although the type of help they had found had not always been appropriate or effective.

Frances also has some trenchant criticisms of the groups, particularly in relation to the lack of formal training for group leaders, inconsistencies in the way they were run, and failure to deliver on promises made at the outset—such as maintaining regular contact with all women partners of men in the groups. But, overall, her assessment is positive, and lends force to the argument that the groups should be considered an important component in the way Australian society confronts men's use of violence against women. Frances' findings also reinforce the view that the existence of such groups has actually contributed to a franker and more open public discussion of domestic violence. According to Dale Hirst, who has been leading men's violence groups in Melbourne for some years, there's been a fundamental shift in community attitudes to violence in the last decade. Hirst says men are now much more likely to seek help for their violence, and are doing so in ever larger numbers. He no longer advertises the groups he runs, because the demand from men who hear about them by word of mouth is already more than he can meet. These impressions from someone working at the 'frontline' of domestic violence are borne out by a study of community attitudes to violence conducted by the Office of the Status of Women. The conspiracy of silence surrounding domestic violence is being broken more and more frequently, and violence against women and children is regarded as unacceptable under any circumstances by a majority of Australians. However, one effect of this heightened awareness of violence and a greater willingness to talk about it openly, has been the emergence of a new topic for debate, one that was previously taboo: women's violence against men.

VIOLENT WOMEN, BATTERED MEN

The victim's face is in shadow. Light pours in from a large window at the back of the room, offering up to the camera the trappings of an anonymous living room in an anonymous suburban home: television, VCR, empty bookshelves, coffee table, empty cups. 'I felt as though I was walking on eggshells the whole time,' he tells us, 'I lived in a constant state of fear.'

Future historians of relations between men and women in Australia may well decide to designate 1996 as the Year of the Battered Man. In the first weeks of the year, Channel 9's *A Current Affair* ran a report featuring testimony from a man who claimed to have been regularly kicked, punched and assaulted in other ways by his former wife. The man in question, Keith Shew, had lodged a complaint with the Human Rights and Equal Opportunity Commission claiming that he had been discriminated against by the Queensland Domestic Violence Resource Council, which he alleged had refused his request for help on the grounds that he was a man. Shew's complaint was dismissed—but he declared he would fight on in the High Court. In the same report on *A Current Affair*, a commentator from a men's rights group in Victoria told the reporter, 'Men are victims too'.[8]

This was, however, not the first time that a battered man had made an appearance in the Australian media. During the broadcast of the *Male Matters* series on Radio National, the original catalyst for this book, we received a number of calls and letters from men and women who felt that in our discussion of domestic violence, the voices of men who'd been assaulted or abused by women were being silenced or ignored. A one-hour talkback on the subject broadcast later in the year generated heated debate, with some callers claiming that the statistics on the incidence of domestic violence were being manipulated by feminists in government and the public service bureaucracies in order to make men look bad. The same claims were put forward again in an article published in the monthly magazine the *Independent* in November 1995.[9]

Domestic violence has emerged as one of the key areas in which some men's rights groups and Victim Masculinists have begun to argue that there is systemic bias against men. Their claims tend to centre on two issues: what statistics tell us about the prevalence of domestic violence and who's doing it; and the lack of support services for men who have been victims of abuse. Broadly speaking, they argue that women are just as likely to be violent in intimate relationships as men, and more likely than men to abuse or assault children. Men, they say, are being demonized and their needs ignored by a society dominated by feminist orthodoxy.

Interestingly, the spirit if not the substance of their claims has received support from one prominent Australian feminist, Beatrice Faust. Faust has argued in her newspaper columns and a recent pamphlet that some sections of the media—in particular *The Age* newspaper—and influential women's lobby groups have exaggerated levels of violence against women. In her view, contemporary feminism's preoccupation with violence and sexual assault runs the risk of turning all women into victims, and obscures concerns—such as poverty, lack of housing and unemployment which she believes are much more central to the well-being of the majority of women in Australia.[10]

It's not surprising that as men and 'men's issues' become part of the mainstream media agenda, violence emerges as a key area of contention, since it is intimately bound up with power. If some groups of men in Australian society want to represent themselves as powerless or disempowered as a consequence of being male, there is arguably no more shocking or provocative way of doing so than portraying themselves as the victims of physical violence inflicted by women. The image of the vulnerable, suffering male seems to be at one level potentially subversive, since it runs counter to a whole set of cultural stereotypes about the nature of masculinity. But just how true are the claims that there's a conspiracy of silence surrounding female violence? And what are the implications of acknowledging that women do batter men?

Debate about domestic violence in Australia is hampered to a certain extent by the fact that there is no comprehensive national statistical survey on the incidence of violence and who does what to whom. Much of the public rhetoric on the subject tends to fall back on evidence from overseas. *Behind Closed Doors: Violence in the American Family* was published in 1980 and updated ten years later, and is still considered to be the major authoritative study of domestic violence. It tells a surprising tale: the men and women interviewed by the authors admitted to roughly equal numbers of acts of physical aggression towards their partners. Moreover, a slightly higher percentage of men reported 'severe violence' committed against them by a female partner—including punching, kicking, hitting with an object, or assaults with a knife or gun—than women who said they'd been severely assaulted by a man.[11]

This pathbreaking study has been criticized on the basis that the authors' definition of violence was so broad it included behaviour such as 'raising one's voice', and consequently may have obscured actual levels of serious physical violence. However, its findings about gender equality in the ways that men and women use violence and experience it in their intimate relationships have not been widely publicized.

If we look at a breakdown of the data available in Australia, we can begin to understand the pitfalls in interpreting the findings of *Behind Closed Doors*. Beginning with the most serious form of domestic violence in which one partner kills the other, we can see that women make up 90 per cent of victims, according to figures gathered by the Victorian State Coroner. Deaths due to domestic violence also make up a much higher percentage of the total number of deaths due to violent assault among women than they do among men.[12]

Turning now to non-fatal injuries inflicted as a result of domestic violence, women still clearly and unambiguously outnumber men. A study run over three years by the Monash University Accident Research Centre, using information from the Victorian Injury Surveillance System, surveyed people who came into the casualty departments of a number of major Melbourne hospitals for treatment. According to this study, five times as many women as men presented with injuries they reported as having been inflicted by their partner. Injuries were broken down into categories. In cases where patients specifically identified their partner as the assailant, 90 per cent of those patients who'd been hit by the other person (or by an object wielded by them) were women and 10 per cent were men. Nearly 100 per cent of patients with injuries incurred by being pushed or thrown were women. However, in the case of injuries caused by being 'grazed, abraded, lacerated or punctured by an object', 64 per cent of victims were men. The weapon used in inflicting these injuries was most often a knife or window glass. Overall, women with injuries inflicted by a domestic partner outnumbered men by five to one. However, three times as many men as women were admitted to hospital as a result of those injuries.

This figure has been seized on by advocates of the 'feminist conspiracy' theory as evidence that women can be as prone to committing acts of violence as men, and are indeed more likely to inflict serious injury on their victims than men. John Coochey, an economist in the federal public service, wrote in the *Independent* that the Monash study showed 'surprisingly high levels of admissions for men who were victims of domestic violence'.

In some senses, this figure is surprising. However, set against the figures for murder and manslaughter included in the same survey (and conveniently ignored by Coochey) it suggests that women are much less likely than men to resort to violence that does not involve a weapon. Where weapons are used, women are much less effective than men at inflicting fatal injury.

Given the ways in which statistics can be used and abused for political ends, it's important that the statistical basis for public debate about domestic violence be as clear and reliable as possible. However, there's something profoundly distasteful about the recriminative approach adopted by Coochey and his supporters. In my view, it is in the interests of both men and women to recognize that women do engage in abusive behaviour in intimate relationships and that women are sometimes violent. But this does not make male violence any more acceptable. In Dave's story, which opens this chapter, his partner actually 'threw a few punches' before he threw her a right hook. However, Dave doesn't believe that this justified his retaliation, for the simple reason that sheer superiority of physical strength meant that he could do a great deal more damage to his partner than she could do to him. This is a recurrent theme in the stories of the men I spoke to, men who had themselves been violent: men's greater strength and stature not only gives them more power to harm with their bare hands than women, but also a greater capacity to intimidate. It's pernicious to ignore this imbalance when comparing men's and women's engagement in violent or abusive behaviour towards their partners.

Nevertheless, I think there are a number of reasons why a more open acknowledgement that women are sometimes violent and men are sometimes victims would benefit both sexes. To begin with, we might avert the danger of forcing women back into the sexual straitjacket from which they have spent a large part of the last hundred years escaping. Unlike Beatrice Faust, I do not believe that generating greater public awareness about women's experience of domestic violence will make all women into victims. If Dr Faust had spent more time in community health centres, district courts and women's housing services, she would have found that the majority of workers there direct their efforts towards getting women out of a 'victim mentality' and trying to provide them with the concrete means either to leave an abusive relationship, or to confront the abusive behaviour of their partner in a way that will lead to change.

However, as Faust points out, the media's predilection for apocalyptic language—speaking, for example, of a 'War Against Women' or an 'epidemic' of domestic violence—is not doing women any favours. The subtle danger of stirring up a moral panic that casts men always in the role of perpetrators of violence, and women always as victims, is that women are put back on their nineteenth-century pedestal. By portraying women as innately nurturing, non-aggressive and peace-loving, some 'essentialist' strands of the women's movement have been complicit in this tendency.

Contemporary feminism has largely left essentialism behind, but some pro-feminist men seem, with the best of intentions, to have taken it on in their tendency to morally idealize women and demonize men. To deny women's capacity for violence and aggression is to deny their participation in the full repertoire of human possibility and complexity, and to truncate their existence as moral beings. Anne Campbell, a criminologist and psychologist who has spent 20 years studying female aggression among girls in remand homes and street gangs, makes this point forcefully in a recent book:

> However distasteful it may be politically to some ideological stakeholders, women are not only victims. They

> are as capable as men of being aggressors. What is perhaps surprising is the absence of domestic aggression by the vast majority of women who are subject to the double and conflicting demands of work and home, with initiative and competitiveness demanded by one and subservience and co-operation required by the other. To deny the legitimacy of studying women's aggression in the home is a sad loss for our understanding of aggression, but, equally important, it does a grave injustice to women to recognize them only as victims rather than as active agents. By sterotyping them as helpless and passive, we sorely underestimate and oversimplify their complex and often conflicted sense of their own rights.[13]

Another reason for a more open approach to the issue of female aggression is the possibility that the testimonies of men who've suffered abuse by a female partner may elicit from other men a greater understanding of what it's like to be on the receiving end of violence, and result in a greater empathy with women who suffer in this way. The danger is that such openness may encourage point-scoring exercises such as those engaged in by people like John Coochey, which are as much about denying the scope and seriousness of women's experience of violence as they are about acknowledging the reality of the battered man. Interestingly, though they are as yet only in their infancy, support services for gay men who've been assaulted by their male partners are starting to emerge—as well as support services for lesbians who've suffered violence at the hands of their female partners or been violent themselves. There's already recognition that abuse and violence occur in the context of both gay and lesbian relationships. There is no reason why we should not begin to provide services for heterosexual men who've been victims of domestic violence, rather than portraying them as 'wimps' simply because they choose to speak openly about their experiences.

As we've seen, men's violence groups work on the assumption that violence and abuse are tied up with power. As people begin to speak more openly about women's use of violence in intimate relationships, they will need to address the ways in which women exercise power in those relationships when they become abusive. This will also involve a recognition that women sometimes engage in psychological abuse of their male (or female) partners, as well as actual physical violence. One step in this direction is to seek a better understanding of what different meanings may be attached to the ways that men and women use aggression.

MEN, WOMEN AND THE MEANINGS OF AGGRESSION

> I done it. I was the only one in the house so I obviously done it. I did admit to them that yes I did hit him in the head with the axe but if my life depended on it I couldn't tell them how many times, because I just don't know.
>
> He didn't treat me like a wife, he treated me like I was a dog. His exact words were that because I was his wife I had to do everything that he said when he said I had to do it. It's not very nice and I don't want it written in the papers but I know youse are probably going to write it anyway . . . he used to rape me if he wanted sex, and if I didn't want it he would just rape me anyway. To him because I was his wife I was his property and he owned me, that was his exact words, I was his wife and he owned me.

Sheree Lee Seakins was charged with the murder of her husband in Darwin in 1993, after admitting she'd struck him several times with the blunt end of an axe. The Northern Territory's Director of Public Prosecutions subsequently dropped the charges, citing 'insufficient evidence', despite Seakins' admission that she had administered the blows.[14]

The Seakins case is worth recalling because it throws into sharp relief the different ways in which men and women experience violence in intimate relationships, and the differing circumstances that lead them to assault a partner with deadly force. Very few men experience repeated rape or sexual assault by a female partner. For women in long-term abusive relationships, however, rape or the routine use of sexual coercion by their male partner is a commonly reported experience. Moreover, in nearly all cases where a woman kills her husband, she has been subjected to a period of protracted abuse beforehand.[15] Very few men are routinely threatened with guns by their wives, and very few husbands are told by their wives that they are property, like a domestic animal, and must consequently be obedient at all times or be punished. Yet the testimonies of women who've been in violent relationships reveal that these kinds of abuse crop up again and again.

What these testimonies and Sheree Lee Seakins' account of her own marriage make very clear—a point that's been stressed throughout this chapter—is that aggression and violence are deployed by men as a means of asserting control. In other words, men have an *instrumental* understanding of violence: it is a means, or instrument, used to achieve an end. According to Anne Campbell, there is a fundamental difference in the way men and women understand the meaning of aggression, because it performs different functions.

Campbell argues that men learn the instrumental use of aggression as boys in the schoolyard, where fighting, threats and displays of bravado regulate the pecking order, and establish status and popularity. They learn by example that aggression, strategically deployed, pays dividends and, conversely, that challenges to their autonomy or control over their lives must be met with reciprocal aggression.

For women, by contrast, aggression has an expressive function. Rather than being a means to an end, it is an end in itself, a cathartic release of tension and frustration. We can understand this better if we look at the differing ways in which men and women respond to stress. Campbell cites a study that charted the relationship between levels of stress (caused by factors such as losing one's job, children getting into trouble at school, illness and so on) and the use of violence by men and women in relationships. The study found that while men's levels of aggression rose steadily in proportion to the amount of stress they were under, women's aggression remained low until stress became intense, at which point women's aggression would characteristically 'explode'. Women, says Campbell, are socialized to control their own aggression and keep a much tighter rein on it than men. When they actually express it physically or, more often, verbally, their anger functions as a kind of expressive code for a number of other emotions that are being expressed at the same time: frustration, desperation, depression, and also insecurity and a desire for sympathy and support.

The problem, according to Campbell, is that men and women misread each other's codes, because they assume that the meaning of aggression is the same for the opposite sex as it is for their own. Thus women tend to interpret men's aggression as an expression of irritation or frustration, and often look for the source of this within themselves. Men, on the other hand, interpret aggression from their female partner as a challenge to their authority, and react by going on the offensive themselves.[16] This mutual misreading can lead to a cycle of escalating aggression in which both partners become physically violent. However, in abusive relationships, the more common pattern is that the woman's self-confidence and sense of autonomy are eroded by the man's aggression, causing her to become more and more cautious and controlled, while the man reads any sign of dissatisfaction as a direct threat to his authority. In the most severe cases, this pattern can lead to a situation such as the one in which Sheree Lee Seakins killed her husband: an intense expressive outburst of aggression under extreme duress. Men's use of fatal violence follows a different script. For a man who kills 'habituated to violence as a means of controlling his wife and maintaining self-esteem, her death is the final stop on a tragic journey from intimacy to isolation and from dependence to ultimate power'.[17]

There are, of course, a whole set of social and cultural mechanisms that teach men and women to put checks and balances on aggression. But, Campbell argues, intimate relationships pose a dilemma for men because the achievement of intimacy involves a surrender of control. Most men manage to achieve a balance between these two imperatives, and are able to enter into a world where emotions and actions cease to be purely instrumental. Abusive men, while possessing a strong need for intimacy, find this world too threatening, and tend to return quickly to the world of ends and means, where the calculated use of aggression enables them to maintain control over the person with whom they are intimate.

Anne Campbell's work offers a range of illuminating insights into the different ways in which men and women use and understand violence. There's a danger, however, that in applying these insights too rigidly, we may simply create a new set of gender stereotypes, a point illustrated vividly by the following story.

Steve was arrested by police in the northern suburbs of Melbourne after going on what he describes as a 'rampage'. Married for 12 years and the father of four children, when I met him he was living at Phoenix House, a community house set up by the Uniting Church with state government assistance to provide accommodation for men who've been violent, in order that their families won't have to leave their homes. Steve has spent his adult life moving in and out of paid work, drinking and smoking a lot of marijuana. He's in his mid-30s, long and lean, with tattoos swimming up and down his biceps and a sense of suppressed energy about the way he holds himself. His body and manner of speech suggest a jack-in-the-box who's spent too long coiled up inside the box. Here's how he described the way he ended up at Phoenix House:

> My wife stopped me drinking. She comes from a non-drinking family and she couldn't cope with it. My mates

were coming round, we had a brand new billiard table, and they'd ask, 'You don't mind me drinking, do you?'

I'd say, nah, it's sweet, but pretty soon I started sneaking it out the back of the house. My wife cottoned on to me, smelt it on my breath, straight away she went off her head, told me to get out.

So I took off up to Mt Disappointment, where I normally go when I'm told to get out, because I like my freedom, took a slab and a bottle of Bundy, started drinking, walked round up there in the dark and fell off a cliff. It wasn't very steep, and I ended up in a creek, then I was walking around in the dark for three hours, saturated, couldn't find my car.

Eventually I found me car, drove back down to town and went on a rampage through Melbourne. I knew I was going crazy, I would have done some damage, I was going against traffic down the Sydney Road, I was going to kill someone with my car, it was the weapon. Then I pulled up, ranting and raving at this place I used to work, a panelbeater's. I saw this bloke I knew, I was yelling out hit me, you have to hit me, 'cause I knew he was a wild bloke.

I was getting really angry, trying to get people to beat me up, doing all the sorts of things that'd make someone think, I'll give him a hiding, but no-one would beat me up.

I ended up going back home, my wife wouldn't let me in. I kicked the front door but didn't really damage it, she called the police, I went to the boot of the car, grabbed my cans, the police come, followed me up the middle of the road. I kept telling them to stay back, stay back. They ended up putting me down about half a kilometre away, and arrested me.

Given the recent record of the Victorian Police Force, Steve is probably lucky to be still above ground. What's remarkable about this odyssey of self-destruction is the way in which it combines 'instrumental' and 'expressive' aggression. Steve has a long history of violence in the home. He admits to having hit his wife on a few isolated occasions (once he broke an acoustic guitar over her head), but most often, by his own account, his aggression took other forms.

> I do a lot of verbal abuse, I'll smash the house, but won't touch the family. One time I was stoking the fire, she told me, she said, 'Kids, your dad's started drinking again, watch him smash the house up'. Normally I smash holes in the walls, but I had the iron in the fire, and I started burning down my arm. It took the steam out, it was all starting to build up, from what she was saying, and I thought I was going to explode and do what she was saying to the kids, but I thought, I'll try this method instead, I started burning me arms and it just pulled me down straight away, felt like I got the sort of pleasure I would have got when I smashed the house up.

There's plainly an element of instrumental, controlling aggression in Steve's propensity to smash the house up. But his description of the 'steam' building up, and his discovery that he could release it and achieve catharsis by burning himself, indicates that for him aggression also has a strong expressive function, and acts as a cry for recognition of his inner pain. This came out even more strongly when I asked him why, in the course of his rampage, he'd tried to get himself beaten up:

> It would have let out something inside me, it was just like something was inside me and I needed to be kicked senseless, just to let out my anger.

It's a commonplace among social workers who work with delinquent youth that boys tend to express alienation, frustration and aggression by 'acting out', seeking attention through publicly destructive behaviour, while girls are much more likely to harm themselves. Steve's story shows us both kinds of behaviour side-by-side.

The presence of both instrumental and expressive elements in Steve's use of aggression may not be of much practical comfort to Steve's wife and children, who have to put up with his outbreaks of violence. However, his story suggests that working with men who use violence by focusing only on issues related to power and control—

the instrumental dimension—may not go far enough. Confronting men with their need to control, and exposing the belief system that leads them to think they are entitled to do so, is the first step towards insight—the shock of recognition that makes the scales fall from their eyes. It's also a crucial element in ensuring the safety of their partners and children. But, also, we need to pay attention to the expressive elements in their aggression, to give them strategies for dealing with the greater vulnerability the surrender of control carries with it.

The need for such strategies is already beginning to be recognized in the changing orientation of groups such as the one I visited in Doveton. Men who come to the group seeking help for their violence begin by attending two five-week units on stopping violence. They can then continue with a further 30 weeks of group work covering areas such as assertiveness, sexuality and grief, self-confidence and self-esteem. These units are also open to men who don't have a problem with violence. Between 40 and 50 men attend the groups at Doveton every Thursday night and according to Rod Greenaway, who co-ordinates the courses and has been working with men for a decade, the demand far outstrips the number of places they are able to supply.

To close this chapter, I want to return to the question posed earlier: whether or not we can justifiably see the men who attend these groups as 'trailblazers' and, if so, what their pioneering work means for the much larger body of men who have not yet set out along the trail and who may see no need to do so, since they themselves are not violent. Greenaway believes that the work done in men's violence groups can be, and has already proved to be, a catalyst for a greater awareness of the factors that cause men to lead lives exiled from their own emotions, at once needful and fearful of intimacy, with no language to articulate these needs and fears except the language of aggression. In this sense, I would argue, the men who attend such groups can rightfully be seen as trailblazers, since the questions they confront are at the core of transforming not only the relationships between men and women, but those between men and men as well. Moreover, the overwhelmingly positive ways in which men talk about the atmosphere in the groups, the sense of revelation at experiencing a powerful solidarity between men—what Ruth Frances refers to somewhat cheekily as 'mateship without the beer'—can provide a stimulus to men to confront broader issues of power and privilege in our society.

In another sense, the issues raised in men's violence groups have a very real bearing on the lives and experience of men who may not be violent themselves, but who are involved in relationships with women. As we've seen, the groups work on the principle that there are many forms of abuse, but all of them revolve around power and all of them need to be challenged. Issues of power raise the interesting question of whether or not *any* relationship can be truly 'abuse-free'. Most of us, at some point, are guilty of engaging in 'abusive' behaviour towards our partners. All of us, in certain situations, will try to manipulate our partners, threaten them or undermine them in order to get what we want or assert our control. Moreover, this is a game played by both sexes: women are just as capable as men are of engaging in controlling and manipulative behaviour, of undermining their partner's sense of self-respect and self-esteem, and of belittling and humiliating them.

To imagine relationships entirely free of abuse is, in one sense, to imagine relationships in which there is no exercise of power by either partner. On the one hand, it's difficult to imagine such unions surviving, since the contest between partners over power is often what lends a relationship its energy, and its potential for change and growth. However, many of the power struggles enacted between men and women in relationships are purely destructive, compulsive cycles repeated again and again because the participants know no way of breaking out of them. Our culture offers men and women very few resources for coming to understand the patterns of power and domination in intimate relationships, or indeed many practical tools for changing these patterns. It's by no means impossible for women and men to create relationships based on a fundamental respect for the integrity of the other person, and on that person's right to be considered an equal with their own legitimate needs, values and aspirations. More democracy in our intimate lives does not mean relationships will be less dynamic, either emotionally or sexually. However, we have very few models for how a genuine 'intimate democracy' might be achieved. The next chapter explores how we might begin to create such models.

5

Intimate experiments

> I think there's a lack of support for men from women. Women say they want men to be softer, to express their feelings—but at the same time, speaking from personal experience, if you drop the tough image, the armour—that's not what they want at all—they want someone they can hang off. I think there has to be a reassessment of who men and women are—not who we think they should be.

Bill's bewilderment (expressed during an interview with the author) is typical of many men of his age and background—mid-30s, middle-class, and in the midst of a deep confusion about their intimate relationships with women. Quietly spoken, articulate, a former Olympic sportsman, Bill holds an engineering degree and now works as an environmental consultant. He describes his early adulthood as driven by a fierce competitiveness and a distrust of the emotions. Recently, he's become involved in men's support and self-therapy groups. Bill believes that men's desire for change has arisen not only as a reaction to the demands of women, but from a deeply felt disinclination on the part of men like him to go on preserving the façade of conventional masculinity. Yet, as he would put it, he feels that women have not sufficiently 'honoured' men's attempts to fashion a new kind of manhood. A similar confusion was expressed by many of the men I spoke to in the course of writing this book.

In the foregoing chapters I've argued that this confusion arises partly out of a fundamental shift in the balance of power within the family and its place in society—the shift from an industrial to a post-industrial model of the family. However, the changing nature of the family is only part of the story. Not all men and women live in families, and those who do, or aspire to, have to negotiate a complex set of social and sexual codes in order to get there. Moreover, once they are there, it is less and less clear what they should be doing and how they should behave towards one another. This, among other things, may well account for the popular revival of Jane Austen's fiction in the cinema and on television: Austen's characters inhabit a world in which social relations between men and women are governed by a strict set of codes and conventions, designed primarily to guide them into the arms of a suitable partner. Once this has been achieved, the curtain falls: what goes on between a man and woman after they are married is assumed to be entirely unproblematic.

In our own time, it is often what happens once a man and a woman come together as partners that proves to be most problematic of all. The codes that govern our intimate relations are becoming less and less clearly defined. This is why bookshops are full of a seemingly ever-expanding number of self-help handbooks and manuals, which set out to explain to one sex what it is the other sex wants, is thinking, or thinks it wants. Our collective hunger for guidance in matters of the heart has made men like John Gray, the author of *Men Are from Mars, Women Are from Venus*, into wealthy celebrities. Many people find these books extremely useful as a way of understanding and changing patterns of conflict and miscommunication in their relationships. However, the majority of these manuals take it for granted that whatever cracks have appeared in the heterosexual-pair bond can be fixed up with some judicious alterations and renovations. They assure us that the needs and aspirations of men and women can be brought to some common denominator, if only we can learn to communicate better.

Very few of the self-help manuals entertain the possibility that the whole edifice of the pair bond itself is crumbling as its foundations come adrift. Rarely does anyone pause to entertain the possibility that in fact families that are 'functional' for men may be dysfunctional for women and children—or vice versa—or that we may not be able to arrive at some harmonious accommodation of men's and women's needs because they are now different and, in some cases, diametrically opposed.

In Chapter 4 we considered some accounts of what happens when violence enters intimate relationships as a way of gaining and retaining power over one's partner—accounts of the heterosexual-pair bond under extreme stress. Violence is not part of the everyday reality of most men's and women's relationships with each other, but power and the contest for power are. If we want to understand better the sorts of practical, everyday difficulties Bill describes, we need to begin unravelling the complex and shifting dynamics of power, attachment and sexual desire lying behind them; dynamics that have been thrown into an unprecedented state of unpredictable and mercurial fluidity by the end of the industrial era. In particular, we need to understand what happens when men begin to give up certain kinds of power in their relationships, as some of the men in the anti-violence groups have done.

Addressing these questions, Anthony Giddens has developed a very useful and practical notion—the idea that, faced with the sorts of social changes I've outlined, we are forced to conduct 'everyday social experiments' in our own lives in order to deal with them.[1] Giddens bases many of his arguments on British and American research on changing attitudes to sexuality, marriage and relationships, but his arguments are no less applicable to Australia. The value of his idea is that it stresses the improvised nature of modern relationships, the sense that we make them up as we go along, in response to the broader social changes that surround us yet, at the same time, developing new modes of feeling and forms of relationship in individual and practical ways.

Giddens sees men as largely on the back foot in this process, reacting to women's initiatives rather than initiating experiments themselves—a view that concords with the testimonies of many of the men I've interviewed. This is hardly surprising, since most often such experiments require men to give up power and privileges within a relationship. In Chapter 4 we met Tim, who was violent with his wife Alison for ten years before joining an anti-violence group. Tim has been forced to reassess completely all of his assumptions about who was entitled to hold power in their relationship, and to relinquish the control he'd exercised over Alison's life. This is how Tim describes the experiment on which he's embarked:

> Women have changed their expectations. They know what they want out of a relationship and they go and get it. Men I think are a little bit slow—more set in their ways.
>
> I haven't got a right role model to say that's right and that's wrong—I've got to do it all myself—and there's the danger that some of this is politically correct—and it mightn't be right.
>
> That's the scary part. You've thrown it all up in the air, and you've got to pick up the right ones, leave the ones on the floor that are wrong.

The sense of a lack of rules and guidelines, of entering uncharted territory, Tim expresses here is a common sentiment among the men interviewed for this book. In the short term, it would be surprising if our experiments with new ways of engaging with one another were not fraught with disappointment and misunderstanding—as the sad case of the SNAG makes plain.

'YOU DON'T MAKE ME FEEL LIKE I'M A WOMAN ANY MORE'

One of the more extraordinary scenes that presented itself to the devotee of the Australian pub rock circuit during the late 1980s could be witnessed usually about halfway through any show by the Hunters and Collectors, at that time at the height of their fame and fortune. On the stage, the band sweated it out in singlets like a gang of engine stokers, while singer Mark Seymour climbed up onto the mighty locomotive of the music, body taut and face contorted with an almost unbearable intensity of desire to get it out, express, make his very soul visible in the smoky radiance of the stage lights. Out in the room, a mostly male crowd—tightly packed together and rocking from the waist up in worship, stubbies of beer cradled to their chests—gazed, rapt, at the band. All of a sudden, the drummer and the bass player would kick into a brutal backbeat, the horn section coming over the top as if they were trying to blast their way through solid granite, and when Seymour hit the chorus two or three hundred male voices out in the crowd would be raised in unison with him:

> You don't make me feel
> You don't make me feel
> You don't make me feel
> Like I'm a woman anymore

There was something touching about watching all these blokes sing along. They meant it. Whatever it was Seymour and the band were touching there, it brought an instinctive response, a rare moment of shared male recognition. It certainly wasn't an audience full of SNAGs, but the moment Seymour describes in the song—when his girlfriend 'jabs him in the breastbone' with her finger and says those words that make up the chorus—these guys had been there too.

If we were to speak of a malaise among Australian men in the 1990s, this sensation would be one of the primary symptoms—a nagging feeling in the back of men's minds that they don't really know any more how to make themselves desirable to women. The only new male role model the sexual revolution of the last 30 years has produced, the Sensitive New Age Guy, has not proved to be an entirely successful experiment. Martin, a marine biologist who has now become a full-time father looking after his small son, spent a long time trying to work out why:

> I sincerely feel there is a great deal of denial in modern feminists—about what they want intellectually in a man and what they want emotionally. As they see me strive to make myself more and more what they want me to be . . . they lose interest . . . they move on . . . yet they can't describe what it is they're missing.
>
> I've striven to be as sensitive as I thought the women in my life wanted me to be, and I wasn't comfortable myself, but I also sensed I wasn't providing the women in my life what they really needed.
>
> No other sets of roles were handed to me. What I was is no longer acceptable—but there were no substitute roles . . .

Martin now lives in a long-term relationship with the mother of his son but, as he says, both he and his partner have to strive constantly towards a balance in their relationship, and in doing so they have to overcome the 'inappropriate scripts' each has inherited about what their roles should be. In other words, they are engaged in an 'everyday social experiment'—which takes a great deal of effort and commitment to maintain.

The acronym SNAG is a uniquely Australian epithet. However, the male type it describes seems to be an international phenomenon. Hollywood, with a sure instinct for the emerging cultural stereotype, chose to slip the knife into the SNAG in Peter Weir's romantic comedy *Green Card*. Ebullient, temperamental, hard-drinking and heavy-smoking Gérard Dépardieu steals the heart of Andy MacDowell from her soft, sensitive, correct-line vegetarian boyfriend. In one sense, the cultural clichés Weir's film manipulates are old ones: the artist vanquishes the bourgeois and life triumphs over orthodoxy— MacDowell's SNAGgy boyfriend represents a new kind of orthodoxy. Ultimately, it seems, it's Dépardieu's sheer unashamed maleness that wins out, exemplified in the moment he dismisses the boyfriend as a sexual competitor with a single derisive exclamation: 'Cucumber!'.

Of course, Dépardieu's character is a stereotype. However, if we pause for a moment and ask ourselves what we mean by his maleness, it's clear that it resides in our feeling that he's comfortable, at ease with his body, his sexuality and himself. The 'Cucumber', by contrast, seems a rather pale and vapid creature, lacking a strong sense of who he is. It's as though he were putting on an act, but lacks the conviction to make the part come alive.

This feeling that the SNAG is somehow unauthentic, a con-man not entirely to be trusted, is a response common to both men and women. From a woman's point of view, this is hardly surprising—after all, what's in it for a man to give up power? Surely he must have some ulterior motive? Very often, of course, he does. Scratch a sensitive, sympathetic type and not too infrequently there will be an old-fashioned sexual predator underneath.

However, the more serious charge against the SNAG is that he has no sex appeal. The Australian rock journalist and editor of *Australian Style* magazine, Mark Mordue lays out the case in 'Mad Men', an angry piece of polemic written for, of all things, *New Woman*.[2] Mordue is angry because he feels that women have put one over on men. They've told men they want them to be more tender, sensitive, empathetic and gentle, but then they run off with the bad guys, outlaw types like Tex Perkins (singer with the highly successful band, The Cruel Sea) who exude what Mordue calls 'Dark Male Sexuality'.

Reading 'Mad Men', it's easy to mistake Mordue's tone for one of male self-pity and to overlook the genuine confusion that lies beneath it. Mordue claims to know a lot of men who've rejected the tough, sexually nomadic, love 'em and leave 'em ethos, which he sees exemplified in figures like Perkins. Perkins himself has written a song that captures this ethos, though not without a hint of self-irony. The scenario is familiar: it's half-past five in the morning, he's in some nameless hotel, 'half-alive', and he needs to talk to someone:

So I give her a call
And she says, Oh it's you
I know what you want
But what I need is a heart that's true
So I told her that I loved her
But I lied
'Cause sometimes you gotta fake that emotion
Sometimes you gotta lie about your devotion
Sometimes you gotta lie about your intentions
'Cause there are some things you'd be wise not to mention[3]

In fact, there's a certain vulnerability beneath the tough-guy Perkins persona, which comes to light in another song from the same album, in which he declares that he'd give 'anything in my miserable world/Just to show you where I've been scarred'.[4] Mordue's complaint, however, is that those men who choose not to bury their vulnerability so deep and reveal their 'scars' may find themselves spurned. He shares many of the sentiments expressed by Bill at the beginning of this chapter: the feeling that men have done what women asked them to, only to find that women are no longer interested. Mordue is inclined to lay the blame for the double-bind in which such men find themselves at the feet of feminism. There's a double standard at work here, he argues: feminists demonize Dark Male Sexuality in public, but are quite prepared to embrace it in the privacy of the bedroom.

In one sense, this is a phenomenon not tied to the particular moment in which we live. Qualities such as confidence, insouciance and self-possession are attractive in both men and women, and there is no shortage of examples in our literary and cultural traditions to suggest that the Dark Male Sexuality personified, in Mark Mordue's view, by a Tex Perkins or a Dennis Hopper, is anything other than a reincarnation of the magnetism of Don Juan. But it's the frame within which the Don Juan figure and his antithesis, the SNAG, make their appearance that is important here. We can get a better understanding of this if we move for a moment outside of the context of Australian sexual culture.

In her excellent book *XY: On Masculine Identity*, the French philosopher Elisabeth Badinter charts the rise and fall of the 'soft man' in contemporary Europe. The soft man first appeared in the Scandinavian countries, an invention of 'certain men . . . who, in order to please women who were castigating the macho man in the 1970s . . . felt they had to abandon all virility and adopt the most traditional female values and behaviours'.[5] Quoting the Danish novelist Herdis Moellehave, Badinter describes the genesis of the soft man as an alternative to the 'knot-man', the stereotypical traditional male, 'obsessed by competition, attached to his intellectual and sexual performance, handicapped emotionally, pleased with and sure of himself, aggressive, alcoholic and incapable of committing himself to other people'.[6] The soft man, by contrast, gives up all forms of male power and privilege, devotes himself to his partner's career rather than his own and participates fully in the running of the household. In his most extreme manifestation, he tends towards passivity and complaisance.

However, the European soft man appears to have been a very short-lived species. Over a decade ago, his demise was announced at a UNESCO conference on changing gender roles by Merete Gerlach-Nielsen, who had been studying masculine role models in Denmark. Gerlach-Nielsen reported that Scandinavian women were fed up with the soft man: 'even the women most responsive to gentleness on the part of men want nothing more to do with these men, who are ersatz traditional women . . . In 1984, the death of the soft-man was proclaimed.'[7]

Elisabeth Badinter is careful to point out that it may be somewhat premature to order wreaths for the soft man, noting that he appears to be alive and well on the other side of the Atlantic. However, her excursion into the sexual culture of the Scandinavian countries is illuminating, because it throws into sharp relief the reasons why women rejected this particular experiment with a new form of masculinity. Plainly, the adoption by men of 'feminine' values and virtues, particularly those such as passivity, which most women would no longer wish to espouse, was not a satisfactory alternative to the tyranny of the traditional knot-man.

What also begins to become apparent here is that men's responses to the challenge of feminism and the shifting balance of power between the sexes take on different forms and accents in different cultures. The SNAG as we know him is not necessarily identical to the soft man, nor do his brothers and cousins necessarily exist everywhere. According to Badinter, the soft man 'had so few followers in France that one cannot consider him a social phenomenon there'.[8] *Vive le Départdieu!* There may be the faintest tinge of good old-fashioned French nationalism in this statement. Badinter cites a female character in the novel *Les Samourais* by her feminist compatriot Julia Kristeva, who declares that 'a man, a real man, is a rare phenomenon in the United States'.[9] The qualities that make a real man in France also come as a surprise. A survey that asked French men about the personal qualities they thought most important in a man found that they valued honesty, determination and tenderness above all, followed by intelligence, good manners and seductiveness, with virility at the bottom of the list. Plainly the unpopularity of the soft man does not spring from the fact that all Frenchmen are unreconstructed chauvinists. The reasons Badinter gives are more complex and interesting.

She argues that it has not been necessary to create the soft man in France, because the enmity between men and women has never reached the same heights of intensity as it has in the English-speaking countries. The explanation for this, she believes, lies in the distinctive nature of French sexual culture: 'the importance we have always given to seduction, as well as our relationship to our bodies, our almost total ignorance of puritanism, our representation of the role of the mother . . . has resulted in the absence of any war between the sexes.'[10] These traditions, says Badinter, have also shaped the ways in which feminism has evolved in France. French feminism has, in her view, been less radical and uncompromising in tenor than its Anglo-Saxon or German counterparts, less inclined to polarization. Even in the heat of polemical battle, 'the Frenchwoman has never completely broken off her dialogue with her accomplice'. Consequently, Badinter believes, 'the solidarity between the sexes has survived everything, including the periods of sharpest questioning. Virility is less contested on this side of the Atlantic; the men here are not as violent, they have less fear of women, and vice versa. As a result, the problem of masculinity is less acute in France than elsewhere, though that does not stop it from plaguing all of us, men and women.'[11]

Subjective though these perceptions are, Badinter puts her finger on something deeply revealing: the extent to which masculinity may feel itself more threatened in some cultures than others. In a sense, she is saying the public and private assault on men's power has been a great deal fiercer in the United States than it has been in Europe. At the same time, she suggests, women and men were more alienated from each other in the first place in American society. Interestingly, too, she links men's fear of women in the United States with an ingrained puritanism about sexual matters—as well she might. It's instructive to compare, for example, the obsessive prurience with which the US media pursues the sexual indiscretions of its politicians, and the relaxed urbanity of the French. It was common knowledge that François Mitterand had a mistress for all of the time that he was President, and she attended his state funeral along with his wife.

Do Badinter's observations apply also to Australian men? We have no means of measuring the relative degrees of hostility between the sexes in France and Australia, or knowing whether men and women really understand each other any better in Lyon than they do in Lismore. But the degree of polarization between the sexes Badinter perceives in US society is echoed in the observations of Australian men like Bill:

> As we go through this new phase of men saying, 'Hey, I don't want to be this any more, this is not me,' there's bound to be some backlash. No-one likes change. I think there's bound to be a lot more polarization, we haven't started to see that yet, but after that there'll be a much healthier period ahead.

We can only hope. I think, though, that Bill goes to the heart of the matter in predicting that the divisions between the sexes are likely to get worse before they get better. I'm inclined to think also that some of the characteristics Elisabeth Badinter ascribes to American masculinity apply also in an Australian context, at least in the eyes of Australian women. Many of the women I spoke to in the course of writing this book expressed a feeling that their male compatriots find it difficult to relate to them as equals and were not at ease in the company of women.

It would be easy to brush this off as just another manifestation of the cultural cringe. Yet examples of open sexual hostility towards women in Australian culture are, sadly, not difficult to find. One notorious case in the North Queensland town of Ingham during the 1970s involved regular and ritualized pack rapes of one or two women by over 30 men. These rapes took place up to four times a week. It was common knowledge in the town that they were occurring, and yet there was no intervention from the police. Julianne Schultz, who investigated the Ingham case for the *National Times*, wrote afterwards of an extraordinary degree of resistance and denial among male journalists, who refused to take reports of the rapes seriously.[12] Yet at the same time, 'women were ringing in to a talkback program on 4AY Townsville to confirm the horrific extent of the allegations'.[13]

There's a more contemporary example in Nick

Enright's highly successful play *Black Rock*, which has also been made into a film. Based on real events surrounding the rape and murder of a young girl by some teenage boys at a surf club in Newcastle, *Black Rock* grew out of intensive workshops at a local youth theatre group. As such, we can assume it's a reasonably accurate document of attitudes of adolescent Australian males to women and their sexuality. Two emotions stand out in roughly equal measures: contempt and fear. The dead girl quickly becomes an object in the eyes of the male characters, who more or less believe she got what was coming to her. She and her female contemporaries are common sexual property, to be used and discarded at will. Yet, beneath the boys' ugly bravado, there's a current of terror, a suppressed awareness of their own emotional vulnerability, and the threat to it that any kind of equal or feeling relationship with the opposite sex represents.

In a way, the success of *Black Rock* and the fact that it could be written at all, attests to how much public attitudes to rape have changed, and how much more ready we are as a culture to engage with and confront the negative and destructive aspects of Australian masculinity. I don't believe for a moment that the majority of Australian men are chauvinists or misogynists. However, I do think there is some truth in the observation that our sexual culture has not encouraged equal and friendly relations between boys and girls, or men and women.

That it has not may have much to do with the early history of Australian society and its development during the nineteenth century. A stark imbalance between the sexes in the early years of colonisation, the absence of women in the settler towns on the frontier, and an ethos of 'untrammelled bachelorhood' led, according to the historian Raymond Evans, to a society in which 'men's physical and emotional absence from the home environment was validated, as they bonded with other males in a wifeless work and leisured world'.[14] During the later nineteenth century, the dominant Victorian middle-class ethos of 'Christian manliness' was gradually replaced by a new cult of 'muscular manliness' more suited to the needs and values of the colonial era, and this too had its influence on the development of Australian masculinity. This 'muscular manliness' is parodied in a memorable scene from the film *Sunday Too Far Away*, in which the shearers confront one of their number, a solitary type not given to joining in the drinking and general merriment. He's writing a letter when the character played by Jack Thompson, along with a number of the other men, ambles up to him and ask him who he's writing to. 'My wife,' he replies. This answer is greeted by hoots of derision, and a further question from Thompson: 'What are you? A poofter or something?'

Our society has, of course, changed out of all recognition in the course of the last century, not least because the dominance of Anglo-Saxon and Anglo-Celtic cultural traditions has been substantially eroded by immigration from continental Europe, the Middle East and Asia. In many ways, Australia has proved to be something of a social laboratory, both in its experiment with multiculturalism, and now, I would argue, in the field of gender relations. The familiar image of the suburban barbecue, where the men stand in one group all evening and the women in another, may be beginning to outwear its usefulness. But there's still a tendency for mainstream Anglo-Australian culture to produce Abashed Men, who feel discomfort, shame or even fear in the presence of women, and this can't be good for women or men.

In some ways, this tendency may also contribute to the failure of the SNAG as a viable male alternative. Men deal with their fear of women in a myriad of ways, but as we've seen from the previous chapter, many of their methods involve asserting and maintaining power over their female partners. The SNAG, often with the best of intentions, believes that he can redress the balance of power between the sexes by doing whatever it is he thinks women want him to do. Feminism has very successfully seized the moral high ground and the SNAG practices a kind of appeasement. But appeasement does not command respect. Moreover, for women this form of appeasement is in some ways profoundly frustrating, because it amounts to a strategy of avoidance. The man who cedes total moral authority to the woman in his life is choosing not to engage fully with her as a person, or with his own confused and contradictory attitudes to sex, love and power. Once again, he is renouncing responsibility.

However, the SNAG is not only afraid of women. He is also afraid of his own sexuality. He is less and less sure about what is appropriate sexual etiquette, or even about what kinds of behaviour may be construed as sexual. At the same time, he is receiving strong cultural messages from a number of sources that tell him that male sexuality is by nature predatory, exploitative, and inseparable from a desire for domination, which may spill over into violence at any moment. It is hardly surprising that some men who take these messages seriously begin to regard their sexuality as something alien, profoundly at odds with their desire for relationships with women that are equal, open and tender.

We might ask ourselves to what extent this portrait of male sexuality as demonic and destructive—which to many men and women will look very much like a caricature—is the reverse image or alter ego of that Dark Male Sexuality exemplified by the Tex Perkinses, James Deans and Robert De Niros of this world. Can we separate the two? Of course, not all men, or indeed most men, embody the kind of sexuality exuded by these hipster heros, or even necessarily want to. Nor does every woman want such a man as a mate. They are fantasy images, but fantasies are important precisely because they express desires we may not want to admit to, or even act out in real life. What these fantasies tell us is that sexual fascination is bound up with a certain kind of power: elusive, mercurial, careless of itself and others.

The mistake Mark Mordue makes is to assume that

this kind of power is acquired and wielded in only one way. Mordue falls victim to yet another male stereotype about what it is that 'women want', assuming that the sexual conqueror is always the man possessed of what used to be known as 'animal magnetism'. Plainly, both women and men wield sexual power as much through the exercise of such faculties as charm, humour, wit, intelligence—and, in some cases, by virtue of possessing actual power in the social and economic world.

Part of men's and women's difficulty in navigating the turbulent and murky waters of contemporary heterosexual relations springs, I think, from our ambivalent feelings about sexual power. We are troubled by the whole notion that power should play a role in what we conceive to be our most intimate experience of ourselves and others. At other times in history, and today in cultures other than our own, human beings have developed elaborate codes that lay out a series of—usually unspoken—rules on how sexual power is to be exercised—forms of sexual etiquette, we might call them.[15] In the Australia of the 1990s, all but the vestiges of such codes have disappeared. In a world in which the sexual economy has been largely de-regulated, some of us may long for the return of laws of desire. However, most women—and an increasing number of men—would not wish to return to the rigidly defined gender roles with which such laws were identified, or the kinds of power relations between the sexes they often encoded. The challenge for men now is to discover new forms of sexual engagement with women, and new sources of sexual power. As one woman put it to me, in a tone of mild exasperation: 'Men have to find some new way of making themselves attractive!' Yet, as Martin remarked earlier in this chapter, men are in a real dilemma in this regard, and often seem to receive little encouragement from women in their tentative strivings toward some new balance. Martin himself declares that he is searching for a model of the 'perfect man', one who can combine traditionally 'masculine' qualities of strength, courage and humour with 'feminine' qualities such as sensitivity, openness and emotional sophistication. The search to identify just what it is that makes a 'perfect man' is not a new one, nor is the attempt to set out some principles he should follow when wooing his love.

MANUALS FOR OLD AND NEW MEN

> Therefore in my view when the courtier wishes to declare his love he should do so by his actions rather than by speech, for a man's feelings are sometimes more clearly revealed by a sigh, a gesture of respect or a certain shyness than by volumes of words. . . . [But] those men who are too hasty and make their advances too presumptuously, with a kind of stubborn impetuosity, often lose these favours, and with good reason. For a true lady always considers she is being insulted when someone shows a lack of respect by seeking to gain her love before he has served her.[16]

This advice to men is given by the Magnifico, one of the central characters in *The Book of the Courtier*, a manual of Renaissance etiquette and philosophy published in 1528 by Baldesar Castiglione. Castiglione was himself a courtier and diplomat who spent most of his life in the Italian city of Urbino. His book is a compendium of all the qualities essential to a perfect Renaissance man, many of which Castiglione himself seems to have exemplified. On hearing news of his death, the Emperor Charles V of Spain is reported to have exclaimed 'one of the finest gentlemen of the world is dead'.

The Book of the Courtier takes the form of a conversation and disputation which unfolds over a numer of days at an imaginary Italian court, presided over by the beautiful and accomplished Signora Emilia. A number of characters gather each night and converse about almost everything under the sun, from the importance of skill with arms to the art of painting, and the relative virtues of monarchy and republicanism. One whole section is devoted to the relations between men and women, the nature of their differences, and, most importantly, the proper ways in which the courtier should comport himself in the service of women and in the art of love.

Somewhat surprisingly, *The Book of the Courtier* reads in many ways like a sixteenth-century manual of feminism. The Magnifico, the wisest and most perspicacious of the characters and the one who seems to represent the voice of the author, is forever defending women against the assaults on their character and behaviour delivered by his fellow characters, and admonishing men to change their attitudes. Yet the Magnifico is no member of the Sackcloth-and-Ashes Brigade, denouncing his own sex. At one point he exclaims, in a mood of exasperation, 'I don't want to abuse men as gratuitously as they have abused women'.[17] The burden of his message, in which he is supported by Signora Emilia, is that men must learn to serve and please the women they love.

The Book of the Courtier is a work of philosophy, but it is also, in modern parlance, a self-help manual, a book of etiquette for Renaissance students of the laws of desire. It offers practical advice to men on how to win a lady's favour, and how to retain it, stressing the importance of a considerate nature, skill as a conversationalist, virtue, modesty and a desire 'to please the woman he loves and avoid offending her'.[18] It is tempting to think of the Magnifico as a sixteenth-century SNAG, but we should recall that, despite his emphasis on the need for a gentleman to bend his will to that of his beloved, he is writing about a world in which women effectively had very little power or control over their lives.

Nearly 500 years later, we encounter an explosion of self-help manuals on relationships, some of which also advise men on how best to go about pleasing a woman. It would appear that men need this kind of advice more than ever. Today's self-help manuals attempt to fill a gap left by the collapse of social norms, the written and unwritten laws that have governed men's and women's relations with one another for the best part of two centuries. It's in this context, in a world in which these laws have lost much of their authority and legitimacy, that we conduct our 'everyday social experiments', seeking new ways for men and women to engage with one another.

The extraordinary popularity of self-help literature such as *Men Are from Mars, Women Are from Venus*, reveals how hungry men and women are for new guidelines, new methods for their experiments. The one thing all such books have in common is that they take for granted the notion that we need to *work* on our relationships, and indeed on ourselves. Life with one's partner becomes a project, one we need to engage in in a conscious fashion. As Anthony Giddens points out, this in itself is a very new notion, no more than 20 or 30 years old at the most.[19] Nor is it one which all of us find agreeable:

> *Susan*: Mark hardly ever says he loves me. Whenever I want to work on our relationship, he would rather read or watch television. I feel like we have grown apart. Oh yeah, we see eye to eye about raising the kids, and our sex is still great, but why won't Mark talk to me?
>
> *Mark*: I'm not the sort of person who can say 'I love you; I love you' every minute. How can Susan question my feelings? I've done everything I could to help her. I work two jobs so she can go back to school and I do a lot around the house . . . This business about talking about our relationship—What is there to talk about? I love her; I don't want to get into a fight.[20]

According to American research, women tend to evaluate their intimate relationships more negatively than men.[21] While we need to take such research with a grain of salt, especially when applying it in an Australian context, it seems to fit broadly with the observations of Peter Jordan about the couples he counsels in the Family Court and similar observations made by Australian counsellors who work with couples who are not in such severe crisis. As we heard in Chapter 3, the discrepancies between the way a man and a woman see the quality of their relationship may be so great that the man may not be aware that anything is wrong until the woman walks out. Typically, it is women who try to initiate 'work' on the relationship, often to be met with responses similar to those of Mark above.

Susan and Mark may by now have joined the happy throng of couples who testify enthusiastically about how John Gray's book or one of his workshops saved their relationship. Or they may not. In some senses, the strength of such self-help manuals is also their greatest limitation. *Men Are from Mars, Women Are from Venus* attributes the problems men and women experience in their relationships to their *differences*—in communicative styles, emotional make-up and strategies for dealing with conflict. Once we have understood this and accepted it, in a cheerful Californian way, the frequency of divorces will decrease and the number of happy marriages will increase—or so says Gray, at any rate.

Unfortunately, there's a catch. Gray has a great deal to say about difference, but almost nothing to say about inequality. His recipe for happy marriages assumes that in any given couple, the man and the woman will both hold equal amounts of power. Moreover, his analysis of what goes wrong with marriage is completely disconnected from any wider notion of the structures of power and inequality within which men and women live in Gray's own or indeed *any* society.

Of course, it would be foolish and pedantic to expect a popular self-help manual to deliver a radical analysis of the political economy of gender. Here again, we confront a paradox: the kind of perspective I've tried to open up in Chapter 3, which does attempt to look at the underlying economic and social reasons for the crisis of masculinity, tells us very little about how we might deal with the practical consequences of that crisis in our everyday lives. Yet, conversely, our struggles, negotiations and accommodations with our partner do not happen in a vacuum, in some timeless suburbia of the emotions. The battle for power between men and women that is going on at a broader social level, in our workplaces and institutions, reaches into our kitchens and bedrooms. And the everyday social experiments we make in our relationships are also skirmishes in that battle, contributing to its ambit and trajectory.

The literature of self-help has, in the past, been largely directed at women. Marriage manuals not only instructed women on how to be a good wife, but placed the responsibility for the maintenance of a successful marriage fairly and squarely in the female domain. Not surprisingly, there were very few books published advising men on how to be a good husband. Books such as John Gray's would lead us to believe that our notions about whose job it is to keep a relationship in good running order have become more democratic, but the majority of these books are still bought by women.

Recently, however, we have seen the emergence of a whole genre of self-help literature devoted to men. In Australia, by far the most succesful exemplar of this trend is Steve Biddulph's *Manhood*.

Unlike John Gray, Biddulph doesn't shy away from talking about power—whether in the immediate context of men's and women's everyday relationships with one another, or at a broader social level. He's at great pains to let readers know that he does not have an anti-feminist agenda, but wants to offer men positive ways of responding to the feminist challenge. In his chapter on men and women, he explores the failure of the SNAG, telling readers that many strong, capable feminist women confide in him that they are bored stiff with the SNAG in their lives.[22] Biddulph's solution is to exhort men to stand up to their wives and partners as equals, to have a proper sense of themselves, and to seek an adult relationship with the woman in their lives, one not constrained by sexual and emotional dependence. All eminently sensible and practical advice; but it's when he moves to the larger social world that Biddulph really lets his argument and his readers down. In a chapter entitled 'Swimming in a Feminist Sea', he takes issue with the assumption that 'men were somehow the winners in a power struggle and that power was what life was all about'. Rather, he believes, it is 'more realistic' to say that both men and women were 'trapped in a system which damaged them both'.[23]

This is terrible nonsense. Men have received all sorts of benefits from their power over women and continue to do so. Moreover, there is no reason to believe that they would have woken up to the fact that they were 'damaged' by the existing 'system' and begun to search for alternatives unless women had taken the initiative and challenged their power in the first place. To pretend that is not the case is simply bad faith, and does a disservice to both women and men. Men do not need to join the Sackcloth-and-Ashes Brigade, apologize for their masculinity or surrender moral and sexual authority to women. Nor is there much point in men castigating themselves in order to atone for women's oppression, past or present. What they do need to do is to acknowledge honestly that inequality and imbalance of power are not the product of some impersonal and implacable 'system' that oppresses both sexes equally, but of a set of social and economic relations in which men have held power and, in many areas, continue to do so.

To speak of empowering men, as Biddulph does, is a piece of empty rhetoric unless we are prepared to come clean about the real issue at stake, namely, that men will have to become a great deal more active in changing the economic conditions of their lives and attacking entrenched social attitudes before they can hope for more equal, fulfilling and democratic relationships with their partners. Nowhere in his book does Biddulph suggest that men join a trade union or lobby group agitating for more 'family-friendly' workplaces and work practices, or indeed do anything about changing the 'system' that has 'damaged' them. Surely, the 'strong, capable feminist' women

Biddulph speaks of will thank and respect men if they learn to stand up for themselves, articulate their needs and desires, and listen to those of their partner. But women might thank and respect them even more if men set about attacking the crucial, wearying, intractable things that most affect the everyday conditions of men's and women's lives: work, pay, child-care, housework and a fair go in the corridors of power.

Having said this, it would be unjust and unrealistic to ascribe to men the sole responsibility for creating the conditions under which 'intimate democracy' might flourish. It is women, the 'emotional revolutionaries of modernity',[24] in Anthony Giddens' striking phrase, who have led the way towards the democratic 'pure' relationship as a mutual project of self-realization. But to see women as the experts in intimacy, whom men should simply learn to emulate, is not necessarily the correct path for men to take towards intimate democracy. Nor are men the only ones who have 'problems' with intimacy. As Giddens points out, women themselves often have very complex and contradictory responses to male power, particularly in sexual relationships. For some women, 'the demand for equality may jostle psychologically with the search for a male figure who is emotionally remote and authoritative'.[25] Women, too, may need to give up certain 'double standards' where sex and sexuality are concerned, or at least acknowledge more openly that they exist.

Throughout this chapter, I've tried to make some broad connections between the 'everyday social experiments' we make in our intimate relationships and the larger social canvas against which we act them out. Sketching out a set of new rules or guidelines for these experiments, new 'laws of desire', as the self-help manuals seek to do, may give us some practical help, but leaves the underlying issues unaddressed. There is, however, one area on which self-help literature offers advice to men that I have not touched on, an area most men consider of prime importance in their intimate relationships: sex.

WHY MEN CAN'T GET IT RIGHT IN BED

In 1984, a previously unknown British band called Frankie Goes to Hollywood went rocketing up the British and Australian pop charts with their first hit, 'Relax'. This bombastic, lavishly produced anthem with its grinding bass beat sent the music industry into a frenzy of hype. However, 'Relax' was not a prophetic prefiguration from the Mother Country of John Howard's vision of a relaxed and comfortable Australia. It was a song devoted to the theme of premature ejaculation.

'Relax' was an unashamedly gay anthem by an unashamedly gay band. The filmclip featured a lot of leather and a few coy references to S&M, but the message that Holly Johnston and his band of merry men wished to get across was direct and unequivocal: don't shoot your bolt too soon.

Had he not been quite clearly claiming allegiance to a decidedly non-hetero sexual culture, his fans could have been forgiven for thinking, in retrospect, that Holly had been studying one of a number of manuals for straight men on how to be a better lover. Many of these manuals place a great deal of stress on delaying orgasm and controlling ejaculation as a matter of prime necessity in satisfying a woman sexually. Most of the New Age variety draw on Tantric or other Eastern sexual practices in advising men on how to control ejaculation. *Sexual Secrets for Men*, written by two Australians, Kerry and Diane Riley, who run workshops on 'relationships and sensual loving', devotes a whole chapter to muscle control and breathing techniques. In the foreword, Kerry Riley tells us that he believes there is a new man in the world today, one who 'wants to experience sex at its full potential' and 'open the door to the greatest joy for his loved one and himself'.[26] What this involves is a lot of massage, structured techniques to improve communication (such as the 'Bonding Process'), and the practice of a fairly rigorous sexual discipline, all with the aim of transforming sex into a deep and powerful spiritual experience. Among other things, the authors recommend that couples should practice a 'daily devotion', which involves placing 'lingam in yoni' for five minutes every day: 'Man and woman have the potential to harmonise as a couple again every time lingam is in yoni.'[27] In fact, they recommend making sure that you have lingam in yoni whether you are feeling in a frisky mood or not, along the lines of the German proverb which says appetite comes with eating.

If you are not of a New Age persuasion you may find all of this silly, embarrassing or just downright laughable. Some people may find it highly erotic. I wouldn't want to deny for a moment that the sorts of techniques Kerry and Diane Riley recommend, and the stress they place on relaxation and 'being in the body', might not make many men's (and women's) sex lives more rewarding and fulfilling. Yet, in a curious way, stripped of its New Age trappings, this manual on how a man can become 'an extraordinary lover' is mostly about technique. What is intriguing is what it leaves out. There's no mention at all of sexual fantasy and the place it may have in people's sex lives. Instead, sex becomes a discipline, a form of religious experience rather than something people do for fun. Moreover, the script for these devotees of 'spiritual sex' is always about 'honouring', 'affirming' and 'loving'; it is never rude or raunchy or sleazy.

Woody Allen was once asked in an interview if he thought sex was dirty. Allen reflected for a moment, then replied, 'Only if it's done properly'. By contrast, sex in the New Age manuals for men tends to be a sanitized affair, which is all the more surprising when we compare them with similar sexual self-help texts for women, which are much more explicit in advocating that women give a free rein to their fantasies. Consider this example from Olivia St Claire's *Unleashing the Sex Goddess in Every Woman*, one of a number of fantasies St Claire offers to readers:

> One night, while out dancing in a tight red dress, I am suddenly grabbed by three men who blindfold me and

> throw me into the back of a van . . . later, I find myself standing on the auction block of a white slave market. The auctioneer . . . rips away my robes, exposing my entire naked body; the audience gasps in excited approval. Several customers, men dressed in long robes and turbans, come up and bounce my breasts between their hands, pinch my nipples and grab my bottom . . . Though I should feel humiliated and angry, I find myself feeling haughty and sexy instead, because I can see that every one of these men has a huge erection jutting out under his robe. I start gyrating my hips, squeezing my own tits, and massaging my pussy . . . [eventually] the man in the blue sash . . . sticks his stone-hard member straight up my pussy and fucks me hard, fast and deep, right there in front of everybody, and I explode in uncontrollable spasms. I select him as my lucky owner and lead him off to demand more fucking.[28]

It's illuminating to consider for a moment what our reaction would be if this little story were written from the point of view of the man in the blue sash, or one of the other men at the auction. Would we be shocked and disgusted at the elements of domination and subjugation that are involved? Would we condemn the author as a sadist and pervert? Plainly, there's a certain erotic charge generated for the fantasizing woman as she imagines being carried off as a slave. Where that charge comes from is also clear, from the dynamic of power that's at play, the feeling that she has no choice but to surrender to the power of the man who is carrying her off. In her fantasy, there's a delicate balance between his power over her and the sexual respect with which he treats her. He is not a cruel or sadistic rapist.

We know, of course, that it *is* a fantasy, that the author has no desire to actually act it out. Indeed, this is precisely what constitutes the erotic appeal of fantasy. Fantasy is a domain of sexual freedom, a place where we can experience our sexuality in ways that we cannot or would not choose to do in everyday life. It is a world in which we can play at domination and subjugation without experiencing the consequences. It is also a world we may choose to share with our lovers and sexual partners, creating a particular kind of intimacy by admitting them into our secrets.

Of course, many people do choose to act out these fantasies in the form of bondage and discipline, S&M and other kinds of kinky sex. In gay and lesbian subcultures, these kinds of sexual practices have become popular and also highly politicized, in the sense that their devotees sometimes depict themselves as part of a sexual avant-garde which is confronting head-on the nexus between sex and power. Whether most heterosexuals who go in for bondage and S&M see themselves as making a political statement is less clear. In the early 1990s, kinky sex enjoyed a brief period of notoriety in Australian magazines as the latest 'lifestyle' trend for straight couples, but if the sexual tastes of those couples are as fickle as the interests of the magazine writers, the handcuffs and ropes are now likely to be gathering dust.

Nevertheless, S&M and bondage and discipline do have the useful quality of making the erotic dynamics of power concrete and clearly visible. For Olivia St Claire, these dynamics can happily remain in the realm of fantasy, as the activities of devotees of consensual S&M remain behind the closed doors of the bedroom. Questions about the relationship between sex and power, however, are very much out in the open today, and I think St Claire's harmless fantasy shows us that there is a certain gender asymmetry in the way we think about them.

It's extremely difficult to imagine, for example, that a similar fantasy written from the male point of view could have been published in a self-help book exhorting men to explore their sexual fantasies without attracting all sorts of criticism and outrage. This is hardly surprising. We are now so used to being confronted with the predatory, violent and coercive aspects of male sexuality that we are more than likely to feel a certain squeamishness about any erotic narrative involving a man using physical force to carry off a woman. However, cordoning-off certain aspects of sexuality and declaring them out-of-bounds to men may also have undesirable consequences. The sanitization of sex in self-help manuals for men certainly has this effect. *Sexual Secrets for Men* gets through a whole 268 pages without once mentioning the word 'underwear'. Books like these simply don't reflect the diversity—and, one might add, perversity—of men's and women's sexual experience. They, and the New Age sexual ethic that runs through them, lock men into another kind of sexual straitjacket. Moreover, at the same time, we as a society are in the process of creating a whole new set of taboos about male sexuality, and all of these taboos revolve, in one way or another, around men exercising power in a sexual relationship.

This set of circumstances puts heterosexual men in something of a spot. As we saw in the case of the SNAG, his lack of sexual appeal for women seems to have been tied up with a lack of spine and substance, his willingness to simply hand over power to the woman in his life without putting up any kind of fight or challenging her right to take it. One might object that there is a difference between the negotiation over power that goes on every day in a relationship and the power we assume or surrender in the bedroom, but, in fact, the two are intimately linked. As we saw in the previous chapter, in extreme circumstances men may seek, through violence or sexual coercion, to exercise over women the power they lack or feel they are losing in other areas of the relationship, or in other areas of their lives. Anthony Giddens goes so far as to see this behaviour as a growing social phenomenon. In his view, as men lose the sexual control over women they've been accustomed to in the past, their sexual insecurity manifests itself in a rising tide of male violence towards women.[29]

The challenge in the bedroom for straight men is to find a form of sexuality that embraces playfulness, fantasy and imagination, and not simply technique. The challenge also involves a recognition that sex, in many ways, is a kind of theatre in which we can act out narratives of power and surrender without diminishing our respect for the autonomy and selfhood of our lovers. It's worth reflecting that the sense of sexual openness and confidence that runs through Olivia St Claire's fantasy is in many ways the result of a 30-year struggle on the part of women to wrest control of their sexuality from men and explore new attitudes to their bodies, their sexuality and their desires. It may be that men have an even longer struggle ahead in moulding new forms of sexual identity not founded on fear and shame. As we'll see in Chapter 6, the private and the public aspects of this process are very much interlinked.

WHAT DOES A MAN WANT?

One interesting question still deserves consideration: what is it that men want from their sexual relationships? On the one hand, it appears that they do want to be better lovers, better able to please women sexually. But, how much do they want to please themselves? After all, the things women seem to want from men in their intimate relationships—more communication, more playfulness and imagination, more awareness of their partner's and their own body and feelings—may not necessarily be what men want. To reiterate a point made earlier in another context, we should be wary of directing men to become more like women, in bed or anywhere else.

Some interesting insights into just what men do want from sex reveal themselves in a study of 667 male clients of sex workers conducted in Sydney.[30] Although the study was carried out primarily to investigate the attitudes of the men to safe sex practices, it contains much fascinating information about why men visit prostitutes and what they like to do with them. Most of the men were aged between 22 and 45, and slightly less than half were married. They came from a variety of social classes, had an above-average level of education and some attended church regularly (the study draws attention to the high proportion of Catholic men in their sample). On the whole, the men tended to visit a sex worker about once every one or two months.

When asked why they visited sex workers, a fifth of the men replied that they liked their company. A third said that sex with prostitutes was 'less complicated', and about the same proportion said they liked to have sex with a variety of women. As one man put it, 'You can't eat spaghetti every night'. Ten per cent said that their regular partner did not provide enough sex, while slightly over 10 per cent of the men said that sex with sex workers was the only sex available to them.

When it came to what the men liked to do with the workers they visited, the survey showed very little difference between the kinds of sexual practices they paid for and what they did with other sexual partners. Penetrative sex came in first place in both categories, with oral sex a close second. Sado-masochism proved to be very much a minority interest, with only 1.2 per cent of the men reporting that they engaged in it with sex workers, as opposed to 0.6 with other partners. Fantasy sex was more popular; 7.5 per cent practised it with workers, while only 2.5 per cent did it outside of the paid trade.

The overall picture that emerges from these statistics is an intriguing one. Plainly, there is not a huge demand for kinky sex from prostitutes. The vast majority of men are interested in 'straight' sex. Close to 45 per cent of the men questioned were either married or in long-term monogamous relationships and they did not have sex with anyone else apart from prostitutes. Seventy-two per cent of these men said they were having sex with their wife or partner at least once a week, and in some cases much more often. For these men, the overwhelming reason for visiting sex workers was a desire for variety in their sex lives rather than a lack of satisfaction with the quantity of sex available 'at home'.

Naturally, we should be cautious about drawing any overly dramatic conclusions from this evidence. Men who visit sex workers are not necessarily representative of the male population at large—although the authors of the study observed that the participants 'do not appear to be very different to the average man'.[31] However, the results seem to me to suggest that a substantial percentage of the men surveyed make an interesting compromise with monogamy and the limits of the pair bond. They maintain a commitment to emotional monogamy, choosing not to pursue romantic or emotional attachment to anyone other than their wife or partner. At the same time, they find exclusive sexual monogamy too restrictive. Visiting a sex worker, where the nature and limits of the sexual exchange are clearly defined and the possibility of emotional involvement is low, is a pragmatic solution to this dilemma.

I shall have more to say on monogamy and its limits in Chapter 10. In the meantime, we might wish to consider what implication this pragmatic compromise might have for our view of male sexuality. Men's ability or tendency to separate sex from love, to see their sexuality in a purely instrumental way, or as a form of recreation, is often decried. Yet it may be that if we wish to create more open, equal and rewarding relationships between men and women—in other words, to take the pair bond into another stage of development—we may need to think about how tightly we draw the sexual boundaries around these relationships. We may also have to revise some of our conventional notions about what it is that men actually want from sex. Although the Australian study cited above does not seem to suggest so, overseas research suggests that many men have fantasies of being sexually dominated by women. Indeed, one study which also surveyed sex workers and their male clients concluded that a 'common feature of men's sexual activity with prostitutes is the opportunity it provides to escape conventional male heterosexual roles with their heavy emphasis on masculine prowess and dominance'.[32] One man put it like this: 'I go there because I know I can lie down and just leave it to the girls'.[33] All of the men surveyed were married, and it is fascinating to speculate why these men apparently felt unable to act out with their wives the same fantasies or desires which they enjoyed experiencing with prostitutes. On the basis of this and other evidence, the feminist author Lynne Segal attacks what she believes are 'myths of the inevitable link between sexuality and male dominance'.[34] Indeed, Segal argues, 'for many men it is precisely through sex that they experience their greatest uncertainties, dependence and deference in relation to women—in stark contrast, quite often, with their experience of authority and independence in the public world'.[35] For some men, surrendering control in their sexual relations with women may be a source of pleasure, while for others it involves terror. Both of these possibilities should lead us to think carefully about the way our own private, intimate experiments with each other as men and women relate to the larger dramas of power and sexuality which unfold around us in our public lives.

6

The end of sex?

In the 1940s, the American humorist James Thurber published a sequence of cartoons entitled *The War between Men and Women.* Loosely modelled on the American Civil War, the sequence depicted such events as 'The Fight in the Grocery', 'Capture of Three Physics Professors', 'Surrender of Three Blondes' and 'Gettysburg'. With the exception of the blondes, the women appear calm, businesslike and staunchly resolute in battle, the men by turns are nonplussed and apprehensive. Ultimately, however, the men rally and turn the tables, and the sequence ends with the surrender of the women, whose leader hands over a baseball bat to the commander of the men.

Throughout his career as a writer, Thurber published many stories and cartoons portraying the comedy of 'modern' relations between men and women, satirizing women's growing confidence and self-sufficiency, and men's bemused and often alarmed responses. One sequence of cartoons, *The Masculine Approach*, explores a wide variety of masculine approaches to courtship, among them The Let 'Em Wait and Wonder Plan, The Pawing System, The I'm Not Good Enough for You Announcement, and perhaps the most unorthodox, The Harpo Marx Attack.

Thurber is a very funny cartoonist, but there's an element of melancholy and anxiety in many of these cartoons, as though the men in them were all pondering the answer to Freud's famous question 'What does a woman want?' and becoming even more confused about the answer in the process. (Thurber spent a lot of time taking the mickey out of serious psycho-analytical tracts on sex.) His choice of the American Civil War as the historical backdrop for *The War between Men and Women* is not purely arbitrary. The Civil War was known for having set father against son and brother against brother, and it's often been remarked that civil wars are particularly vicious because the people fighting them are in many ways like each other, united by ties of language, culture and kinship.

For Thurber, the battle of the sexes was still a comedy, though a dark one. In the 1990s, the same metaphor of violent conflict between men and women is frequently employed, with decidely less comic overtones. In 1993, *The Age* newspaper in Melbourne published a series of articles entitled 'War against Women', dealing with rape, incest and domestic violence in Victoria. While *The Age* series quite unequivocally portrayed women as victims and men as aggressors in this war, the British journalist Neil Lyndon took a quite different tack in his book *No More Sex War*, published in Australia in the same year. Lyndon, who has written for the *Times*, the *Sunday Times* and the *Independent*, paints a gaudy, sensational picture of men vilified, persecuted and pursued to the last ditch by 'totalitarian feminism'.

There is hyperbole and sensationalism in both these examples. Yet it seems to me that the underlying assumption in both—that men and women as cohesive groups or classes are engaged in combat with one another—carries a grain of truth in it. Many readers will find this suggestion just plain silly. After all, millions of men and women in Australia live and work together in relative harmony, make love, raise children and play bowls. Where are the organizations mobilizing them for battle? Where are the generals planning the battle strategy and giving the orders to the troops to open fire?

The war between men and women is not being fought in the way that we're accustomed to thinking of social conflicts being played out, such as the way power struggles between organized groups like unions and employers are conducted. Nevertheless, it is a real and potent social drama, in which conflicts between individuals or individuals and institutions become magnified and seize the public imagination as symbols of much larger clashes of principle or interest. Typically, this drama revolves around sex, and the most common context in which it unfolds is in sexual harassment cases. The controversy unleashed by Helen Garner's book *The First Stone* shows what a deep nerve such cases touch, and how intensely they engage people's attitudes and sympathies. *The First Stone* deals with an alleged case of sexual harassment at Ormond College, a prestigious, highly traditional college at the University of Melbourne. In 1992, the Master of the college was charged with indecent assault after a female student alleged that he had put his hand on her breast while they were dancing at a college function. Reading about the case in the newspaper, Garner was shocked, and overcome by a feeling that the punishment was out of all proportion to the crime. On an impulse, she wrote a letter to the Master:

> I want you to know that there are plenty of women out here who step back in dismay from the kind of treatment you have received, and who still hope that men and women, for all our foolishness and mistakes, can behave towards each other with kindness, rather than being engaged in this kind of warfare.[1]

Garner quite explicitly employs the image of 'warfare' in her letter. One of the reasons why her book sparked off such a heated public debate—and sold so well—lies in these few lines of her letter, dashed off on the spur of the moment, before she had any idea that she would write a book about the case. She sensed that the incident at Ormond College evokes a much larger drama, which draws in not just an individual man and woman, but 'men' and 'women' as separate and distinct groups, which can choose to behave towards each other with kindness, or treat each other as mutual antagonists in warfare.

Sex is the battleground of this war—and what gives *The First Stone* such force is Garner's intuition that the implications of the Ormond College case, fought out publicly in the ritualized theatre of the courts, spill over into the private lives of men and women, into the most intimate recesses of their sexual relations with one another. She believes that the delicate dynamics of 'ordinary', consensual heterosexual relations—what she elegantly calls 'the little God Eros, flickering and flashing through the plod of our ordinary working lives'—are suffering collateral damage from the public warfare between men and women.[2] And, though she never spells this out, there's a strong implication in her story that men are suffering from this damage more than women. It's not simply the sexual ethics of a particular man that were under scrutiny in the public discussion of the Ormond College case, she suggests, but men as a sex who were on trial.

As I'll make clear later in this chapter, I happen not to agree with Helen Garner about her overall interpretation of what went on at Ormond College. However, some of the issues she raises in *The First Stone* do help to highlight the confusion felt by many Australian men—men like Gary, from the Shoalhaven Men's Group—about what is appropriate sexual behaviour both inside and outside the bedroom.

> Some women . . . when I go out with them, I don't know how they want me to act . . . I don't know if they want me to kiss them or whatever . . . and yet with others I know they're willing to go as far as they want . . . like they're really easy and that. I know a lot of women, I just don't know how to act around them.

Gary belongs to the category of Australian men I've described as 'abashed'. Though they are abashed generally in their relations with women, they are particularly abashed in their sexuality. In Chapter 5, I suggested that part of the reason for this is the disappearance of the kinds of codes of sexual etiquette that helped men (and women) in earlier times negotiate courtship and what we would now call 'extramarital' sex. To borrow a metaphor from economics, we might say that whereas previously sexual transactions between people were regulated and shaped by these codes, the sexual economy has now been almost totally de-regulated, and we are living in a sexual free market.[3] However, 'de-regulation' doesn't adequately account for men's abashment, their feeling that sex is a minefield through which they must tread with care.

This feeling relates primarily to the courtship stage, when, as men or women, we are trying to induce someone to go to bed with us, rather than to what actually goes on in the bedroom. Here, too, I've heard men express doubts and misgivings about what they should or shouldn't be doing in bed, how much they should 'let themselves go'. Some of these doubts are picked up by women, who feel that men are not at ease with their sexuality, particularly its more 'animal' aspects. Here again, the unfortunate SNAG, trying desperately to be a sexually sensitive 'excellent lover' takes a further pasting. One woman, a little ruefully, put it to me like this: 'What women want,' she said, 'is a man who's a SNAG in the kitchen and a tiger in the bedroom. But it's hard to find both in the one man.'

As we saw in Chapter 5, this dilemma is a real one for men, and much of it revolves around the relationship between sexual attraction and power. Helen Garner also sets out to ask some questions about sex and power in *The First Stone*. Although the answers she comes up with purport to offer a more complex picture of what this relationship might be, ultimately they fall back on some very tired old sexual stereotypes. Despite this, the great merit of her book is to suggest that men's private dilemmas about their sexual relations with women and the social drama of 'warfare' between men and women played out in areas such as sexual harassment cases are closely interlinked. In order to see how and why this is so, it's useful to consider exactly what's at stake in our notions of sexual harassment.

A TOWN LIKE NORMAL

> I think America is very schizophrenic when it comes to sex. On one level it's very puritanical, you know, we don't want nudie pictures and magazines, no bare-breasted sunbathing on beaches; and so on. But on the other hand there are many aspects of American life that are just full of sex. You know, in sort of more covert ways. In many workplaces the level of raunchiness is very high indeed. So it may be that in a country that was less schizophrenic, you might have less extreme on the raunchiness side, and therefore need less in the way of remedies.
>
> Professor Mary Becker, University of Chicago[4]

The town of Normal is about 150 miles south-west of Chicago, in central Illinois. Over the last 18 months, Normal has been the setting for one of the most spectacular sexual harassment cases in the world. The United States Federal Equal Employment Opportunity Council has launched a class action for sexual harassment against Mitsubishi on behalf of hundreds of women workers at the Mitsubishi auto plant in Normal. The case is interesting for a number of reasons.

To begin with, it goes beyond commonplace notions of sexual harassment, which presume an individual harasser and another individual who has been harassed. The Normal case rests on the assertion that women at the Mitsubishi plant have been subjected to a climate of harassment, rather than sexual advances or pestering by particular persons. Under US law, it's illegal for an employer to permit a working environment in his or her workplace that is 'significantly and pervasively and seriously hostile towards women'.[5] The case against Mitsubishi, which grew out of a private legal action taken by 28 women workers, brings into play a number of federal and state laws in order to argue that the company allowed such a hostile environment to exist, and did nothing to remedy the conditions being experienced by the women at the plant. According to press accounts of the trial, the complaints made by the women included 'somebody grabbing you . . . somebody blocking your way so that you can't get through an aisle, somebody following you to a bar at night and asking you to go out even though they know you don't want to go out'. The women claimed that they were afraid to go to work on account of these kinds of harassment, and that their pride and self-esteem were being affected.

What is also interesting about the Normal case is the fact that the women were complaining about the behaviour of fellow workers of the same status and position as them, and not just the actions of superiors seeking to use their power over the women to extract sexual favours. Not only this, the climate of sexual harassment and hostility the women experienced is seen as extending beyond the boundaries of the workplace itself, to situations where the women are being 'followed to a bar at night' and subjected to unwelcome sexual attentions there as well as at work.

The complainants in the case have also been exposed to considerable antagonism and hostility since they took up their legal action. Those who are still working at the plant are shunned by fellow workers and some have received anonymous notes with messages such as 'Die, bitch, you'll be sorry'.

Following on from the initial private action taken by the 28 workers against Mitsubishi, the Federal Equal Employment Opportunity Council is now seeking compensation from Mitsubishi on behalf of 700 women who work, or used to work at the Normal plant. The women who launched the initial action against Mitsubishi are factory workers, working-class women without a great deal of formal education. They are not the kind of modern middle-class feminists Helen Garner accuses of being 'priggish, disingenuous, unforgiving' in their attitudes to men and sexual harassment.[6]

Quite apart from the sheer scale of the legal action, the interest it has generated in the media and the fact that the defendant is a large multinational company, the Normal case is fascinating because it represents a public drama, a powerful collective protest by a group of women against the attitudes and behaviour of men. It's a drama that has elicited an equally powerful reaction from the men who are 'on trial'—though, in point of fact, it is Mitsubishi that is on trial by proxy. Mary Becker, a Professor of Law at the University of Chicago and an expert on sexual harassment legislation, argues that the death threats show the seriousness of the battle and the interests that are felt to be at stake.

Similar levels of hostility and aggression were evident in one of the more notorious sexual harassment cases in Australia in recent years, to which I referred in Chapter 1. Julieanne Ashton, a trader's assistant in her early 20s at the Sydney Futures Exchange, took legal action against her employer, Bankers Trust, claiming that she'd been subjected to sexual discrimination and victimisation. She told the Equal Opportunity Tribunal that when she complained about this behaviour to one of the managers at Bankers Trust, her complaint was ignored, and that the same manager afterwards made negative written comments about her work.

During the hearings, one of Ashton's colleagues admitted to calling her a slut, but argued that this was normal behaviour on the trading floor or 'pit', and that Ashton had not been treated any differently from a man. The sexual innuendo and 'forms of embarrassment' used by himself and the other men towards Ashton, he said, were part of a process of initiation, which younger employees in the pit were put through as a matter of course.[7]

Bankers Trust initially denied the allegations, but subsequently settled out of court, making a formal apology to Julieanne Ashton and paying her an undisclosed amount in damages. According to Ann Sherry, a human resources policy manager at Westpac, the problems Ashton had experienced were by no means unusual in the banking and finance sector, which in her view was still condoning practices that had been 'stamped out of blue-collar workplaces five or ten years ago'.[8]

Julieanne Ashton's complaint against Bankers Trust has some elements in common with the Normal case. She felt she had experienced a climate of harassment, rather than unwanted sexual attentions from a particular individual. In her case, this climate was quite clearly intended to intimidate and humiliate her. Over and above this, it sent a signal that if she, as a woman, expected to work in a space dominated by men, she would have to play by their rules. Sex itself is plainly secondary here. There was no real suggestion that any of Ashton's male colleagues were sexually attracted to her or wanted to initiate some kind of erotic liaison with her. Rather, sex was being used as a way of asserting power, an attempt on the part of the men either to force Ashton out of the 'pit' or to become one of the boys.

Why were these men, and the men in the Mitsubishi plant in Normal, so hostile to the presence of women in their workplace? Cases such as these generate an extraordinary amount of aggression and recrimination on both sides. They represent a type of theatre, a public drama in which men's and women's private experience of the dynamics of power and control in their intimate relationships are writ large, focused and magnified. The initial impetus for the action by the 28 women in Normal was a conversation between one woman and the lawyer who was handling her divorce. During the conversation, the woman happened to mention the climate at work and her feelings about it to the lawyer, who told her that there were laws prohibiting behaviour of that kind in the workplace—something of which the woman had previously been unaware.

It is not surprising that such dramas or conflicts should occur when the balance of power between men and women is shifting, or that they should generate intense interest and controversy among people who are not directly involved—as happened with the Ormond College case. However, the idea that our intimate relationships and the delicate mechanisms of desire are suffering collateral damage as a result is based on a misapprehension. These larger conflicts *grow out of* the uncertainties, fears and insecurities men and women experience in their everyday relationships with one another—rather than the other way around. They would not capture the public imagination in the way they do if they were not emblematic of questions we are forced to grapple with in the 'micropolitics' of everyday life. Our difficulties in untangling these questions, and our confusion in trying to arrive at some new idea of a sexual ethics for men and women based on equality and respect for the integrity of the other person, spring from many sources. One of them is a very modern confusion about the nature of seduction.

SEDUCTION

Let's return for a moment to some remarks of Elisabeth Badinter's quoted in Chapter 5. Badinter believes that the war between men and women has never reached the same pitch in France as it has in the Anglo-Saxon countries, at least partly because of what she claims is 'the importance we have always given to seduction, as well as our relationship to our bodies'. This apparently inconsequential remark takes on a wealth of significance in an Anglo-Saxon context. Anyone who has watched a few French films is familiar with the conventions of seduction in the style of the French. Seduction is an art practised by both men and women, an art that involves the exercise of a certain kind of power or fascination over the object of one's desire. It is also an art practised according to a set of unspoken rules of which both parties are more or less aware. Love is a game and some of the most common metaphors for sexual and romantic attraction have themes of games, gambling and intrigue. Most importantly, for Gallic lovers, the act of seduction—or being seduced—is not necessarily regarded as morally reprehensible. French culture, Badinter proclaims, is almost totally ignorant of puritanism.[9]

Anglo-Saxon culture, on the other hand, knows all about puritanism and not very much about seduction. Indeed, seduction is a particularly unpopular, almost scandalous notion in late twentieth-century Anglo-Saxon cultures. The *Shorter Oxford Dictionary* says that seduction is both 'the condition of being led astray' and 'the action of inducing (a woman) to surrender her chastity', the 'act . . . of seducing (a person) to err in conduct or belief' and 'an allurement'. In and between each of these gradations of meaning there is a tension, the blurring of a line between the deliberate exercise of one person's will to bend another to his or her purpose, and the surrender of oneself to another. When we are seduced, we allow ourselves to be led astray, we suspend our own will and give ourselves up to the will of the seducer. Put simply, we allow ourselves to give up control. But there is an element of volition in this surrender. We are more or less aware—though we may not want to admit to ourselves—that our surrender to the other person is something we are choosing.

The themes of seduction and surrender run through erotic literature of all ages and cultures, from *Tom Jones* to the novels of the Japanese writers Shusaku Endo and Junichiro Tanizaki, from Marvell's seventeenth-century poem *To His Coy Mistress*, to the love lyrics of the English pop singer P.J. Harvey.

Seduction and surrender are part of the enlivening energy of desire itself. In giving up control over ourselves—'losing ourselves'—we feel, paradoxically, that we come closer to ourselves, experiencing ourselves, however fleetingly, in a way we don't have access to while we carry the burden of will. It's this experience Lynne Segal celebrates in her recent book *Straight Sex*:

> It is never really 'me, myself, alone', but always thoughts of being desired by, dominated by, or variously handled by others, thoughts of desiring, subordinating or variously using others, that excite us . . . It is those special others, real or imaginary, who arouse us with . . . . at least as I experience it . . . a fairly constant and chronic desire just to be held close, and to hold, to smell, to taste, to kiss, to stroke and to feel some particular person inside our arms, mouth, cunt . . . It is the very greatest of joys, as I experience it.[10]

Straight Sex is a passionate defence of heterosexual sexuality, and the positive possibilities of sex, love, desire and companionship between a woman and a man. It might seem extraordinary that Segal should feel the need to defend something the majority of people practise. However, as a committed feminist and a distinguished writer and scholar, she is impelled by a strongly felt conviction that a certain kind of feminism, exemplified by the American authors Andrea Dworkin and Catharine MacKinnon, is attempting to proscribe women's pleasure in sex with men and portray all women who have sex with men, or engage in sexual and companionable relationships with men, as collaborators in the systematic oppression of women.

For feminists of Dworkin's and MacKinnon's persuasion, penetrative sex is, by its very essence, an act of exploitation and oppression. Here is how Andrea Dworkin describes 'intercourse':

> He has to *push in past boundaries*. There is never a real privacy of the body that can co-exist with intercourse: with being entered. The vagina itself is muscled and the muscles have to be pushed apart. The thrusting is persistent invasion.[11]

It follows, then, that seduction is quite beyond the pale. Most practising heterosexuals may find it easy to shrug off this particular brand of feminism as a product of the rarefied atmosphere of the academies, without any real influence on the everyday lives of the majority of men and women. This would be a mistake. In fact, the attitude to heterosexual sexuality espoused by Dworkin and MacKinnon is only the extreme form of a much more general anxiety about straight sex, which runs through the mainstream of late twentieth-century Anglo-Saxon culture.

This anxiety is crystallized by the experience of seduction, because seduction, by its very nature, throws into question the autonomy of the self and the state of 'self-possession', which means we are in control of our actions and motivations, and free to shape our lives as we choose. Feminists like Dworkin and MacKinnon place an absolute premium on the autonomy of the self, which for them resides above all in the 'privacy of the body'. This is why penetrative sex is so objectionable to them, because it represents an invasion of that privacy. For this reason, there is little, in their eyes, to distinguish consensual penetrative sex from rape. It both embodies and symbolizes the subjugation of a woman by a man. It is, by its very nature, coercive. It does not matter whether the woman has consented to the man entering her body. The mere fact that he has done so is an expression of his power over her and, as such—for Dworkin and MacKinnon—a denial of her autonomy as a human being.

Not surprisingly, practising heterosexual feminists like Segal find this argument offensive. Segal happens to like penetrative sex, and is not afraid to say so. Moreover, she thinks Dworkin's and MacKinnon's arguments are patronizing to women, and has mounted a powerful and spirited theoretical challenge to them in *Straight Sex*. This theoretical debate about sex and the autonomy of the self has practical consequences in women's and men's everyday lives. In the United States, the question of 'date rape' has provided fodder to journalists and exercised the popular conscience of the white middle classes since the late 1980s. There has even been serious discussion of the notion that young people should fill out forms before going out on a date, specifying exactly which kinds of sexual contact or congress they wish to consent to, so that there can be no uncertainty before one or the other makes an advance and no question of litigation the morning after.

Moral panic about date rape has never made much of an impact in Australia. The whole notion of date rape, and the 'solution' proposed for American teenagers, raises some interesting conundrums about the everyday conventions of our sexual lives. Under such a system there could never be any question of seduction. We would have to be entirely clear in our own minds before we consented to a trip to the pictures, dinner for two or a moonlit walk on the beach whether we wished to have sex with the person concerned, should the situation arise. Yet, as anyone who has ever been seduced knows, we may not be aware, or indeed *wish to be aware*, that we want to have sex with someone until it happens. The quiver of desire may take us by surprise. There is also a certain sense in which we are deliberately not being frank with ourselves when we allow ourselves to be seduced, 'led astray'. We pretend to ourselves that we are in control in the very moment we collude with the stratagems of the seducer. Similarly, anyone who has ever been a seducer knows that seduction is a game in which we do seek to exercise sexual power over the person we desire, to have him or her surrender to us, a game in which there is always *also* the possibility that we may be seduced and fall under the power of the other.

This delicate interplay of control and surrender is integral to sexual desire, to what Helen Garner calls Eros, 'the spark that ignites and connects'.[12] But as Garner suggests, Eros poses a problem for feminists. Much of the project of feminism since the late 1960s has revolved around stressing women's need for and right to autonomy. As we've seen in Chapter 5, this autonomy is not some abstract theoretical principle. It's a struggle many women in Australia have had to fight again and again in their everyday lives, over things many people take for granted: the right to have a job; to have one's own friends; and even to decide when and for how long one goes for a walk on one's own.

And, as I've been arguing throughout this book, a measure of real autonomy for women has come only as a result of concrete social, economic and technological changes: access to employment and higher education for women of all classes, the availability of child-care and reliable contraception. For the Dworkin/MacKinnon brand of feminism, this autonomy is in many ways a purely private affair, located first and foremost in the body itself. Sexual desire is deeply problematic for them, not simply because it involves the 'invasion' of the body, but because to give oneself up to desire for another person involves the surrender of a certain degree of one's own autonomy. We speak of placing ourselves in the power of another person when we give ourselves to them sexually, and this is precisely what Dworkin and MacKinnon find so objectionable. Indeed, for them any kind of power differential between the partners in a sexual relationship is necessarily exploitative and thus proscribed. In their terms, *any* sexual relationship between a man and a woman will always be exploitative, because men will always be the ones who hold power. It does not matter whether the man is a company director or an unemployed plumber.

This is one thread in the tangled fabric of attitudes to sex and power I'm attempting to unravel in this chapter. It is important because it represents an attempt to create a powerful new taboo, to re-regulate the sexual economy according to extremely rigid principles that injure both men and women. However, the arguments of the most radical 'free marketeers' are not necessarily an attractive alternative. At the opposite end of the feminist spectrum in the 1990s is Camille Paglia, who not only acknowledges power as an integral component of sexual desire, but indeed celebrates it. As we'll see in a moment, these two implacably antagonistic tendencies in contemporary feminism actually have a great deal more in common than we might think.

THE MARRIAGE OF FEMINISM AND ECONOMIC RATIONALISM OR SEX IN THE FREE MARKET

> I'm saying that sex is a surging power thing between the sexes. It's a sex war . . . It's up to women to realize it's dangerous. Sex is dangerous—it's a dangerous sport.
>
> Camille Paglia, *Sex, Art and American Culture: Essays*, p. 68

Paglia's great cry—one which has been the basis of her career as a popular intellectual—is that women must throw off the garments of victim feminism and claim their sexual power. Rather than complaining about sexual harassment and stigmatizing men's sexuality and their own, Paglia believes that women should recognize their sexual attractiveness to men for what it is: a bargaining chip, a medium of exchange, a subtle and flexible way of obtaining 'leverage' in their dealings with men.

It might be said of this particular version of female sexual power that Madonna is its divine personification and Camille Paglia her prophet. Paglia celebrates Madonna as a woman who is 'in control' of her sexuality, able to slip in and out of sexual personae as a snake sheds skins, to be one moment dominant and the next submissive, now alluring and the next moment cool and distant—but always as a matter of choice. For Paglia, this is a sign of freedom, a woman's freedom to choose who she is sexually and in all other matters. If sexual submission to another man or woman turns her on, well and good. It is what she has chosen of her own free will. Tomorrow she may choose to be the dominatrix.

Paglia is a libertarian. Like Segal, she does not take kindly to being told what she should or should not be doing in the privacy of her own bedroom. Unlike Segal, however, she sees women's right to sexual freedom as bestowing on them a certain kind of power, which it is perfectly legitimate to exercise outside of the bedroom in women's everyday negotiations with men. Questions of sexual harassment are largely irrelevant for Paglia. In any situation where a man has power over a woman in a public setting—as an employer, boss, or teacher—and tries to use it to induce her to have sex with him, she can fight fire with fire, using her sexual power over him to manipulate him as she wishes.

Power, however, is always bought at a cost, and in this case the cost is one that cements women in the role of sexual puppeteer and men in the role of the puppet, the prisoners of their lust—unable to exercise responsibility or sexual autonomy. Paglia's argument, presented as a modern, post-feminist response to women's situation is in fact an old and familiar one, and deeply reactionary at that. It is also offensive to men, because it celebrates women's 'freedom' at the expense of men's supposed inability to be anything other than 'dick-driven', to use a popular and vividly succinct colloquialism. Moreover, it cements once and for all a purely instrumental view of sexuality. If we choose to see sexual relations between men and women primarily in terms of power, we must live with the consequences. If women want the rewards that sexual power brings, they must be prepared to be consistent, and to some extent ruthless in the exercise of that power, and also prepared to accept its cost: that men will continue to be content to explain their own behaviour as if their sexual responses were not within their own power. This particular myth of male sexuality is one in which some women are only too happy to collude. It serves as a kind of alibi for both sexes. If men have power over women in nearly every sphere of everyday life, women's power over men in the sexual sphere is supposed to provide some kind of compensation.

There are, however, serious flaws in this argument. To begin with, the implicit backdrop is the jungle, rather than the suburban bedroom or urban street. Sexuality here is a matter of predator and prey, a kind of state of nature in which the strong woman will survive by remaining 'in control of her sexuality'. However, as I've tried to suggest, it is not only the complex game of power that makes sexual intimacy between people as intense, absorbing and pleasurable as it can be, but also the experience of vulnerability. The knowledge of ourselves into which we enter in our vulnerability before another's power—knowledge that is surely a component of what Garner calls the 'movement of Eros'—is something that can only be achieved through a surrender of control. This surrender cannot come easily to the woman for whom sexuality is instrumental, a means to an end. Nor should it surprise us that so many men, having internalized the kind of sexual script that tells them they are *not in control* of their sexuality, should respond with feelings of fear and anxiety about sex. These feelings fuel a hostility towards women and female sexuality that we know all too well—a hostility documented in chilling detail in Nick Enright's play *Black Rock*.

A further problem with Camille Paglia's approach to sexual power is that power is not distributed equally among women—or men, for that matter. Not all women have the kind of 'daring beauty', and the power that comes with it, which Garner describes in Elizabeth Rosen, one of the two young women in the Ormond College case. As Garner suggests, we can live in awe of such beauty; but we must also be aware that possession of such beauty or power is arbitrary, neither fair nor just. Some women and men have it and some do not. This is the 'injustice' Kurt Vonnegut Jr alludes to in a darkly satirical story in his collection *Welcome to the Monkey House*. Vonnegut conjures up an America in which everyone is truly equal: the beautiful are forced to wear masks and other appurtenances that disguise or disfigure them; ballerinas must carry weights; and the overly intelligent are fitted with headsets that fill their ears with periodic squeals and stop them thinking too hard. Presiding over this America of the twenty-first century is the forbidding figure of Diana Moon Glampers, the United States Handicapper General, whose role it is to ensure that 'nobody was smarter than anybody else . . . nobody was better looking than anybody else . . . nobody was stronger or quicker than anybody else . . . they were equal every which way'.[13]

We do not need to live in the world Vonnegut imagines to know that among both women and men, the distribution of sexual power is profoundly undemocratic. Paglia's argument that women should reclaim their power and cease behaving like victims is laced with a stiff shot of sexual Darwinism: more power to the young, the glamorous and the beautiful and bad luck to the ugly, the old and the fat.

This gives us another hint at what it is that really unites Paglia and those who would appear to be her intellectual antagonists, Dworkin and MacKinnon, namely, a profoundly individualistic view of human relations and human experience, in which the self is always at the centre. In Paglia's case it is the controlling self, the self for whom other people are only objects, accessories to our desires and designs. For Dworkin and MacKinnon, it is the self as victim, defined by the need to repel sexual 'invasion' and assert the primacy of individual autonomy as an absolute principle. Either way, what we are offered is an emotionally claustrophobic and intellectually shabby view of the world, which betrays a limited compehension of the depth and complexity of men's and women's sexual experience of themselves and each other—in other words, an *adolescent* view of the world.

Moreover, both these apparently opposed views prescribe a limited range of roles and moral possibilities for men. Men are either a kind of 'collective perpetrator', oppressing all women at all times, or the prisoners of their penises, driven by their relentless sexual urges and thus susceptible to sexual control by the wily, self-aware woman. In fact, there is very little to separate these two portraits. Neither of them allows any room for the possibility that men might be capable of real intimacy, trust or companionship with women, or that they might desire it.

These are the possibilities Helen Garner seeks to defend in her letter to the Master of Ormond College, and indeed the whole of her book: the capacity of men and women to behave towards each other with 'kindness'. Yet, in her desire to shield intimate relations between the sexes and men, in particular, from gender warfare, she comes perilously close to espousing a similar position to Paglia's. At one point in the book she describes a conversation with the women's officer at Melbourne University, a young student activist to whom she gives the pseudonym Christine G-. Christine G- insists on the need to punish academics who sexually harass their students. Garner, who believes conciliation would have been a more human approach, uses the word 'ferocity' to describe the way the young women who claimed to have been harassed and their supporters had wanted such punishment meted out. Both she and Christine G- become increasingly angry, until Garner decides to lay it on the line:

> 'As you get older,' I said, . . . 'you begin to understand that a lot of men in these harassment situations are weak. You realise that behind what you saw as force, all these years, there's actually a sort of terrible pathos. Blokes who come on to girls are putting themselves out on a limb—their *self* is at risk. You start to learn that women have got a particular power of their own, if they knew how to use it'.[14]

There is a 'terrible pathos' about this passage, but not the kind Garner herself alludes to. What is pathetic about it is the way in which Garner is prepared to infantilize male sexuality, or rather to perpetuate the existence of a certain kind of infantile male sexuality, as if she were in some way doing men—and women—a favour. Why should a man's 'self' be at risk every time he makes a pass at a woman he is attracted to? Do we really want to perpetuate the chronic lack of sexual confidence, self-worth and dignity this passage suggests as the distinguishing features of Australian male sexuality?

Garner identifies some things that are true about many men's sexuality. She points to the fragility of conventional masculinity—its underlying vulnerability, panic about sexual potency, and fear of women's sexual power. Yet she seems content to preserve the status quo, arguing that men's sexual vulnerability places women in a special position of power. Thus, she reasons, when one of the young women in the Ormond College case stated that the alleged harassment had made her feel like 'a worthless sexual object', Garner dismisses this as a 'bit of feminist sabre-rattling on behalf of a young woman who has not taken the responsibility of learning how to handle the effects, on men, of her beauty and her erotic style of self-presentation'. This young woman, Garner believes, must expect to take on the responsibility that beauty endows; she must realize 'what a powerful anima figure she is to the men she encounters in her life'.[15]

Why should women have to take responsibility for men's sexual responses to them? This expectation simply reinforces the split built into the gender contract: women take responsibility for the 'private' world of feelings and intimacy—in which sex plays a central role—and men take responsibility for the 'public' world of work, money and power. This split condemns men to a state of permanent emotional adolescence. In this public world, becoming an adult involves taking on responsibility; so too, in the world of the feelings, emotional maturity means becoming responsible for our own feelings and needs, and the impact they have on the needs and feelings of others.

Portraying men, as Garner and Paglia do, as somehow at the mercy of women's 'erotic style of self-presentation', as the *objects* of women's power to fascinate, precludes them from taking responsibility for their own sexual feelings. Of course, the way we feel about someone sexually, and the dynamics of control and surrender involved in whether or not we decide to go to bed with them are subtle and complex. We take control and give up control all the time when we're having sex, often without having made a conscious decision to do so. But responsibility is a different thing from control. It is not a matter of men exercising more sexual 'self-control', in the Victorian sense, but of being aware of the nature of their feelings and aware that it is their choice as to how they act on them—or don't act on them.

Garner's argument that women should recognize that they have 'a particular power of their own, if they knew how to use it'—words almost identical to those used by Camille Paglia[16]—is all the more disturbing because it implicitly reinforces a whole set of attitudes to women's and men's sexuality, which her generation of feminists worked very hard to break down. The notion that men are driven by an insatiable sex drive of which they are not the masters goes hand in hand with the view that women are somehow less sexual than men, less susceptible to desire, and less sensual and passionate in their enjoyment of sexual pleasure. This was a view that became common in nineteenth-century Europe, especially in Victorian England, where physicians wrote learned treatises on the differences between male and female sexual behaviour. Dr William Acton, one of the leading experts of the time on sex and sexual disorders, wrote that 'the majority of women (happily for them) are not very much troubled with sexual feeling of any kind', and that even when these feelings were roused, they were 'very moderate compared with [those of] the male'.[17]

Before the nineteenth century, women's sexual desires were generally considered to be as strong as men's, or if anything, stronger. One strand of Christian thought dating back to the early church fathers tended to identify women with sex and sex with the fallen, sinful side of Man's nature. Eve, the first woman, was considered responsible for the Fall because she had tempted Adam to eat the fruit from the tree of the knowledge of good and evil.

This original temptation became linked with the sexual temptation represented by all women—in the eyes of the church fathers. They passed on to Western Christianity a strong tradition of male sexual disgust at what they saw as women's uncontrollable lust—all the more remarkable since Jesus' chosen companion in the latter part of his life was the prostitute Mary Magdalen.

However, this strongly moralistic view of women's sexuality was by no means dominant in pre-modern Europe. Chaucer's *Canterbury Tales* and Boccaccio's *Decameron* are full of stories of women with strong and enthusiastic sexual appetites, who are not condemned or vilified by the authors for their delight in desire. Indeed, as the historian Thomas Laquer has shown, until the eighteenth century, women's sexual pleasure was considered to be an essential part of reproduction. It was broadly believed by medical science that women could not conceive without first having an orgasm. During the eighteenth century, however, physicians and philosophers began to record cases of women who had been impregnated in their sleep, or some form of coma, and to speculate about how this might have happened. Before long, medical science had established that orgasm in women was only incidental to conception (though, as we know now, it actually helps). Once this link was broken, women's sexual pleasure became effectively redundant. Within the utilitarian ethos of emerging capitalism, the sexual fulfilment of wives was no longer likely to figure as a high priority for husbands, since it no longer served a useful purpose. It was only a small step from there to believing that women had no 'sexual feelings', as Dr Acton put it. Science played midwife to a process that moved European sexual sensibility from the playful and uninhibited eroticism of Fielding's *Tom Jones* to the repressed refinement of Jane Austen in the space of a generation. In so doing, it helped to install a set of sexual stereotypes that persisted well into this century. It was these stereotypes, at least as they related to women, that the feminism of the 1960s and 1970s rejected—but which Dworkin, Paglia and Helen Garner, from their own different perspectives, and despite their own different agendas, seem quite happy to revive in relation to men's sexuality.[18]

In many ways, especially during the Victorian period, these stereotypes were linked to the sexual double standard. Sex with more than one woman before and during marriage was considered acceptable for a man, because he 'couldn't help himself'. Women, however, were expected to have only one sexual partner: if they chose to have more, it was considered a sign of either vice or illness. Lawrence Stone, the great British historian of marriage and divorce, points out that the double standard is closely bound up with the protection of property and the legal principles of inheritance. When a woman committed adultery, says Stone, her action was regarded as 'an unpardonable breach of the law of property and idea of hereditary descent', and was severely punished by the law. Male philandering, by contrast, was seen as 'a regrettable but understandable foible'.[19]

Of course, the double standard goes back a long way before the Victorian era. It is one of the subjects of a conversation in Castiglione's *Book of the Courtier*. In the course of a discussion on the character of women, Signor Gaspare remarks that 'countless evils' arise from the sexual incontinence of women, and that this is why it is more important for a woman to preserve her 'one virtue of chastity' than a man. Otherwise, he argues,

> there would be doubts about one's children, and the bond which binds the whole world on account of blood, and of each man's natural love for his own offspring, would be dissolved. So women are more sternly forbidden a more dissolute way of life than men, whose bodies do not bear their children for nine months.

Ever ready to spring to women's defence, the Magnifico replies that

> we [men] have granted ourselves the license by which we want the same sins that are trivial and sometimes

> even praiseworthy when committed by men to be so damnable in women that they cannot be punished enough, save by a shameful death, or at least everlasting infamy.[20]

Whether the setting is Italy in the early sixteenth century or Victorian England, the message is clear: men's desire to control women's sexuality is bound up with a belief that both women and children are property. This belief was enshrined in the laws of many European countries until the latter part of the nineteenth century. Under it wives (and children) were considered to be the legal property of husbands. Implicitly, wives were also sexual property, to be used according to the will of husbands, and jealously guarded against the sexual encroachment of other men.

Just how strongly this notion of women as sexual property has survived up to the present day is evident from the testimony of Sheree Lea Seakins, quoted in Chapter 4. Explaining that she had killed her husband, Seakins described how, among other things, 'he used to rape me if he wanted sex, and if I didn't want it he would just rape me anyway. To him because I was his wife I was his property and he owned me, that was his exact words, I was his wife and he owned me.'[21] The converse of this belief is that any woman who is not identifiably the property of a man must be a kind of sexual *terra nullius*, fair game for the sexual advances of men, whether wanted or unwanted.

It's precisely these attitudes to women and their sexuality—attitudes that spring from the view that men have a right to sexual gratification from women—that are being challenged by the availability of sexual harassment procedures. While our notions of rights and entitlements are very closely bound up with property, they are also bound up with power. If a man has power over a woman by virtue of his superior status or position, whether it is in a factory, an office, a university or any other 'public' setting, and if he believes that he has a right to sexual access to her, he may seek to exercise that right whether she wants it or not. In a more extreme variation of this attitude, men may believe that if they have the right to control over a certain public space—a workplace or institution they've been accustomed to dominate—they also have the right to sexual control over women who venture into that space. Or, conversely, they may try to use sex itself as a way of re-asserting control over their territory. This is plainly what's at stake in the Australian Futures Exchange and the town of Normal. The intensity and vengefulness of men's responses in both these cases can, I think, be at least partly explained by the fact that women's 'intrusion' into their territory has happened so recently and so quickly, and that women now have some recourse to the law in a way they never had before.

It's all the more perplexing, then, that Helen Garner should deplore the 'ferocity' with which the Ormond College women pursued their alleged harasser. Garner is forgetting a part of recent history. Women—and men—have only had the option of complaining formally about sexual harassment, or taking legal action over it, for a little over a decade. Having been a student at an Australian university at a time when procedures for dealing with sexual harassment were first being introduced, I can vividly remember the extent of academic opposition to making such procedures official university policy. Equally vivid is the memory of certain male academics privately bemoaning to me the fact that they would no longer be able to extract sexual favours from their 18- and 19-year-old female students, which they had done previously by suggesting to the young women in private meetings that their marks would suffer if they did not 'come across'. These men believed that sex with students was an entitlement, a perk that went with the job. There were good reasons for introducing sexual harassment guidelines at universities, and good reasons for prosecuting academics who transgressed them, which remain relevant.

In some cases, however, students do want to go to

bed with their lecturers, and may even initiate a sexual relationship with them. Many academics are happily married to former students. To proscribe such marriages or relationships, or argue that they are somehow oppressive to women or men, is patronizing and paternalistic. It denies to women—and men—the ability to make choices about their emotional and sexual lives as adult human beings. Moreover, it entrenches the kind of view of sexual relations that informs Andrea Dworkin's tirades against intercourse, namely, that any kind of power differential between partners in a sexual relationship is morally wrong. Yet this is precisely what some universities are now attempting to do, by introducing regulations that would prohibit any kind of intimate relations between staff and students.

Solutions that try to impose some kind of simplistic moral clarity on the complex interactions of sex and power will not help us bring a halt to the warfare between men and women or encourage 'warmer relations' between them. As I've suggested, we need to see disputes over sexual harassment not as individual cases, but as part of a much larger drama, in which women are challenging men's sexual control over them in a whole range of arenas, both private and public. As in any major shift in the balance of power in a society, there are bound to be injustices and excesses, but this does not mean that the process of change and challenge will not, or should not, proceed. Men will continue to be angry with women and women will no doubt continue to be angry with men. Rather than trying to end the hostilities by cordoning off the sexual battlefield and imposing on men and women a whole new set of sexual taboos, we would do better to institute some confidence-building measures.

Confidence-building measures require good faith and a willingness to compromise on both sides. Of course, it's somewhat fanciful to speak of men and women as 'sides' in a conflict when they are not organized as such, and when there is no sign of any great solidarity in either group. Yet it's precisely in the case of the sorts of conflicts I've been discussing in this chapter that men and women start to see themselves as separate groups with separate interests. And although we cannot really imagine something like a charter or treaty between men and women, we can at least imagine what such a charter might include.

Concessions will have to be made by both men and women. The most obvious and practical concession that men will need to make is to acknowledge that the 'unwritten laws' about what is and isn't appropriate sexual behaviour towards women are a great deal clearer than many men are prepared to admit. The vast majority of cases of sexual harassment involve men and women who have not been to bed together. Helen Garner seems to feel that cases like the Ormond College one are somehow making courtship or seduction more difficult and fraught with danger, particularly for men. This is disingenuous in the extreme. I make no comment on the veracity of anyone's account of what happened at Ormond College when I say that it ought to be very clear to an adult man that putting one's hand on a woman's breast before she has given you any indication that she is sexually interested in you, kissed you, or been physically affectionate in another way is clumsy and inappropriate. A woman who is setting out to seduce a man does not usually grab him by the crotch or pinch his nipples as an opening gambit. Successful seduction is as much a matter of manners, patience and consideration, as it is of passion and animal magnetism, and there is no reason why men should find it more difficult to learn these things in a sexual context than in any other.

Similarly, men will have to be prepared to give up the old excuse that they are somehow rendered powerless, deprived of any control over their sexual urges by a woman who is displaying her sexual attractiveness in an open way. Here Helen Garner makes a telling and useful point when she says that men have no 'language of appreciation' for women's beauty or sexual radiance. Is this perhaps because they have no language of appreciation for their own? Women are quite capable of admiring and appreciating the sexual attractiveness of other women—whereas for heterosexual men, at least in the Christian West, acknowledgement of the beauty of the male form is strictly taboo. Perhaps straight men might become more comfortable with the sexual radiance of women if they were able to experience themselves and their bodies as 'objects of desire'—for both women *and* men. Whatever the case, the pretence that men become passive victims of a woman's beauty and sexual confidence, is something ultimately demeaning to men.

A small example from the television comedy *Seinfeld* helps to illustrate this point. In one episode, George, who lives with his parents, is caught 'doing it with himself' by his mother when she returns unexpectedly from shopping. George tells his friends about this embarrassing episode and says he has taken a vow to give up the solitary vice altogether and remain 'master of his domain'. This prompts the four friends to a contest in which they bet on who can remain 'master' for longest. But, almost immediately, the three males are confronted with a sore test of their resolve: a beautiful woman, who lives in the building opposite, and whose window is clearly visible from Jerry Seinfeld's apartment, has taken to wandering around her own flat naked. Kramer sets up a pair of binoculars at the window. Shortly afterwards, all four are in Jerry's apartment when the voluptuous neighbour makes her appearance. While Jerry and George groan and contort with sexual frustration, Kramer disappears, only to return less than two minutes later—relaxed, loose-limbed, but clearly no longer master of his domain.

Kramer's response to his own feelings of sexual excitement is a pragmatic and sensible one. Sadly, some men seem to be affronted by women who display their beauty and sexual attractiveness openly. I think this feeling stems from their lack of sexual confidence, their alienation from their own bodies, and above all their simultaneous need for, and fear of, emotional intimacy. For many men, sex is the primary way in which they feel they can have access to such intimacy and, at the same time, the surrender of control that intimacy involves represents a powerful threat to their own sense of autonomy.

It seems to me, that women will need to exercise enormous patience with men—patience that is not simply a matter of condescension to men's less well-developed understanding of their own feelings and their often 'inarticulate speech of the heart', to quote Van Morrison. If women truly want men to engage with them as equals and adults, they will have to acknowledge that men's task in constructing a form of masculinity that will allow them to do this is a long and difficult one. It is not simply a matter of men doing more housework, learning some new sexual techniques, or attending a bit of therapy. The task for men is to achieve a degree of emotional self-reliance that will enable them to meet women as equals, rather than as eternal sexual and emotional supplicants. Men are used to being emotionally self-reliant in contexts such as war, where they are capable of displaying extraordinary emotional courage and fortitude. Discovering such qualities on the sexual battlefield may, in some ways, prove a more difficult challenge. This challenge is made all the more complicated when not only men's sexuality, but masculinity itself is on trial.

7

The case against masculinity

Masculinity is in trouble. In contemporary Australia, it leads a double life, a schizophrenic existence in the shadowy and ambiguous world of our cultural fantasies. Occasionally, the contours of this life are thrown into sharp relief. Reading the accounts of Martin Bryant's murderous rampage in Port Arthur, during which he cold-bloodedly shot mothers and small children in the head at close range, one could be forgiven for thinking that there was something uniquely and pathologically masculine about the act. There are no similar instances of women embarking on a killing spree in our recent history. Yet, as a columnist in the *Sydney Morning Herald* pointed out in the week following the Port Arthur murders, the bloody spectacle also revealed another side of masculinity. A number of Bryant's male victims died shielding their wives and children with their own bodies, throwing themselves in the path of the bullets by sheer reflex action.

Port Arthur shows us the extremes of masculinity in action: narcissistic and self-centred brutality on the one hand, and extraordinary courage and self-sacrifice on the other. In the much less extreme and dramatic circumstances of everyday life, our attitudes to manhood and what it means are also deeply divided. The 'new father' has entered the media mainstream, and is regularly celebrated in advertising and the newspaper commentaries of Steve Biddulph and other custodians of the middle-class conscience. Men are adjured to spend more time with their children, to become more involved with parenting and more 'in touch' with the nurturing emotions. At the same time, an opposing and no less powerful series of images surrounding men's relationship to children circulates in the media and popular culture. Behind the warm and comforting figure of the new father lurks the shadow of his alter-ego, the pederast and perpetrator of physical and sexual abuse.

This is particularly clear in the case of men who stand in for fathers or mothers in caring for children. In early 1996, Qantas issued an internal directive that male flight attendants would no longer be allowed to take care of children travelling unaccompanied on their flights. Not surprisingly, male flight attendants were not impressed, and passed details of the directive on to the media. 'They're very upset,' reported Caroline Andoven, a union official, 'because of the question mark this places on their character'.[1] Shortly afterwards, an even more remarkable aspect of Qantas policy came to light. In a 1995 edition of *Cabin Crew News*, the airline's internal newsletter, it was stated that unaccompanied children must not be seated next to male passengers. Now it was the entire sex that, unsupervised, could not be trusted.

It is, of course, all too easy to hold up examples such as this as evidence of a deep-seated social prejudice against men. One might reasonably suppose that Qantas was simply protecting itself from a possible lawsuit, at a time when Australians are becoming more litigious, and an institution as venerable as the Catholic Church itself is facing legal action because of child sexual abuse by members of the clergy. In all sorts of other contexts, however, a generalized anxiety about the potentially predatory nature of male sexuality makes itself felt—not least in the minds of men. Male child-care workers report that they regularly find themselves in a dilemma as to how much physical contact they should have with, and how much affection they should express for, the children they look after. However, the deep ambiguity in our attitude to the nurturing male is at its clearest in the cult of the naked father.

It's become a commonplace of contemporary photography in popular magazines that if you are going to take a picture of Dad and the kids, Dad should be wearing as little as possible. So, for example, the 24 April 1996 edition of *Who Weekly* features a colour photo of footballer Andrew Ettinghausen dandling his two infant daughters on his knee. The daughters are wearing white nighties; Ettinghausen is clad in a pair of boxer shorts and nothing else. There is nothing remarkable about this image. Since the late 1980s, we've seen hundreds of similar images in advertising, TV, films and poster shops. It's interesting to reflect, however, on precisely what it says and doesn't say. Where, for example, is Mum? If she were included in the picture, would she also be dressed only in her underwear? And if so, would she be accused—as psychologists regularly accused mothers in the 1960s and 1970s—of 'sexualising' the mother–child relationship?

I don't want to suggest that there is necessarily anything in the least bit sinister or prurient in such images of the naked father (though, as I'll suggest in a later chapter, I'm inclined to suspect that they are profoundly narcissistic). In one sense, there's no doubt that we ought to encourage images of male physicality associated with warmth and nurture rather than power. The prevalence of these images, though, suggests that they actually represent something else—a foil or counterpoint to our anxiety about the predatory and demonic aspects of male sexuality, particularly as it relates to children. As a long-term strategy, this is unlikely to be successful. The trouble that heterosexual masculinity is in is too deep.

In this book, I am trying to argue for a sympathetic response to this trouble, but one that does not provide alibis for either men or women. Feminism has opened up a space in which to talk about the demonic aspects of masculinity. Without feminism, the conspiracy of silence about child sexual abuse would not have been broken, and without feminism sexual abuse could not have been exposed as something that inheres in the nuclear family itself, rather than being the domain of lone perverts and sexual outcasts. Yet feminism has also opened the space for a cultural conversation about new and positive possibilities for masculinity. It has precipitated an urgent desire on the part of women that men take more responsibility for the care of their children—a desire that has been answered, to a certain extent, by men themselves. As a culture, we continue to be deeply unsure what it is we expect of men. A welter of confused and conflicting images of masculinity exist.

Sex and sexuality act as a focus, magnifying deeper, yet less clearly defined cultural anxieties about masculinity. In recent years, one particular branch of feminist thought has mounted a powerful critique of contemporary masculinity, one which goes beyond attacking men's responsibility for the oppression of women, and argues that it is masculinity itself that is responsible for the destruction of the natural world, colonial exploitation, war and poverty. In this chapter, I shall explore the nature and origins of this case against masculinity, the extent of its significance, and its relevance to men.

THE EMPEROR'S NEW CLOTHES

As we've seen in Chapter 2, a crisis of masculinity occurred both in European and in American culture roughly a century ago. This crisis was precipitated in large part by women's demands for legal and economic rights, and their very modest progress towards attaining these—but also by other, less tangible cultural anxieties about the 'feminization of men'. There is, however, one important difference about the contemporary dilemma of manhood, one which distinguishes it clearly from previous crises. Whereas the primary concern of writers at the end of the nineteenth century was that men were being emasculated, whether through the onslaughts of the bluestockings, or the insidious influence of an effete and decadent culture—typified by the figure of the dandy—the problem for contemporary masculinity is quite the reverse. The crisis of masculinity in our time arises out of a call for *even more* emasculation, rather than a revivification of manhood. Never before has the whole moral legitimacy of masculinity *as a way of being in the world* come under such concerted assault. More and more, in the late twentieth century, masculinity has come to be seen as a destructive force. Images of violation and domination are applied to men's treatment of the natural world and their own species: the devastation of the environment and the stockpiling of weapons of mass destruction are attributed to their desire to subjugate and control.

Even in such conservative domains as the Catholic Church, there is a growing and influential body of radical theology, which argues that Christians have been the victims of a patriarchal hoax. Through close scrutiny of the original biblical texts, scholars have shown that many of the qualities attributed to the God of the Old Testament were in fact feminine. The distortion of this original tradition by the church fathers from St Augustine onwards, it is argued, has produced a faith and a doctrine hostile to the creative and nurturing energies of women and femininity, hostile, indeed, to creation itself.[2]

At a cultural level, masculinity is undergoing what the German philosopher Jürgen Habermas has called a crisis of legitimation, a moment in the life of a society, or a political regime, when the right of those who hold power to hold it is suddenly called into question and is no longer acknowledged by the broad mass of the population. It's that moment in which people begin to admit to themselves and each other that the emperor is not wearing any clothes. As we'll see, criticism of traditional masculinity is a characteristic of many of the new social movements that have sprung up since the 1960s, most particularly the peace movement and the environmental movement. Yet a perception that masculinity is innately threatening and destructive is part of the experience of many of the men I've spoken to in the course of writing this book. We'll encounter some of these men in the following chapter. Bill, the Olympic sportsman we met in Chapter 5, describes his feelings about masculinity like this:

> I had a belief that men were dangerous, that stepping into the masculine meant you got hurt. What we see in the wider society, the violence, is big boys who haven't grown up, haven't accepted their power, their responsibility.

We are dealing here with a further aspect of the 'power paradox' I posed at the beginning of this book, one that cannot simply be explained in terms of economic change and the demise of men's role as breadwinner within the nuclear family. How are we to explain this paradox? Partly, at least, as the symptom of a crisis of legitimation, an intimation that the moral foundations of masculinity are rotten.

This is the key to understanding the paradox I've outlined above. Since the 'Second Wave' feminism of the 1960s, a certain section of the women's movement has progressed from simple demands that women be given equality with men, to a much more radical critique of masculinity itself. This radical critique has been surprisingly successful in gaining cultural influence. Not only have the moral underpinnings of men's power in the world been attacked: feminists have launched a powerful case arguing that men and masculinity are responsible for, or complicit in, many of the evils that afflict humanity in the late twentieth century. This crisis of masculinity is part of a much larger cultural crisis, a crisis in our attitude to the modern world itself.

THE VICTORY OF THE EUNUCHS

> I think there is a strong impulse towards emasculation in all men, particularly today.
>
> Obviously men are on the back foot and very much

> conscious of the fact at the moment. Masculinity, and I mean that in the broadest possible sense—the generally masculine attitude—which has got us I guess in so much trouble—the macho attitude towards knowledge and nature . . . if that is masculinity then I think most of the problems of the world can be sheeted home to it. That's a factor that no matter how aggressively masculine you wish to remain you can't ignore.
>
> David Foster, speaking on *Books and Writing*, ABC Radio National, 12 April 1996

David Foster made these remarks apropos the publication of his novel *The Glade within the Grove*, a huge, rambling comic epic about a 1960s commune in the Southern Highlands of New South Wales in which a number of the men decide to emasculate themselves and become eunuchs. Foster, who has written a number of novels about some of the more aggressively masculine aspects of Australian culture and who has worked as a prawn fisherman and postman, is not what you could call a feminist or a SNAG. Yet the whole thesis of the novel—that there is something destructive about masculinity, and indeed about our whole culture, and that nothing less than a collective act of spiritual, if not literal emasculation will save us from self-destruction—shares a great deal with certain branches of contemporary feminism, in particular what has come to be known as eco-feminism.[3]

Eco-feminism began to emerge as a significant current within the environmental movement in the late 1970s. Women were heavily involved in the peace movements and campaigns against nuclear energy in Germany, Britain, the Netherlands and some other neighbouring countries. They drew links between the proliferation of weapons of mass destruction, the nuclear industry, and male domination of governments and political structures. 'Take the toys from the boys' was a slogan often seen on banners at peace marches in Europe in the early 1980s. It was, for many people living in Europe at the time—including myself—a slogan easy to sympathise with. During the two years I spent studying in a small town in the south of Germany,

President Reagan announced that it might be necessary to fight a limited nuclear war in central Europe in order to contain the threat of Communism and NATO decided to deploy a new generation of medium-range missiles with nuclear warheads on German soil. Watching the political and military leaders of West and East discussing the need for ever more, newer and better nuclear weapons, the idea of taking the toys from the boys seemed eminently sensible, if utopian. The presence of Mrs Thatcher among their ranks, herself one of the most ardent supporters of the nuclear deterrent, should perhaps have raised more doubts than it did at the time about whether or not women would be less hawk-like if they, and not the boys, were in charge of the toys.

Eco-feminism developed out of the immediate context of the peace and anti-nuclear movements into a broad philosophical vision, which rests on the assumption that there is an explicit link between the oppression of nature and the oppression of women.[4] The early manifestos of eco-feminism argued that solutions to environmental problems could not be achieved without the inclusion of a feminist perspective, and a feminist critique of the connections between men's power over women and men's power over nature. More recently, the scope of eco-feminism has expanded, drawing links with the struggles of women in the Third World against what they see as the continuing colonial domination of the West, driven by the 'European project of so-called modernity or progress'.[5] A recent book on eco-feminism, a collaboration between an Indian and a German feminist, describes the guiding principles of eco-feminism like this:

> Wherever women acted against ecological destruction or/and the threat of atomic annihilation, they immediately became aware of the connection between patriarchal violence against women, other people and nature, and that: In defying this patriarchy we are loyal to future generations and to life and this planet itself. We have a deep and particular understanding of this both through our natures and our experience as women.[6]

One of the principal proponents of eco-feminism is an Australian philosopher, Val Plumwood, whose concern for nature has survived a severe, almost fatal, mauling from a crocodile in the Northern Territory. Plumwood broadens the scope of the eco-feminist thesis to embrace a critique of what she sees as the male-centred nature of the whole tradition of modern Western thought.

According to Plumwood, ever since the rise of scientific rationalism—exemplified by the philosophy of Descartes—Western thought has divided the world up into sets of opposing categories, distinguished, above all, by gender. On the one side is the masculine sphere, the domain of science, rationality and order—the dwelling place of the mind. This masculine sphere is also the public sphere, the place in which political and social conflicts are played out, and the social world in which the way we live is shaped. By contrast, the feminine sphere is the domain of emotion, intuition and the body. It is, above all, the domain of nature rather than culture. In this view, women and the feminine have no role to play in social or political life. Their concern is with reproduction and the purely private world of the family. These two spheres exist in a relationship of hierarchy: the masculine is superior to the feminine; science and rationality are superior to intuition and emotion; culture is superior to nature. Because of this superiority, the masculine sphere may legitimately exercise power over the feminine, in order to shape it to more rational ends. This assumption of a right to dominate, says Plumwood, is at the core of masculinity and the core of the Western civilisation of the Enlightenment.[7]

This critique of 'masculine' thought is by no means exclusive to eco-feminism. Much contemporary feminist theory draws attention to what it calls the 'gendered' nature of knowledge in Western science and Western culture. Even abstract and theoretical ways of understanding the world, such as philosophy, have a gender, feminists argue, because they tend to assume that 'the citizen' or the 'the individual' is always male.[8]

Indeed, the very creation of knowledge itself has largely depended on the sexual division of labour; until recently, the vast majority of male scientists, philosophers, writers and artists have had their dinners cooked, their children cared for and their shirts ironed by wives or female servants, while they 'got on with their work'.

Eco-feminism, however, does not stop at pointing out that knowledge is gendered. It draws a direct line from the Enlightenment to Hiroshima and Chernobyl, and ascribes the blame for these catastrophes to men. The arrogance of science and scientists, their unswerving belief in the value of rationality and technological progress, are seen as directly responsible for the devastation of the environment and the rape of nature. The metaphor is chosen quite deliberately, for, in the eco-feminist analysis, the destructive propensities of technology, hand-in-glove with the ruthless energies of capitalism and imperialism, are propelled by a distinctively male lust for power and dominion over the earth and all its creatures.

At least one eco-feminist philosopher has suggested that the roots of this pathological need to dominate and control lie in men's inability to bear children.[9] The argument runs as follows: men cannot create life within their own bodies. As a consequence, they experience their own mortality in a very different way from women—who can, to a certain extent, overcome their own mortality through giving birth to children. Men try to confront or escape from their mortality in different ways. This may involve withdrawing from the life of the body into the life of the mind, or seeking to understand and control the primal energies of nature with which women are more directly in touch. In its most extreme form, this form of masculine desire gives rise to the Frankenstein complex—the attempt to outdo nature by bringing forth life artificially, out of the womb of the intellect rather than the body. Recent developments in genetics and biotechnology suggest that it may not be long before this fantasy becomes a reality.[10]

We need to be quite clear about the implications of this argument. It is masculinity itself—or more accurately, a particularly Western, capitalist, late-industrial version of masculinity that stands accused, and the charges against it are manifold: the destruction of forests and lands and the creatures that live in them, the befoulment of the oceans and the air, and the terrible suffering inflicted by man on his own kind in the course of war and colonial expansion.

According to the feminist scholar and critic, Rita Felski, this critique of masculinity has now become part of the 'common sense' of mainstream feminist thought, which sees fundamental characteristics of the modern world, shaped by men, as inimical to the interests and concerns of women. Mainstream feminism, she writes, is permeated by 'a belief that such phenomena as industry, consumerism, the modern city, the mass media, and technology are in some sense fundamentally masculine, and that feminine values of intimacy and authenticity remain outside the dehumanizing and alienating logic of modernity.[11] Felski herself believes that this view of the modern world does women no favours, since it makes them into purely passive participants in the shaping of social and political reality and thereby effectively 'writes them out of history'.[12]

As Felski says, however, the comprehensive case against masculinity mounted by eco-feminism and related branches of feminist thought has become remarkably influential; and not only among feminists. It has found its way into places as diverse as David Foster's novel and radical theology, as well as increasingly permeating global popular culture.

Consider the two *Terminator* films, which appeared in the 1980s and were enormously successful with audiences around the world. Both films carry an explicitly feminist message, one which strikes at the moral foundation of masculinity itself.

In the first film, this message is more at the level of subtext. After a titanic struggle, Sarah Connor, the female lead, succeeds in destroying the Terminator, a powerful android played by Arnold Schwarzenegger, who has been sent back from the future with the sole mission of killing her. The future Arnie hails from is a post-Holocaust world dominated by machines bent on destroying the human race. In good Frankensteinian fashion these machines have turned on their masters. Built and programmed to survive nuclear attack and continue fighting the enemy at all costs, they have decided, quite reasonably, that the humans who made them now constitute the greatest threat to their survival, and are bent on their eradication. The human resistance is led by one John Connor, and it is his mother whom the Terminator is sent back through time to destroy.[13] At the end of *Terminator*, however, it is she who emerges victorious, the female warrior triumphant in the fashion of Sigourney Weaver in *Alien*.

Terminator II: Judgement Day moves from the celebration of the strong woman to a much more up-front critique of masculinity. Some 12 years have passed, and Sarah's son John is now a rebellious teenager. This time two Terminators are dispatched from the future, one with the task of killing him, and one, which has been re-programmed by the humans, sent back to protect him. The tables are turned. In this version, Arnold Schwarzenegger plays the 'good' Terminator, and in many ways his story is an allegory of masculine redemption, though one achieved only at the cost of his ultimate destruction. Prior to this catharsis, however, men come in for a pretty severe pasting from Sarah. About half-way through the film, she sets out to kill a computer scientist, the unwitting architect of World War III. He is on the point of developing a revolutionary new micro-processor, which will enable computers to become sentient, and ultimately trigger their war against humanity. At the crucial moment, however,

Sarah cannot bring herself to kill him, but instead delivers this panegyric:

> Fucking men like you built the hydrogen bomb. Men like you fired it off.
>
> You think you're so creative. You don't know what it's like to really create something, feel it growing inside you.
>
> All you know how to create is death and destruction.

At another point in the film, Sarah watches Arnold, the good Terminator, playing with her son, and muses:

> Watching John with the machine, it was suddenly so clear. The Terminator would never stop, it would never leave him, never hurt him, never shout at him, never get drunk and hit him, or say it was too busy to spend time with him. It would always be there and it would die to protect him.
>
> Of all the would be fathers who came and went over the years, it was the only one who measured up.

Though they owe a great deal to the genre called into life by Mary Shelley's *Frankenstein*, the Terminator films embody a genuine modern myth, a tragic narrative of the destructive and self-destructive essence of masculinity. Yet these are not art-house movies, tailored to a middle-class, pro-feminist perspective. They are aimed fairly and squarely at the cultural mainstream, a product of the Hollywood dream factory. In this case, the factory has brought forth a nightmare, but one which, in its popularity with audiences, shows that the crisis of masculinity has entered the mainstream, become part of the collective unconscious of late twentieth-century Western capitalism. Moreover, it is a nightmare that neatly turns Montaigne's dictum that 'the sleep of reason gives rise to monsters' on its head. Now it is Reason itself that has brought forth monsters, and the brainchildren of man, which are devouring the earth.

Whether we encounter this depiction of masculinity on the flickering screen, in the lecture theatre, or emblazoned on the banners of the environmental movement, it should be clear that it is not simply masculinity that is on trial, but the modern world itself. Men and masculinity are, in a sense, guilty by association, if not in deed. In many ways, the two are seen as synonymous. The eco-feminist critique of masculinity is, first and foremost, a critique of modernity, the technologized, rational world of industrial capitalism. This, I would argue, is one of the principal reasons why masculinity is in such deep trouble: it is increasingly seen as linked to the depredations of a whole historical epoch, extending roughly from the time of the French Revolution to our own—an epoch out of which we are now passing.

The French philosopher Luc Ferry, in his recent book *The New Ecological Order*, suggests that it would be a mistake to see this critique of masculinity as a fringe phenomenon, a marginal philosophy without any real influence. Eco-feminism, he argues, 'is beginning to occupy a less than negligible place in the heart of American feminism and beyond: it is omnipresent in universities', where, in his view, 'it strongly contributes to the reign of intellectual terror exercised in the name of political correctness'.[14] It's worth pointing out here that Ferry is resolutely a man of the Left. He is a humanist who believes that the ideas of deep ecology and eco-feminism are inimical to Enlightenment notions of justice, equality and human dignity—notions that have shaped modern history ever since the French Revolution. He is by no means anti-feminist, nor is he opposed to the aims of the environmental movement; rather, his concern is to show that eco-feminism and radical ecology run the risk of throwing the baby out with the bathwater—rejecting all aspects of the modern world, including those which have helped to liberate ordinary men and women from poverty, oppression and superstition. Ferry sees the crucial problem with eco-feminism as being its assumption that 'salvation, in effect, can only come from women'.[15] This assumption, he argues, is one that plays into the hands of precisely those conservative forces from which the feminist movement has struggled so hard to liberate women.

> That the eco-feminists hate Western civilisation is their business. That they wish to find natural justifications for this hatred means playing the game of biological determinism, of which, if it is to be taken seriously, all women will suffer the consequences.[16]

I shall return to some critical perspectives on the 'case against masculinity' in the final part of this chapter. It's interesting to note, though, that this anti-modernist attack on masculinity from groups which we're accustomed to thinking of as belonging to the Left—feminists and the environmental movement—is matched by an equal and opposite reaction from the Right.

This reaction comes in the shape of groups such as the Promise Keepers, mentioned in Chapter 2, who hold rallies all over the United States in support of 'traditional family values' and a return to wholesome, clearly-defined gender roles: man as breadwinner and woman as homemaker. The Promise Keepers are also an anti-modernist movement, although the version of modernity they are protesting against is one that begins in the 1960s, and the Golden Age they would like to restore is that of 1950s smalltown America, and not the pre-industrial epoch. Nevertheless, they and the groups like them, which are beginning to emerge in Australia, are a direct reaction to masculinity's crisis of legitimation.

In one sense, the Promise Keepers are not all that different in their motivation from those elements in American society a century ago that decried the arrival of the 'modern woman'. However, if one looks more closely at their rhetoric, it's clear that a large part of what they're objecting to is not so much equal pay and equal rights for women as the rise of 'political correctness'. For groups such as these, 'political correctness' is a catchphrase that covers a multitude of sins, but in this particular context it's seen as a kind of cultural orthodoxy that accords an automatic moral superiority to women and the feminine. Nowhere are the incursions of 'political correctness' felt to be more intrusive and offensive than in the arena of sex—though the attitudes of feminists Catharine MacKinnon and Andrea Dworkin and groups like the Promise Keepers often seem curiously similar in their desire to regulate sexuality and to codify which forms of sexual interaction are 'healthy' and acceptable, and which are not.

In this sense, the extent of the reaction *against* the diverse challenges to masculinity I've been enumerating gives us some notion of the depth and ambit of the crisis. Yet both eco-feminism, on the one hand, and the radical or fundamentalist conservatism of a group like the Promise Keepers, on the other, spring from the same source: a powerful reaction against the nature of the modern world. To understand how it is that eco-feminism and the broader feminist critique of masculinity have become as powerful and pervasive as they have, it's helpful to look back, to a time when the modern world itself was in the process of being born.

THE POWER PARADOX REVISITED

One of the difficulties in understanding the recent change in relations between men and women is that there appear to be no historical precedents with which to compare it. In analysing many of the other major political and economic changes that have taken place this century, historians often have recourse to examples from earlier epochs. In the case of the power struggle between the sexes, however, despite the parallels I've already alluded to between the 1890s and the 1990s, the differences far outweigh the similarities. The gains made by women in our own time are a great deal more far reaching and fundamental than they were a hundred years ago, and are much less likely to be reversed.

If we want to find historical precedents for the rise of feminism and its impact on mainstream cultural values, we need to look beyond the immediate context of gender relations. If, as I've suggested, feminism has managed successfully to challenge the legitimacy of male power, we may be able to better understand this success by comparing it with other junctures in history where relatively powerless groups have taken on the powerful and won. One illuminating parallel presents itself in an unlikely place—in late eighteenth-century Germany, in the years preceding the French Revolution.

By comparison with England and France at the time, Germany was both politically and economically backward. There was no great German metropolis to match Paris or London, no industry to speak of, and the German middle class was still in its infancy. In England, the merchant middle classes were becoming rich and politically influential. In Germany, by contrast, trade was still firmly in the grip of feudal rulers, and members of what middle class there was eked out an existence as tutors to their rulers' children or petty officials in their service. They were, by and large, completely excluded from any kind of real political or economic power.

Some years ago, a historian called Reinhart Koselleck set out to answer a perplexing question about German history: how was it that this marginalized middle class had nevertheless managed to exert a very considerable influence over the rulers of the time and bring about political reforms to their own advantage?[17] Koselleck's answer, arrived at after lengthy study of the philosophy and social history of the period, was that these middle-class scholars, writers and pamphleteers had managed, subtly, to change the rules of the political game. They transformed the nature of political discourse by introducing into it questions of morality, and questioning the moral authority of those in power.

It's difficult to understand, from our perspective, just what a revolutionary notion this was. Previously, the kings and princes of Europe had claimed their right to power on the basis of lineage, the grace of God, sheer brute force—or a combination of all three. The idea that they should have to justify themselves, or submit themselves to the rule of law would have struck them as bizarre. Power was power, and their right to it was absolute: the notion that they ruled by consent of their subjects, or that they were morally accountable to them, never entered their heads.

It's only with the spread of Enlightenment ideas about individual liberty and equality that this assumption was challenged. If all men were born equal, what right did one man have to rule over others, except with their free consent? Did he not have to earn that right, through just rule, wisdom, and compassion? The rulers of late eighteenth-century Germany could, of course, have simply ignored these protestations, or clamped those who made them in irons. In fact, however, they proved remarkably receptive to the criticisms made of their power. Frederick the Great of Prussia went so far as to refer to himself as 'the first servant of the state' and instituted wide-ranging social reforms.

Even though Germany did not experience a revolution as did France, Koselleck points out that the moral critique levelled against Germany's feudal rulers was remarkably successful because it did not pose a direct challenge to their power. Rather than a call to open revolt, it whittled away at the legitimacy of their right to wield power. By introducing notions of morality and accountability into politics, a small group of marginalized middle-class intellectuals were able—for a while—to change the whole basis on which politics itself were played out. By seizing what we would today call the moral high ground, they created a 'state within the state', which gradually expanded to occupy more and more of the state itself.[18]

What's interesting about this argument, for our purposes, is that it points to moments in the life of society or political system where the rules of the game shift. We might think here of the momentous changes in the former Soviet Union in the wake of Mikhail Gorbachov's introduction of *glasnost* and *perestroika*. What began as an attempt, from within, to reform the Communist Party and its control of the structures of Soviet society took on its own momentum and became a self-perpetuating process which eventually resulted in the collapse, not only of the Party, but also of the Soviet Union itself. The precondition for this process was a crisis of legitimation: the Communist Party had lost moral authority in the eyes of the majority of Soviet citizens, and with it the legitimation of its power. Glasnost and perestroika did not so much expose the true nature of the Soviet system as allow the truth about it to be spoken: all of a sudden, people could admit, without fear of punishment, that the Emperor was naked.

It would be fanciful to suggest that feminism has brought about a revolutionary reversal of the balance of power in Australia, or similar countries, comparable to the downfall of the Communist Party in Soviet Russia. At an institutional level, men still hold the reins of power, but the legitimacy of that power is crumbling. Men's moral authority has been challenged by women at many levels, from that of the family through to the courts and parliaments. The principles of equal opportunity are now enshrined in laws governing most of our major institutions and, although these principles are often breached, the essential legitimacy of their claims is seldom disputed publicly. Like the middle-class intellectuals in eighteenth-century Germany, feminism has begun to infiltrate the corridors of power, even if it has not yet gained control of the levers.

As I've been stressing throughout this book, the degree of real power and equality which women have won in the key areas which control our society—government, the banks and large corporations, the judiciary and the media—is still very limited. Feminists such as Eva Cox argue that the women's movement must redouble its efforts to get women into positions of power and authority, and to value qualities of leadership in women once they get there. Whether this will actually change the nature and culture of the dominant institutions of our society is another question. It seems to me, however, that in certain areas, such as the recognition of sexual abuse in all its forms, women have managed to change the moral agenda and achieve a position of moral authority which exceeds the extent of their actual 'power base'.

The moral critique of masculinity, whose outlines I have sketched above, goes a great deal further than this. In his book *Masculinities*, by far the most comprehensive study of masculinity in Australia to date, Bob Connell has drawn attention to 'crisis tendencies' in contemporary masculinity, brought about by what he describes as 'a historic collapse of the legitimacy of patriarchal power and a global movement for the emancipation of women'.[19] When it comes to recommending what part men should play in this process, however, Connell seems deeply uncertain. He is profoundly suspicious of any attempts to organise a men's movement, since he seems to feel that any attempt to assert that there are positive aspects to masculinity is necessarily anti-feminist and reactionary.[20] I do not believe that this is a helpful position for either men or women; and it seems to me that a good measure of Connell's ambivalence about what form a 'men's politics' ought to take comes from an unwillingness to admit that there are any elements of the case against masculinity which are unjust and unconstructive.

COUNSEL FOR THE DEFENCE

It should be clear that contemporary feminism derives a great deal of its continuing force from the moral critique of masculinity—a critique which extends far beyond a simple demand for equality. What is also clear, both from debates in the public arena and my own conversations in the course of writing this book, is that this moral critique, in certain forms, elicits a particularly angry and negative response from men. Particularly inflammatory is the assumption that men as a sex are morally abject—an assumption which runs through much eco-feminist writing, and often informs feminist positions on sexual abuse.

Anger against what is perceived as 'an indictment against a whole people', in Edmund Burke's phrase, or in this case a whole gender, is by no means confined to men. A female speaker at a pro-gun rally in rural Queensland in 1996 spoke on ABC television of the need for wives of gun owners to state publicly that 'our husbands are normal men, who have normal, healthy relationships with their wives and children. They're not monsters just because they own guns'.[21] Evidently, the speaker felt that in some way men themselves were on trial.

A case against masculinity which rests on the belief that all men are moral outcasts, or at least morally inferior to women, is not something which men should accept. Such a belief is profoundly inimical to the whole basis of liberal society, in which we assume—however naively—that we are equal before the law, and entitled to be judged according to our own individual merits and defects, not pre-judged on the basis of belonging to a particular group within society.

The real problem with the case against masculinity is that it runs the risk of strapping men—and, perhaps more significantly, women—back into the sexual straitjackets from which a century of feminist endeavour has been so concerned to liberate them. By equating masculinity with the destructive, demonic aspects of the modern world, and femininity with the creative and nurturing values, it sets up a rigidly dualistic view of gender which constrains both women and men. Some Australian feminists, such as Lynne Segal and Moira Gatens, are highly critical of this 'essentialist' approach to gender relations. They argue that such an approach, which assumes that there is something natural and essential about women's propensity to nurture, strays dangerously close to the kind of conservative notions about women, motherhood and the 'finer feelings' which formed the basis of the bourgeois nuclear family.[22] Indeed, precisely these kinds of notions are enjoying a comeback in the 1990s, in the views on child-rearing of Penelope Leach and others.

One of the more interesting paradoxes about essentialist feminism, of which eco-feminism is a prime example, is that it shares a great deal of common ground with the 'hard' sciences of which it is often so critical. Over the last 20 years, in areas such as genetics and the new branches of evolutionary theory, such as 'evolutionary psychology', science has moved further away from the idea that it is nurture which shapes our development as human beings, and more towards an insistence that we are prisoners of our genetic programming. A swathe of books has been published, arguing that whole areas of complex human motivation and emotion, from love to guilt, shame and the desire for justice, are no more than evolutionary reflexes disguised as moral behaviour.[23] Significantly, though, a great deal of this theory concentrates on human sexuality and gender difference, and what it tells us is—as Robert Wright, author of *The Moral Animal*, happily admits—not all that different from what the Victorians thought about men and women and their inclinations, desires and aspirations. Men, according to Wright, are programmed by their evolutionary psychology to want 'as many sex-providing and child-making machines as they can comfortably afford', while women are less interested in sex and want above all to 'maximise the resources available to their children'.[24] Men are naturally polygamous and unfaithful, while women are naturally monogamous and faithful; in fact, women who are promiscuous are denying their genetic programming and are likely to be punished by not being able to get a mate to commit to them, since men are unlikely to 'invest' in a mate who may bear children not his own. The 'Madonna/whore' dichotomy in the way that men see women is, according to Wright, not a product of the

Victorian sexual double standard, but something written into men's genes.[25]

It should be clear that arguments such as these, which assume that not only the behaviour, but also the moral character of men and women is a product of their 'nature', have a great deal in common with the assertions of eco-feminism that masculinity is essentially dominating and destructive, while femininity is essentially nurturing and creative. Eco-feminists, then, are not all that far removed in their view of gender differences from the geneticists and other late twentieth-century pioneers of science whom they so revile.

The task of rebutting the arguments of evolutionary psychology in an intellectually rigorous way is one that has yet to be undertaken. It is not enough to protest that these arguments are offensive; what matters is to show that they are logically and methodologically shoddy, which they are. Only a critique that engages with the actual scientific content of 'evolutionary psychology' will expose its views on gender for what they are: a conservative moral agenda masquerading as biological necessity.[26]

If, however, we want to prevent men and women from being slapped back into the sexual straitjacket by an alliance of eco-feminists and evolutionary biologists we need, among other things, to engage with and reject the eco-feminist critique of masculinity as synonymous with, and responsible for, all the negative aspects of modernity. It is easy enough to point to features of modern scientific rationalism which have brought concrete improvements in the situation of women and children—for example, the simple medical procedures, advances in hygiene and the use of anaesthetics which have dramatically reduced the risks of childbirth, for both mother and child. Conversely, there are many aspects of the modern world, and men's part in its making, which are the rightful objects of criticism. We do not need to wholeheartedly reject the modern world in order to criticise or change it. But this is not really the point. What is more important is to recognise that the kind of moral absolutism which can produce an indictment of a whole civilisation—the 'European project of so-called modernity or progress'—or of a whole gender, is anything but emancipatory, for either women or men. In the same way Rita Felski argues that we should question 'sweeping evaluations of the modern as either a liberating or repressive phenomenon',[27] we should also question assertions that women are any more or less capable of the full spectrum of human behaviours, both good and evil, than are men. We should be glad that the legitimacy of men's power is being challenged, but we should be sorry if a new moral orthodoxy, divided along gender lines, were to arise in its place.

In Chapter 8 I shall explore how one group of men is attempting to create new forms of masculinity and solidarity among men. As we'll see, however, certain aspects of this endeavour bear a surprising similarity to the guiding ideas of the eco-feminists we've encountered in this chapter.

8

The circle of men

It's swelteringly hot under the canvas. Not a breath of a breeze disturbs the heavy noonday haze in this lush valley half-an-hour's drive out of Lismore, in the heart of northern New South Wales' hippy homelands. Under a large open-sided marquee in the middle of a green field 100 men and boys sit, sprawl or lie full-length on the grass, listening while one of their number speaks. Many of them have stripped to the waist in the soupy heat. Some sport dreadlocks and multiple earrings; others have sensible city haircuts and the sleek look of professionals. The oldest man here is 75, the youngest 12. Around a quarter of the bare-chested legion reclining in the shade of the marquee are locals; others have travelled from Sydney, Adelaide, Brisbane and Tasmania to be here, at a gathering of the 'Circle of Men'. It's the third such national gathering, and the theme this year is 'Standing Up Alive—Healing the Masculine Spirit in True Community'.

All morning, one by one, as the heat of the day thickens, these men have been rising to their feet to tell their stories, confessing, seeking catharsis. Now, we are transported by this speaker's tale to another parched summer's day two years ago, on the highway winding up from Sydney into the Blue Mountains.

Fires are slinking through the deep valleys and scrambling their way up steep hillsides, taking wing on the hot dry winds blowing in from the west, beginning to sniff at the edges of towns and swallow outlying houses. In response, an army of strangers has converged on the mountains. Firefighters from the far reaches of the country have come here to defend the homes of people they have never met. Martin, an eloquent narrator, describes them crossing hot deserts to don helmets and wield hoses. In our mind's eyes, we see them smeared with soot and dazed with danger and exhaustion. In our inner ears, we can hear the rhythm of an army's feet, bent to one united purpose.

Martin tells us how, on that day, as he passed the columns of firefighters on the road, again and again he was moved to tears—so much so that he couldn't go on driving, but had to pull over to the side of the road and wait for the tears to leave him. 'I didn't know why I was crying,' he says, 'I don't cry easily. It wasn't until later that I realized what had moved me so much. It was the image of a community of men who'd come together to give help and succour to strangers. I've been accustomed to think of large groups of men as hostile, threatening, prone to arbitrary violence. It's only in wartime that we're used to seeing men perform acts of collective heroism and self-sacrifice. And I thought—is it only in times of crisis and catastrophe that men can come together in this way? Do we have to set fire to the world before we can get men to unite in peace?'

There's a faintly apocalyptic tinge to Martin's story, but no trace of histrionics. Martin has had his own clashes and crises with the world of men. After the early death of his father, he spent his teens in constant trouble with the police—his way, as he sees it now, of seeking contact with, and recognition by strong male authority. Since then he's been a marine biologist, taught at a university on the island of Tonga for five years, and is now looking after his small son full-time while his wife works. He's been a member of a men's group for a year or so, but this is his first 'men's gathering'.

Many of the other men's stories are as dramatic as Martin's in their own way, though they tend to be more purely personal and biographical in their details. Again and again, the same themes recur: unhappy childhoods, violent or distant fathers, adult lives lived in exile from one's own feelings. Often, the men break down and weep openly. It's impossible not to be moved by the sincerity of these displays of emotion, and by their very public character. The storytelling takes on the heightened intensity of theatre or religious ritual. Indeed, we've been told as we arrive for this four-day gathering that we are entering 'ritual space'. At times, though, the intensity of ritual gives way to something more reminiscent of a Scout camp. At one point towards the end of the gathering, the men form a large circle and chant and sway to the rhythm of drums, drums that have been pounding again and again in the course of the weekend. Now, under instruction from one of the 'ritual makers', groups of ten men take it in turns to step forward into the centre of the circle, form a ring within a ring and sink down dancing and chanting onto their haunches, only to spring up again as one with a cry of victory.

There's not much to distinguish this from a pack of Cubs yelling out 'Akela! Akela!' or 'Dib Dib Dob' in unison around the campfire, except that these are adult men in their 30s and 40s doing the yelling, men with mobile phones in their cars and successful careers and businesses of their own. Why are these men here? What has prompted them to travel hundreds of kilometres to spend a long weekend with a bunch of strangers performing strange and often embarrassing rituals, and opening their hearts?

Gatherings such as this are the media-visible face of the 'men's movement', and have attracted much more attention than men's violence groups or the advocates of 'men's rights'. Not surprisingly, the 'spearchuckers', as they are sometimes known colloquially, have also been the subject of a good deal of ridicule from men and suspicion from women, who think—not entirely without cause—that their avowed aim of redeeming and reconstructing masculinity conceals a desire to put women back in their place and restore masculine authority. This seems, however, to be more of a feature of men's gatherings in the United States. There were no spears in evidence at Standing Up Alive, and women were hardly mentioned in the entire four days.

Gatherings of this kind are not particularly widespread in Australia. However, the emotional territory traversed within the Circle of Men is the same as that covered by many men's support groups in both the country and the city. Many of the men who attended the gathering also belong to such groups. These are the Born-Again Blokes of whom I've given a brief portrait in Chapter 2. They see themselves as part of a men's movement dedicated to 'healing the masculine spirit' and creating new forms of masculinity that are strong, positive and compassionate. Gatherings like Standing Up Alive crystallize the ideals and aspirations of the Australian men's movement, and reveal aspects of it that are both progressive and problematic. Whether or not they represent a genuinely new form of male solidarity, which offers possibilities for changing men that may also benefit women, is a question I shall try to answer in the course of this chapter.

THE COMMUNITY OF MEN

> I grew up learning not to trust other men in numbers greater than one. My experience with other men has been that they turned into a pack of wolves—and these were my friends.

There's nothing about Alan's appearance or manner to suggest that he mistrusts his fellow man. He's a big, lean bloke in his mid-20s with an open, friendly demeanour and long black hair. He bears a strong resemblance to a member of the Red Hot Chilli Peppers, an American rock group. Alan spends a lot of his spare time surfing, and makes his living as a body-worker and healer. He's come along to Standing Up Alive at the encouragment of his friend Brendan, who's been involved in the men's movement for some time.

Growing up as a Lebanese Australian kid, Alan says he was teased and taunted by his schoolmates and 'shamed' for the colour of his skin. He describes himself as having had a soft and gentle nature as a boy. Unsure how to defend himself, he quickly learned that peer pressure could turn friends into enemies when they got together in a group. Groups of men, he says, seemed to be organized around the need to shame each other, to be driven by ego, competition and the instinct for survival.

Recently, according to Alan, becoming involved in men's groups has meant a major change in his attitude to men, and enabled him to form close friendships with other men. Yet the feelings and experiences that had shaped his basic assumptions about men are extraordinarily common. Many of the men who, like Alan, spoke out in the course of the gathering said they found it difficult to trust other men or to speak to them about anything remotely personal. Martin said that he had had 'not a great deal of respect for things masculine' and found the ways in which men are accustomed to keeping company with each other foreign and alienating: 'the group of men in the pub, the football—are not situations I feel comfortable with'.

Emotional isolation from others of their own sex was a common feature of the experience of many of the men at the gathering. Bill, a successful Olympic athlete and middle-class professional in his late 30s, whom we met in an earlier chapter described how he'd believed 'that men were dangerous, stepping into the masculine meant you got hurt'. Bill had spent a large part of his working life and leisure time in the company of men. He'd belonged to a number of sporting clubs and spent some time in the Army Reserve. Despite this, he said, he had no close male friends.

A surprisingly large number of men of widely differing backgrounds I've spoken to said the same. Interestingly enough, many of them drew a strong distinction between the conviviality men share at the pub, club or sporting fixture and genuine friendship. Most of them said they would only open their hearts to their partners or a woman friend, if they did so at all. Perhaps for this reason, many men who go along to a men's group for the first time, or to a gathering like Standing Up Alive, find the experience something of a revelation. 'I've never spoken about these things before to anyone' was a statement that recurred with the frequency of a mantra during the four days. It's as though these men are breathing a huge sigh of relief at no longer having to maintain a façade of tough, competent, self-controlled masculinity. As Bill put it:

> If you can get up and speak your fears, you take away some of the energy behind them. It's been interesting how many men have said, here I was thinking I was a unique individual with unique problems, and I'm just normal. That for me was the most important aspect of the weekend, that people can get up and say anything at all and not be judged—but on the contrary, receive pure love—that's been a very important shift for me.

As we've seen, this sense of isolation, mistrust and fear of 'opening up' to other men was also felt by many of the members of men's violence groups. Veterans of the groups speak of the support and comfort they've experienced and continue to experience within a group of men, support and comfort they say they have never received from their 'mates', not least because they weren't able to ask for it. This 'mateship without the beer' is something they regard as very valuable.

It would seem, then, that men in these different settings, from diverse class and educational backgrounds, have a common desire for greater intimacy in their relationships with other men, which is not available to them as part of conventional mateship. Australian popular culture offers men very few alternatives to the ethos of mateship. Moreover, much of the writing about men—particularly by women—tends to see the lack men identify in their relations with other men, especially with those who are supposed to be their mates, as purely a problem of communication. The conventional wisdom has it that when women begin talking together, they will very soon be discussing their personal lives and their relationships with their partners, whereas for men, this is the last topic that will be raised, if it is raised at all. Women are considered to be open, frank and empathetic in their communication with other women, while men are seen as closed, guarded, and either unsympathetic or just plain inarticulate. Often, the remedy prescribed is for men to make their style of communication more like women's: if they would become more open and expressive, and learn to articulate their feelings more, they would be happier and better people.

This prescription led the English newspaper columnist Julie Burchill to remark once that what she liked about men was the fact that they bottled everything up and never talked about their feelings. This meant, according to Burchill, that they were 'full of nasty poisons which made them interesting'. Women, by contrast, were always going on about their feelings and their personal lives, which she found 'tiresome'.

Not many women—or men, I suspect—would share Burchill's views fully. As we've seen, however, asking men to become more like women seems not to make either sex happy in the long run. More importantly, in regard to relationships between men, it misses the point. It's not so much the way in which men communicate, as the *context* in which they do so that makes it difficult for them to talk to each other. For many men, as we've seen, the primary issue is trust—the need to feel that if you unburden yourself to other men or admit that you don't feel in control of your life, you will not be shamed or ridiculed.

Exactly what it is that makes it difficult for men in Australia to feel trust towards one another is a complex question. Clearly, feelings of suspicion and mistrust towards members of one's own sex are not limited to the men in the groups I've been discussing. Reviewing Bill Hayden's autobiography, journalist and long-time member of the Canberra press gallery Alan Ramsey remarked that Hayden had been told by his mother at an early age that 'men are mongrels, all of them', and this seemed to have formed his attitude to other men for the rest of his life. Hayden, wrote Ramsey, who worked for the former Labor leader as a press secretary for five years, was 'one of the most distrusting men I ever knew'. He seemed always more comfortable in the company of women, and had only 'one real intimate', his wife Dallas.[1]

A solitary disposition in a politician is nothing unusual, and perhaps we should not attribute too much influence to the pronouncements of Bill Hayden's mother. Nevertheless, there's an echo of the words 'men are mongrels, all of them' in the way Alan described his perception of other men as 'wolves', and Martin's view of large groups of men as 'hostile, threatening, prone to arbitrary violence'. Until they discovered the men's movement, these men and the man who might have been prime minister had something in common: they experienced relations between men as inherently competitive, a state of war in which the façade of sociability and mateship hides the reality that it's every man for himself.

These men, for their own reasons, seem to have encountered all the negative aspects of Australian mateship and none of its positive aspects: solidarity, loyalty and mutual respect. The tradition of mateship in Australia was shaped by two 'primal scenes': the bush and the battlefield. In both these contexts, men had no choice but to be dependent on each other, and out of this dependence grew an extraordinary capacity for courage, self-sacrifice and devotion in looking after one's mates. This devotion and consideration survive among men in the armed services today. In the *Male Matters* series broadcast on Radio National, the photographer George Gittoes, who has travelled overseas with Australian peace-keeping forces as a 'war artist' on a number of occasions, described how, in many of the units, a sergeant will become 'mother' to the men under his command, preparing special treats for them and showing many small signs of solicitude on their behalf.

We know from the stories of many Australian soldiers just how strong the emotional bonds between men, created by the shared experience of war, can be. Comparable kinds of solidarity between men have existed in the trades union movement. Nowadays, however, the vast majority of Australian men have no direct experience of war—something for which we should be profoundly grateful—and the trades union movement is in a state of serious decline. The only form of solidarity with other men most Australian men experience is playing or watching sport.

Of course, many men—including myself—are fortunate enough to enjoy close friendships with other men, which afford an enormous amount of pleasure, comfort and what Yeats called 'heart-revealing intimacy'. From the testimonies of men whom I spoke to, it would seem that there are many more who desire such close friendships with other men, but have not been able to achieve them. There is an untold story of isolation and emotional poverty at the heart of Australian masculinity—one which prompts men such as those who attended the Standing Up Alive gathering to seek not only closer bonds of friendship with individual men, but a broader sense of masculine community. One of the explicit aims of the Circle of Men is to create an atmosphere—or to use the language preferred by many of the participants, a 'space'—in which men can reveal themselves to other men, 'speak from the heart', and know that they will be supported and their experience 'validated'. Again and again, participants in the gathering spoke of their desire for community—a desire to create a community of men that would be seen as embodying positive 'masculine' values such as courage, fortitude and protectiveness (towards nature and other human beings), as well as 'feminine' qualities of trust, compassion and acceptance. It's a community, in other words, which would unite men in the same purposeful way as the threat of bushfires or war—as Martin put it, 'a community of men who'd come together to give help and succour to strangers'—but without the need for disaster to catalyse its sense of unity and cohesion.

This is a far cry from the image of mud-smeared 'spearchuckers'. 'Community', however, is a term much bandied about in contemporary political debate, and pressed into service by groups on both the Left and the Right. Appeals to the spirit of community carry their own contradictions and unexplored questions with them—and the Circle of Men's avowed aim of 'healing the masculine spirit in true community' is no exception.

DID YE GET HEALED?

> I came mainly for the healing. I was optimistic about the whole thing—I've really enjoyed meeting up with older men, it was quite a shock that some of the stuff I went through as a kid—men who are 40, 50, 60 are dealing with the same stuff I dealt with in my childhood.
>
> Django, age 16

Django is one of the youngest participants at our gathering. He wears his name with pride, as well he might. His namesake, the great gypsy guitarist Django Reinhardt, was a fiery player and musical innovator who has left his stamp on the history of jazz, an untrained genius, an outlaw and a survivor. On the second morning, Django stands before the entire assembly of 100 men and tells his story in a simple, matter-of-fact tone:

> My mum was a chronic alchoholic . . . there was a lot of violence—basically I was really fucked up as a kid

> and my childhood could have been much much better and safer . . . I was just lucky that my Dad kept on hearing me crying over the phone and took me off. Men here have had problems with their Dads and got on fine with their Mums—I was the opposite. I was just lucky he was there to give me all the love and support that I needed. I just consider myself lucky to be this young and being able to deal with it now instead of holding onto it until I'm older—it could build up and build up and be twice as bad.

This is the part of the gathering many of the men here have come for—the open session every day in which any man can get up and speak what's on his mind. A piece of shell carved with figures from Aboriginal mythology lies in a wooden bowl in the centre of our circle. Whoever desires to speak must simply pick up the shell and hold it. He then has the right to speak without interruption for as long or as little as he likes. It might just be a few words, or a whole life's story.

Extraordinary dramas are acted out here and painful memories recalled. Many of the men speak about their fathers: fathers who were violent, fathers who ran away, fathers who never gave their approval, fathers who loved them. The oldest man there, a 75-year-old farmer from central north Queensland, has come along at the request of his son, 50 years his junior. This is his first encounter with the men's movement, and he's been made an honourary elder for the weekend. He rises and tells us how proud he is of his boy, how close he feels to him, even though they now live many hundreds of kilometres apart. The youngest participant, Joseph, a boy of 12, takes the shell and says he's been fighting like cat and dog with his brother for months and he wants to make peace. His brother gets up and they hug each other. There's hardly a dry eye in the whole tent.

Some men break down, and are held and comforted. Others vent their anger. There is something very public about these displays of emotion. In many ways, the men's speeches contain strong elements of performance. Not that this makes the feelings that accompany them any less genuine. There's not necessarily a contradiction between performance and 'speaking from the heart'. Indeed, public performance is one context in which men are permitted to do just that. We're not used to seeing men express emotion, but we are used to seeing them perform it—most commonly on the sports field, where players will weep with exultation or despair before tens of thousands of people. We, the spectators, accept this because it is a part of the spectacle—the tears are no less part of the performance than a high mark or a heroic goal, but this does not mean that they are not genuine expressions of exultation in victory or despair in defeat.

Implicit in the performances given within the Circle of Men is a desire to be recognized in one's authenticity as a man, and more than this, to be *witnessed* in an almost religious sense. Apostolic and radical Protestant churches within the Christian tradition place considerable stress on the individual's profession of faith before God being witnessed by his or her fellow believers, peers and equals, rather than being simply acknowledged by an impersonal religious hierarchy. There is something of the same character to this gathering: men who feel that their individuality, their sufferings and achievements are not recognized by the social hierarchies within which they live and work desire to be recognized by a gathering that understands itself as existing outside of those hierarchies.

In some ways, the Circle of Men is not unlike a sect, or an organization such as the Freemasons, which, in its origins at least, sought to create a closed world with its own values and guiding principles. The principles of the Circle of Men are disarmingly simple: speak from the heart rather than the head, honour and respect other men rather than trying to dominate them, be authentic in yourself and your dealings with others.

Closely linked to the idea that 'dealing from the heart' will redeem men is a pre-occupation with healing. In *Iron John*, Robert Bly talks at length about the emotional or psychic 'wounds' men receive in the course of their lives, and many of the men who attended Standing Up Alive spoke of their wounds and their desire for healing. Like Django, Bill, another of the participants, described his experience of the weekend as having had a deeply therapeutic effect:

> For me it was a big thing to come here. My father was a paranoid schizophrenic, a madman you could say. I had a belief that men were dangerous, that stepping into the masculine meant you got hurt. What I found here was really quite the opposite.
>
> It's been wonderful to see the wisdom which is in the older men—for them to share that—and it was fascinating yesterday to watch a 12-year-old stand up and say something which left many of the older men literally in tears. He had so much honesty, he was so in touch with his feelings.
>
> Here we have men from 12 to 70-odd and all sharing. Maybe some of these guys weren't validated by their fathers—most of us weren't, enough—so to be validated by 100 men—was a wonderful experience.

'Validation' is another word that crops up often during the gathering. Many of the men felt that they had never received enough 'validation' from their fathers, in the sense of sufficient approval, affection and recognition of their individuality. This lack of validation, and the harm it does, is also one of the central themes of *Iron John*. According to Robert Bly, all young men receive wounds from their fathers while they are growing up: 'blows that lacerate self-esteem, puncture our sense of grandeur, pollute enthusiasm, poison and desolate confidence, give the soul black-and-blue marks, undermining and degrading the body-image . . . these all make a defilement'.[2] Bill talks about his 'wounds' in a quite unselfconscious way:

> Everyone experiences a wound in relation to their relationship with their parents. From that wound we create a belief about ourselves—the most common beliefs are that we're unworthy, bad, powerless, that we can't trust our own hearts, or that we must control. The irony is

> we made that belief up about ourselves when we were five years old—and we keep on creating scenarios which confirm it.

Like many of the other men at the gathering, Bill sees the wounds he received in childhood as somehow central to the story of his life, and also like many of the others, with the notable exception of Django, he regards the wounds he got from his father as deeper, more lasting, more injurious to his sense of himself as a man:

> A child coming into the world wants different things from each parent. From his mother, he wants her simply to be there, to pick him up when he falls down, he wants her love. From our father we want something quite different, we want validation for our ideas, our dreams. I didn't get that from mine, so I just tried harder and harder to get that validation. He died 20 years ago and I was still there trying harder, all the time. I represented Australia in two sports, I was on a six-figure salary, and I was quite miserable, it didn't mean anything. I just came to realize yesterday what it was that had been driving me, and I was able to stand up in front of 100 men and say I feel validated here, I don't have to keep trying, enough's enough, I don't have to do anything to be who I am.

Plainly, having his story 'witnessed' by the other men was an important part of the therapeutic process Bill feels he's experienced in the course of the gathering, something that might not have happened had he talked about his 'wounds' on a one-to-one basis with a therapist or counsellor. For many like Bill, the breaking down of their sense of isolation is a powerful factor in this process. It's the discovery that they are not alone in their experience that makes attending groups such as the Circle of Men such an emotional revelation. With this revelation, for Bill, comes an acceptance of the creative contribution our wounds make to our identity and personal growth:

> What we don't acknowledge is that from our wound we get our strength. It's a double-edged sword—if we were

> deprived of love there's a huge amount of love building up in us and waiting to get out. It's important not necessarily to love your wound, but to acknowledge the other side of it.

By their own testimony, all the men I spoke to during the gathering and at its conclusion felt that it had been a positive experience for them. It's difficult to see how the breaking-down of isolation and the sense of 'healing' they reported can be anything but positive. However, we might ask ourselves why it is that 'healing' occupies such a pivotal position in the concerns of these men, and the men's movement more generally.

One fairly obvious reason, I think, is the pervasive influence Robert Bly and his Australian popularizer, Steve Biddulph, have had within the men's movement. Many of the men at Standing Up Alive had obviously read *Iron John* and internalized much of its language and conceptual framework—so much so that when they told their personal stories, it was almost as though Bly himself was talking. One cannot help wondering just how much the common features of the men's stories—unhappy or abusive relationships with fathers, lack of validation, wounding—are themselves shaped and created by the ready-made narrative of redemption Bly offers in his book. I don't want to suggest here that any of the men had simply made up their stories to fit the mould, or that they had not had painful and traumatic experiences in childhood or adult life. Rather, it seems to me, there is a sense in which men may reinterpret their experience in the light of Bly's ideas, so they see the drama of alienation from their fathers and the 'father hunger' that follows it as the defining story of their lives.

I'll have more to say about the notion of father hunger in Chapter 9. In many ways, it is not surprising that Bly's ideas should find such a strong resonance within the men's movement. Their appeal lies precisely in the fact that they offer men a narrative that explains the sources of their 'hurt' and loneliness, their sense of being exiled from their own emotions. Contemporary Anglo-Australian society offers men few alternative narratives that might explain their lives to them. As I've suggested, the central story of masculinity in our culture is one grounded in the experience of war and privation, one which has little continuing relevance for the lives of most Australian men. Linked to this narrative of self-reliance, resilience and loyalty to one's mates is another powerful narrative of sacrifice, not just on the battlefield but on the home front. An ethos of sacrifice is at the heart of many of our cultural images of the male breadwinner, images we have inherited from the post-war culture of the Menzies years. These images show us the figure of the strong, silent provider who worked hard and 'went without' in order that his children might have a better life. In Anglo-Australian culture, he's exemplified by the father in Stephen Sewell's play *The Father We Loved on a Beach by the Sea*: solid, distant, locked in a prison of emotional self-denial.

In a fascinating study of American working-class immigrant cultures in the late 1960s, entitled *The Hidden Injuries of Class*, the historian Richard Sennett argued that notions of sacrifice and self-denial were central to the sense of self of many of the men and women who belonged to such cultures, and to the cohesiveness of their group identity. At the time he wrote, this cohesiveness was beginning to break down, partly because the children of these cultures were no longer prepared to accept this ethos of sacrifice as relevant to their own lives.[3] In many ways, a similar ethos has existed in Australia, both in our own immigrant cultures, and in the culture of the mainstream Anglo-Australian working class. And in Australia, too, it has less and less relevance to the lives of men—and women—in the 1990s. As we've seen, it's no longer predominantly men who are the breadwinners, those making the sacrifice of working long hours for the benefit of their children.[4] Certainly men are working longer and longer hours and in the majority of Australian families, their wives are working too. Moreover, notions of self-sacrifice and self-denial are regarded as increasingly pointless and risible in our society. Unlike their parents, baby-boomers do not see 'leaving something to their children' as an important priority. Their retirement plans focus on maintaining their own levels of comfort and consumption, rather than husbanding the wealth they've accumulated to pass on to their progeny when they die.[5]

It is one of the 'hidden injuries' of Australian masculinity that no new narrative of what it is to be a man has replaced the old story of self-reliance, self-denial and sacrifice. There was nothing particularly positive about this old story, which condemned many Australian men to lives of quiet desperation, but at least it gave them some sense of where they belonged in the world. Interestingly, many men continue to fall back on this story when their wives or partners leave them. They feel that they've been dealt a terrible injustice by women who don't appreciate the sacrifices they've made for the family—as in Peter Jordan's poem 'Even Bastards Care'. Yet, even for men not passing through an immediate crisis such as separation or divorce, feelings of disconnection and disorientation are a common experience.

As I've suggested, Robert Bly's story of men's alienation from their fathers offers an explanation of these feelings, a narrative many men feel resonates with the details of their own life stories. Bly also offers hope, hope that a man can be reconciled with his father and with the 'wounds' he received from his father. In other words, *Iron John* is a book about redemption, but the vision of redemption it offers men is a purely personal one, unconnected with any of the material circumstances in which they live their lives. Not only does it assume that our present sufferings can all be traced back to certain traumatic events in our early lives—a commonplace of pop psychology—it ignores the social and economic world in which men live. For Bly, men's 'hurt' is a purely private matter, one to be dealt with through an individual journey of redemption, albeit one that can be shared with other men in groups such as the Circle of Men.

This prescription for 'healing' men fits very well with some of the broader trends that dominate Australian (and, for that matter, American and British) society at the moment. As we privatize more and more of what used to be considered the common weal, we also privatize the causes of suffering and alienation. The suggestion that men's 'hurt' might have anything to do with the present distribution of work and wealth would be laughed off by the economic rationalists and neo-liberals who run our societies. It was certainly not an idea discussed much at Standing Up Alive.

A pre-occupation with searching for the causes of one's 'wounds' so that one can heal them is by no means confined to the men's movement, nor is it, in itself, necessarily harmful. However, we need to ask ourselves whether the desire for personal redemption can really become the basis of a broad social movement that will unite men in trying to change the conditions of their lives. In one important sense, the men who attended the gathering do have a larger vision of redemption for men, which goes beyond the desire to come to terms with their own personal suffering and isolation. As I've hinted earlier, the Circle of Men in many ways bears more resemblance to a religious community than an activist group. The central concerns of many of the men who attended the Standing Up Alive gathering seem to me to revolve more around a search for new forms of spirituality and communion—in the broadest sense of that word—than they do around a desire to reconstruct masculinity.

DRUMS IN THE NIGHT

> I am in the hands of the unknown God,
> he is breaking me down to his own oblivion
> to send me forth on a new morning, a new man.
>
> D.H. Lawrence, 'Shadows'

Night has fallen and a fat yellow moon has risen over the valley. The muted thrumming of a didgeridoo blends with a single, monotonous chant carried by many voices. From the fire, two lines of men lead down a gentle incline to some flat ground near the creek. Each man holds a lighted candle, and many are naked except for body paint and a headband. As the incantation rises and falls, one by one the men closest to the fire step out and advance between the two lines down a path lit on either side by 100 flickering candles and blazing torches.

This ceremony takes place on the last night of the gathering. Each man who walks the candlelit path must turn when he reaches its end and make a pledge before all of the assembled company to change his life in some way. Many of the men speak their names aloud, and the names of their fathers and grandfathers, and some call on a Great Spirit or Supreme Being to witness and strengthen their resolve.

In itself, this ritual is no more bizarre than rituals acted out every week in thousands of churches around Australia, and at meetings of the Freemasons and Lions Clubs, with the difference that participants in the latter are usually wearing clothes. Yet men's rituals such as the one that marked the climax of our gathering outside Lismore routinely excite the fascinated curiosity and derision of the media and many members of the public. A number of my journalist colleagues declared that they could never bring themselves to attend such a gathering, ever. Why?

Much of the explanation must surely lie in that important and pervasive taboo in Australian society, the taboo against exposing oneself to embarrassment. There's also our sense that we are too grown-up for such activities. Why should we want to take part in anachronistic rituals punctuated by a lot of bad singing, rituals that require us to submerge our individuality in the mass and submit to some nebulous spiritual authority—a Great Spirit—which is totally foreign to us?

One of the conditions of my attending the Circle of Men as an observer was that I participate in all of the activities—including the ritual I have just described. My own reactions to it were mixed. On the one hand, I felt that the whole procedure was ridiculous and artificial, an amalgam of vacuous New Age spirituality and bad theatre. On the other hand I couldn't help but be moved by the willingness of the men who participated to expose themselves—both literally and metaphorically—in ways they would never do in normal life, and by the evident gravity and emotional intensity of their involvement in the ceremony.

My own deeper reservation about this particular ritual was about its heavy reliance on elements of Aboriginal culture and tradition. One criticism frequently levelled at the mythopoetic strand of the men's movement in the United States is that it is fiddling with something that does not belong to it, namely, the traditions of indigenous peoples. Men's gatherings similar to the Circle of Men draw heavily on the ritual practice of American Indians, adapting elements of that practice for use in their own ceremonies. In particular, the American men's movement is fascinated by the rituals that surround the initiation of boys into manhood. Bill spoke to me about this at some length:

> It was fascinating to read some of the great American mythologist Joseph Campbell's work, wherein he reported on the initiation process in one of the American Indian tribes. The boys were taken from the women—a very common aspect of initiation, to break that bond—and taken to the initiation tent where their bodies were skewered and buffalo skulls hung from them. They were then suspended from the teepee ceiling and spun until they lost consciousness, and then dragged around the field until the skulls pulled out. Now we might say that this was totally macabre and outrageous, but there was a really important message there: one, to make it very clear to those boys that they were no longer boys, they were now men; and two, to remind them that a woman

> brought them into the world, she suffered pain as a consequence, and to remember that women experience pain throughout their lives not of their choice. It's this concept of respect, respect the woman, and in turn be respected.

Bill does not believe that we should try this at home, nor was I able to find any member of the Circle of Men who felt that we should adopt circumcision or sub-incision as part of developing new rituals for initiating boys. However, there seemed to be a strong feeling among many of the participants, and certainly among the organizers of Standing Up Alive, that creating ritual and ceremony was an integral part of creating community, inseparable from the process of healing and self-revelation. It's hardly surprising in Australia that participants should look to Aboriginal culture for inspiration. In fact, David Mowaljarlai, a senior Aboriginal man from the Ngarinyin people of the Kimberley, and a Member of the Order of Australia, had already attended a previous gathering. Mowaljarlai was also supposed to be guest of honour at Standing Up Alive (which took its name from his writings), but was unable to attend, a fact that caused some consternation among many of the men. Some declared that the prospect of meeting him had been one of the principal reasons for their making the journey to Lismore in the first place.

Despite Mowaljarlai's absence, repeated references were made in the course of the weekend to Aboriginal people's relationship with the land, the roles of men and women in Aboriginal society, and the 'wunnan' or 'sharing system', which was said to be at the heart of their culture. Some of the organizers and facilitators of the gathering had lived and worked on Aboriginal communities in central Australia, and so had some knowledge of particular Aboriginal cultures. Certainly, in these times especially, one can only applaud any desire on the part of white Australians to know more about Aboriginal tradition and enter into a more sympathetic understanding of Aboriginal people's lives. But how legitimate is it for non-Aboriginal men to extract certain elements of Aboriginal tradition from their cultural context for their own use? Doesn't this amount to appropriation, cultural pillage, at worst—or, at best, the creation of a grotesque pantomime, a kind of spiritual Black and White Minstrel Show?

These are all fair questions, but we should be aware of the background against which they are asked. White middle-class intellectuals are perfectly willing to applaud the continuance of ritual and ceremony in indigenous cultures—provided they conform to their notions of what is 'traditional' or 'tribal'. We routinely lament the destruction of custom and tradition in tribal societies as a consequence of contact with Western culture, assuming that indigenous cultures are somehow 'authentic', repositories of spiritual values that have remained changeless over centuries. There are two powerful and contradictory impulses at work here. One is envy: in indigenous cultures we see what we believe we have lost, namely, community, a close relationship with nature, and a harmonious integration of the spiritual and the everyday. The other is reassurance: we need traditional societies to remain at arm's length, to remain changeless and remote, in order for them to function as a cultural alter ego that reassures us about who *we* are—modern, self-aware, autonomous individuals.

There's a strong element of condescension in both these attitudes. Aboriginal culture, like any other, is a changing, evolving entity. Contemporary Aboriginal culture in Australia offers plenty of examples of how tradition is transformed in a dynamic relationship with 'white' culture. This does not mean that the Aboriginal traditions involved are any less authentic.

Castigating the Circle of Men, or the mythopoetic men's movement as a whole, for appropriating Aboriginal traditions is misunderstanding the nature of tradition itself. It's more fruitful, I think, to see this strand of the men's movement as one more example of a much broader phenomenon—the reaction against the modern world I discussed in Chapter 7. In this sense, groups like the Circle of Men and their American cousins are the discontents of 'masculine' technological civilization itself, sharing a view of modernity similar to that of the ecofeminists, and cherishing a similar nostalgia for the pre-industrial past. This is clear in the writings of Robert Bly:

> To judge by men's lives in New Guinea, Kenya, North Africa, the Pygmy territories, Zulu lands, and in the Arab and Persian culture flavoured by Sufi communities, men have lived together in heart unions and soul connections for hundreds of thousands of years . . . Having no soul union with other men can be the most damaging wound of all.[6]

Precisely what evidence Bly has that men lived in 'heart unions and soul connections' in traditional societies is unclear, and he neglects to mention that those men also slaughtered each other in wars and often enslaved the losers. Certainly Bly and the circle around him in the American men's movement romanticize the place of men in traditional societies, but the real voice we hear in Bly's work is the voice of the American pioneer at the frontier, the pioneer engaged in a struggle with nature and those very indigenous cultures Bly so admires—a struggle that generally resulted in their extinction.

Either way, the message is the same: modernity is what's the matter with men. Hand-in-hand with the belief that men's lives were richer or more meaningful in traditional societies, or in pre-industrial Europe, goes a nostalgia for the spiritual values and sense of 'community' that supposedly existed in these contexts. In many ways, what the Circle of Men is striving for is 'communion', in its older sense of an organic union of persons united by common religious faith and rites.

As such, the Circle of Men embodies the meeting and mingling of a number of trends in post-industrial societies, which have produced a whole range of social movements and quasi-religious groups, some of which can be identified as belonging to the New Age. Clearly, the search for new forms of spirituality arises out of a reaction to the increasing secularization of our society, and the perceived loss of spiritual authority of the established religions. One of the participants in the Circle came from an extremely strict and devout Lutheran family, but had rebelled against the orthodoxy of his background and was seeking spiritual regeneration in closer contact with Aboriginal culture.

Individualism is also an important contributing factor in the rise of groups such as the Circle of Men. Even though their avowed aim is to break down the isolation experienced by individual men, the road of redemption they offer to men is a personal one, an individual journey of self-discovery and reconciliation rather than participation in some kind of collective social action. This is not to minimize the real sense of warmth and solidarity many men obviously experienced within the Circle. The Circle, however, does not provide the basis for any broader activism, but is much more an emotional springboard to personal 'fulfilment'. This is particularly clear in the case of other men's events such as the 'Future Warrior' gathering, which is much less explicitly committed to creating community. The advertising material for one event features testimonials from men such as these: 'It has provided me with a way of focusing my power and still keeping my heart open. I have found a sense of self I never had before', or 'Words cannot describe the experience of Future Warrior. I now know the direction I wish to take. Huge value for me' (the latter from a 'Managing Director'). Clearly, these gatherings are a New Age recharging for the individual rather than any kind of attempt to reform or regenerate masculinity.

The Circle of Men also represents one more manifestation among many of what has come to be known as 'identity politics'. Identity politics is a term coined to explain the emergence over the last 30 years of new kinds of political behaviour and affiliation, not based on traditional divisions between Left and Right. People identify with particular groups, which have quite specific and distinctive interests, rather than seeing themselves as belonging to larger groupings such as the working class. Thus we have seen the emergence of particular political groupings that cater to the needs of gay men and lesbians, ethnic groups, handicapped people, Aboriginal people, women and now men. As the larger allegiances of class and religion, which bound societies together in the past, fracture and fragment, identity politics appear in the cracks.

It is pointless to bewail the disappearance of old certainties and solidarities when there is plainly nothing that will bring them back. However, many groups that rely on identity politics for their existence and cohesion do precisely this, conjuring up an imagined and invented past in which they supposedly lived as part of a larger community, and dreaming of how they might re-create that past in the present. Groups such as the Circle of Men, for all the comfort and healing they provide to the men who belong to them, steadfastly refuse to look the real causes of men's pain and alienation in the eye. Nor do they consider in any depth the issue of men's relationship with women, and the difficult questions of power and responsibility I've been exploring in this book. Indeed, women were hardly mentioned in the entire proceedings of the gathering. Some individuals spoke very positively of their own relationships with their wives or female partners. Any larger issues concerning men and women, and the power relations between them, were simply not discussed. Nor was the question of how groups like the Circle of Men might relate to the gay men's movement given any consideration. Both these silences seem to me to point to the limitations of such groups and, indeed, to the limitations of the 'men's movement' in Australia as a whole. In order for a real process of ‘healing’ to begin, the Born-Again Blokes in the men’s movement will need to move beyond a rhetoric of personal redemption, towards a confrontation with the broader context of men’s power and powerlessness. In the next chapter, I shall explore the key existential and political issue for the men’s movement today: fatherhood.

9

Fatherhood

Jeff is a furniture removalist. He's got his own truck and works on a freelance basis for a small removals business in the northern suburbs of Melbourne. In his early 30s, Jeff used to be a roadie for rock'n'roll bands and drive for interstate removals jobs. Now he's married with two young daughters under five. I met him when he put a load of my furniture into storage. It was around ten on a Sunday morning as we finished packing the furniture into the storage space, and Jeff had another two jobs to go, one in the outer suburbs on the other side of town. 'Do you ever get to see your kids?' I asked him. 'Oh sure,' he replied, 'I try not to work any more than 24 hours a week. We're living on the poverty line, but it's important to me to spend as much time as I can with them while they're young.'

Jeff is not a tertiary-educated inner-city professional who's been exposed to feminism or the men's movement. Nor is he short of work—he told me he could easily be working 40 or 50 hours a week if he wanted. He—and his wife—have made a practical choice to accept a lower standard of living, at least until their children go to school, so that Jeff can have a close relationship with his daughters in their formative years.

Jeff's decision may not seem so remarkable until we consider how unusual it would have been 20, or even ten years ago for a man to consciously choose to spend more time with his children at the expense of his working life. Even today, for many men this would simply not be an option, because their jobs do not allow them the flexibility to work a reduced number of hours. Yet the fact that men such as Jeff are making these kinds of choices is evidence of a major shift in our attitudes to men's and women's roles in the family.

If there is one word that sums up the central concerns of the men's movement, it is fatherhood. As we saw in Chapter 8, many of the men who become involved in groups such as the Circle of Men feel that their lives have been damaged in some way by the lack of a close emotional relationship with their fathers when they were growing up. Much of the work of writers such as Robert Bly and Steve Biddulph focuses on the 'father hunger', which they claim is felt by both boys and adult men. They see a revitalization of fatherhood as essential for healing the wounded nature of modern masculinity.

At the same time, Biddulph stresses the need for men to have a closer relationship with their children and to become more involved in caring for them. Indeed, Biddulph encourages men to do exactly what Jeff has done—spend less time at work and more with the kids.

This is the area in which there would seem to be most convergence between the desires of women and the desires of men. In many ways, fatherhood is the arena in which many of the different issues and concerns I've been exploring come together—in which the twin motivations of creating better relationships with women and new forms of solidarity between men meet and merge. Yet, power and the struggle over power have also been key themes in this book—and fatherhood, too, is an arena in which power is vigorously and sometimes bitterly contested.

My argument here is that the 'new father' is a real phenomenon, and one that is likely to become more pervasive in Australian society. However, the reasons for the rise of the new father are complex, and by no means purely the result of a positive response from men to the demands of feminism. Indeed, in one sense men's heightened interest in child-rearing could be seen as an attempt to claw back some of the power men have lost in other areas by attempting to stake a claim in the domain that has, for the last 200 years at least, been largely the province of women.

How men deal with the complex issues surrounding fatherhood seems to me absolutely crucial to the development of any significant men's movement or to the creation of new forms of masculine identity. It is also crucial to any long-term possibility of 'warmer relations between men and women'.[1] However, unless we understand what is truly at stake, there is a great potential that 'Fatherhood!' will become the catchcry of a socially conservative counter-revolution.

THE F WORD

> I've only recently been able to say yes, I'm a full-time father—I've used the F word for the first time and it's starting to feel comfortable . . . but it's been a long evolution, there's a lot of scripting which I've had to put behind me.

Martin, one of the Circle of Men, has been looking after his small son for four years, since the boy was six months old. He and his wife hadn't exactly planned it that way, but when Martin's contract as a university lecturer in marine biology wasn't renewed and his wife was offered a good job, it seemed a logical step. 'Something in me jumped at the chance,' says Martin. His choice to become a primary care-giver seemed a natural evolution in their relationship and, for him, a new adventure.

At the beginning, this adventure proved to be even more challenging than he'd expected. Something in him wouldn't let go of the belief that if he wasn't fulfilling the roles of protector and provider, he was a failure. When he met other men, the inevitable question would come: 'What do you do?' For a long time, Martin says, he would mention that he was looking after his son, but then quickly change the subject to his research (he was also working on a PhD). Gradually, he became more up-front about using the F word and proclaiming proudly that he was a full-time father.

Martin says full-time fathering has been a 'fabulous' experience for him, one he wouldn't have missed for the world:

> I've seen within myself capabilities I didn't know were there—capabilities I thought were restricted to women . . . nurturing and loving. So often I've heard women say they would willingly give up their life for their child—and now I know, if it ever came to that, there'd be no question for me . . . yes, willingly.
>
> I'm not a particularly patient person, but being around my son has brought out a patience in me I didn't know I had.

He also believes the role reversal has had a positive impact on his relationship with his wife, though here, again, the experiment has not been easy:

> We are striving towards a balance . . . it has to be constantly maintained, and we're both working really hard on it. I really respect her for allowing me to do things which none of the men among her friends and in our neighbourhood are doing.
>
> To a great extent I'm breaking new ground in our little neighbourhood, being the care-giver, although I've got to know the other handful of men who are doing it too—the ones who you see in the supermarket at 11.30 in the morning with the kids. So yes, there are a few others out there.

Just how many men there are 'out there' making the same experiment as Martin is very difficult to say—not least because statisticians have only recently begun to gather detailed information on families like Martin's. A 1993 Australian Bureau of Statistics survey of the labour force states that 5 per cent of married couples with dependants had only a mother in the labour force. Census figures over the last 15 years tell an interesting story: in

1981, there were just over 16 000 families with dependent children under 15 in which the mother was working and the father was not. By 1993, this number had increased to over 90 000.

It seems likely that at least part of this increase is due to the sharp rise in male unemployment during the 1980s rather than an emerging mass movement of new fathers. Since these statistics also include children of school age, we can conclude that a fair proportion of the men in question were not necessarily engaged in full-time child-care. In families where the children are under the age of five, the number of full-time fathers is much smaller—around 12 000.[2] However, these statistics leave out couples who live in de-facto relationships, a sizeable omission, since one in four children are now born out of wedlock, and couples in which the man is working part-time.

There are simply not enough hard facts and figures to tell us how significant a group in the population full-time fathers like Martin are, although we can be fairly confident in saying that they are still a small proportion. It's likely, however, for reasons which we'll come to soon, that there is a larger group of men combining the primary care-giving role with part-time work. One very interesting study of men in this category was carried out in Melbourne by Carol Grbich. Grbich studied a group of 25 men over a period of six years from 1984 to 1990. Each of the men in the group was looking after a child or children of pre-kindergarten age for a minimum of 25 hours a week while their wives worked full-time as the primary breadwinner for the family.

The men came from a broad range of occupations, from labourer to architect, and all but three were of Anglo-Australian origin. On average, they looked after children for 41 hours a week. They also took on the responsibility for the majority of domestic tasks such as cooking, shopping, washing clothes and cleaning, though not necessarily with any great relish. A number of the men expressed views along the lines of, 'Housework is tremendously boring. It is a meaningless repetitive task,' and preferred to concentrate on the nurturing aspects of caring for children.[3] These views about housework are similar to those expressed by women in other studies.

The men's reasons for taking on the role of full-time father varied, but they fell into three broad categories. For about a third, their choice to do so grew out of 'commitment to an ideal of egalitarianism'—in other words, a conscious decision to pursue a more democratic or non-traditional division of roles in the family unit. The men in this category ranged from a nursery worker and a taxi-driver to a land agent and engineer. Forty per cent of the men had negotiated with their partners to take over care of the children because of dissatisfaction with being the breadwinner and working full-time. These men ranged from an agricultural scientist and teacher to a printer and a wood machinist. Finally, about a quarter of the men had made the decision as the result of a crisis of some kind in their employment, either retrenchment, sacking, or the failure of a business venture. Overall, Grbich concluded that the initiative to take over the care-giving role had come primarily from the men.[4]

Carol Grbich interviewed the men regularly during the six-year period and observed them in a number of settings, at home and at a playgroup that the fathers themselves had organized. She describes the men as having a very high level of emotional involvement with their children: 'most fathers coped very well with their children's constant requests for help, food, and drink, showing infinite patience and resourcefulness and responding immediately to demands. Babies were unashamedly loved, kissed and talked to in baby talk.'[5]

One significant aspect of the lives of the entire group of men was that they maintained a connection to the world of work or education while carrying out the care-giving role. Two-thirds of them worked part-time either in home businesses which they planned to expand once the children were at school, or outside the home in the evenings or on weekends. A third studied part-time for trade qualifications or university degrees.

Grbich found that the men generally were happy with the choice they had made, and saw it as having had a positive impact on their lives. Their wives were also very happy with the role reversal, commenting typically on the wonderful job their husbands were doing and declaring that 'he is the best person for the job' or 'he has the worst end of the stick'. None of the wives expressed any desire to return to the care-giving role once they had been away from it for more than a year, though they did grumble occasionally about being the breadwinner: 'Sometimes I get a bit resentful and say to myself "Geez, I'm working my arse off and paying for everything!" '[6]

Outside the home, reactions to these experiments in democratizing family life were not as positive. The parents of the men tended to have particularly negative responses to their sons' choices: 'We spent years on his education, now it's just going down the drain,' or 'Raising children is a woman's job, a man should be out making the money' were typical views expressed. The men themselves described a general attitude of suspicion or incomprehension among their male friends, relatives and former work colleagues. One of the group, an ex-plumber, reported that his brother thought he was 'a bit queer', while another's bikie mates wanted to know, 'What the hell are you doing? What's in it?' However, the men's wives also reported negative comments from other women, either about the impact on the man—'One friend (female) thinks I've taken away my husband's masculinity'—or on the children—'How can you leave your baby with your husband. How will he cope?'[7]

This was not so much of a problem for Phil Cleary, also from Melbourne, though not one of the men Grbich interviewed for her study. Cleary, a champion Australian Rules footballer, schoolteacher and former member of federal parliament in the seat of Wills, spent a period as a full-time father in the early 1980s.

> I did it a decade ago in '84, stayed at home and looked after my two daughters, but I had footy you know. My daughters were three and four, so I was running around, I had them during the day, but I had an escape, three nights a week I'd go to footy training, and then I was playing on the weekends, coaching too . . .
>
> My wife at the time went back to work, it suited me, I was sick of teaching. For one year I didn't teach, then I went part-time. I reckon I was one of the first—but it was easy for me, I was seen as a rough and tumble footballer, I wasn't the soft character in the kaftan who stays at home with his kids, I was seen as an ordinary bloke who played footy, was pretty hard at the ball, but decided to take time off and balance work and domesticity.

Some of the most difficult experiences reported by the men in Carol Grbich's study took place in playgroups or child-care centres:

> There was something on at the crèche. I was sitting there with my daughter and this other little girl who was friendly and demonstrative. She put her arms around me and the mother shot across and dragged her off. She was talking to the little girl about having touched me—it was as though I didn't exist—this horrible man was going to race off the little girl was the message . . . I don't think the reaction would have been the same if I had been a woman.

Although the incident described here is one of the more extreme, in general the men felt difficulty in being accepted in their role, and often experienced the invisible-man syndrome—not being acknowledged or accepted in social contexts by women who were full-time carers. This might take the form of women at a playgroup simply ignoring their presence or not including them in shared activities: 'Women at home can go and play tennis because other women are playing tennis, but being a man, you just can't go and play tennis with the girls.'

In response to these difficulties, ten of the men in the group decided to set up their own fathers' playgroup at a neighbourhood centre in Richmond. This proved to be an important support mechanism for many of the men:

> We've got closer to each other and we talk a lot about ourselves . . . The beauty of it is that the defences are dropped . . . Now we talk about our children, dietary matters, discipline, education, the state of the world and any difficulties we might have. The consciousness of the group has been raised and we don't have to be overtly masculine. We can still be men, but we can also do the soft job of nurturing our children.[8]

Even though it is based on a comparatively small sample of men, Carol Grbich's research is important and illuminating for a number of reasons. It has the great advantage that she has followed the men and their partners through the *process* of role reversal, and documented the changes in attitude and behaviour that took place during that process. Her findings show a clear shift in the pattern of men's involvement in housework as well as nurturing. The men took on a higher proportion of domestic tasks than their predecessors in earlier studies. Unlike the men in earlier studies, few expressed any dissatisfaction with the choice they had made. Perhaps most significantly, Grbich reports that at the end of the five-year research period, all the couples felt that shared work and shared parenting were the ideal option, though only four of the 25 couples had managed to achieve this balance.

Not all of the marriages survived this experiment with role reversal. Five of the couples had separated by the end of the study, and Grbich speculates that this may have been due to strains imposed on their relationships by changing roles and expectations. For the remaining 20 couples, however, the experiment proved successful. Despite difficulties, and an often hostile or uncomprehending response from their social group, they had managed to negotiate a democratization of personal life.[9]

One of the interesting anecdotal impressions Carol Grbich gained from her study was about the class background of the men involved. She felt that, on the whole, the men from more traditional working-class backgrounds or occupational categories seemed to make a stronger and more lasting commitment to this process of democratization than their middle-class fellows. While the more educated middle-class men found the initial transition easier, Grbich says they tended to be more 'chameleon-like' in their attitudes over the long term, slipping into and out of a commitment to domestic democracy.[10]

Placing Grbich's study in the broader context of contemporary Australian society, we need to acknowledge that one swallow does not make a summer. The statistical evidence we have suggests that couples similar to those in the group she studied constitute a very small minority of the child-rearing population. For the vast majority of couples with children, the sharing of child-care and housework occurs in a context where one or both partners are working, with the more common pattern being that the father works full-time and the mother part-time. Moreover, what fathers say and what they actually do may be different things. Anthony McMahon, who has written the best and most comprehensive general study of men and domestic life in Australia, argues that we should be very sceptical about the emergence of the new father as a widespread social phenomenon.[11] As he points out, there is often a substantial gap between both men's and women's attitudes to sharing child-care and housework, and what goes on in practice. While both sexes now generally express support for egalitarian arrangements in the home, the largest scale statistical surveys we have show that, in reality, men's participation has only increased by a very modest amount over the last 20 years. Moreover, the areas where men do more are likely to be the more enjoyable, interactive aspects of looking after children, rather than tasks such as washing the floor or doing laundry.

Carol Grbich's study contradicts the findings of these statistical surveys, showing a much greater level of all-round involvement by the men, who took on nearly half of all the domestic tasks by themselves, and over two-thirds of the child-care. It also sheds some interesting new light on one of the most consistent criticisms Anthony McMahon makes of the media cult of the new father. Often, says McMahon, the academics and journalists who proclaim most enthusiastically that men are taking their share of the housework and child-care burdens do so purely on the basis of anecdotal evidence. Typically, they extrapolate from their own, largely middle-class peer group—or from their own domestic arrangements—to conclude that a social revolution led by fathers in aprons is sweeping the country. They celebrate 'vanguard' examples while conveniently ignoring the domestic realities of mainstream Australia.[12]

However, the group Grbich studied included men from a range of class backgrounds and economic circumstances, with working-class men and men in the 'lower occupational groups' making a strong commitment to what we might call domestic democracy. These men *chose* to embark on a particular experiment and carry it through, not primarily for reasons of economic necessity, but out of a sense that their lives and those of their partners would be enhanced in the process. It's important to bear in mind, though, that the choice these men have made is for a substantial role reversal, rather than an entirely even division of labour where both partners do the same amounts of paid work, child-care and housework—a balance that may be much more difficult to achieve.

As yet, the numbers suggest that full-time fathering is an option that only a small percentage of the male population is prepared to take on. Moreover, as I've suggested in Chapter 3, trends in today's labour market send contradictory messages about whether domestic democracy is likely to become more or less widespread and achievable. The increase in part-time work suggests the potential for greater flexibility and sharing of paid and unpaid work between partners, while the increase in average hours worked by men per week seems to push in the opposite direction, towards a more traditional division of labour. One important piece missing from our jigsaw is any kind of reliable information about the impact of long-term structural unemployment on the way men and women share child-care and housework.

However, some other evidence suggests that it will be some time before men are queueing up to become full-time, or even part-time fathers. According to a survey carried out in 1991, a very high percentage of Australian men—around 85 per cent—believe that men and women should share child-care equally. However, there seems to be a contradiction between this belief and men's attitudes to work. The Australian Family Formation Project, a study carried out by the Australian Institute of Family Studies during 1991/92, revealed that 80 per cent of men in relationships expressed a preference for full-time work. Sixteen per cent of the men questioned said they wanted to work part-time, and only 4 per cent would have preferred not to work at all.

By contrast, 41 per cent of women said they preferred full-time work, 28 per cent opted for part-time employment, and 31 per cent said they would prefer not to work at all. Moreover, women with children were much more likely to opt for part-time work or no work than women without children. For men, however, whether or not they had children made no appreciable difference to their work preferences.

The picture that emerges from these statistics is a clear one. The majority of men still appear to regard work as the central focus of their lives, and only a small proportion—a total of one in five—would opt for a more even balance between work and family commitments through options such as part-time work if they had the choice.

Not surprisingly, women, and especially women with children, are much more likely to favour flexible, part-time working arrangements, even if this means a reduction in earning power.

Of course, these statistics tell us nothing about men's reasons for preferring full-time work, reasons that in many cases may be dictated by economic necessity rather than lack of interest in a closer involvement with children. However, Ilene Wollcott and Helen Glazer, the authors of a major study of work and family life in Australia, believe that even when the workplace does offer men opportunities to take parenting leave, or cut back their working hours, men are much less likely than women to 'identify' with these choices, in other words, to see them as relevant to their own lives. Their findings in the Australian context are borne out by European examples. In Sweden, men can take paid paternity leave for a period of up to 18 months, with ten of those months paid at 80 per cent of their normal earnings, and two months paid at 90 per cent. Despite these extremely generous provisions, only around 44 per cent of fathers avail themselves of this leave, and then only for an average period of seven weeks.[13]

Notwithstanding this evidence, which suggests that we should be sceptical about the emergence of a new father, there are a number of reasons why we should not dismiss him too readily as the fantasy of a few middle-class academics. To begin with, the lack of hard data about fathers in Australia can be largely attributed to the fact that social scientists and statisticians have only very recently begun to regard them as a phenomenon in need of study. There are, for example, no available statistics on the numbers of men like Jeff, who work part-time and also care for children. Research into this area is now beginning to be done in Australia. Elsewhere in the world, and particularly in Europe, fathers and fathering have been very much in the spotlight of social inquiry and public policy research in recent years. In 1995, the Council of Europe asked all of its member countries to respond to a questionnaire on The Status and Role of Fathers. A report prepared for the Institute for Public Policy Research in Britain, a think-tank close to the Labour Party, lists a remarkable number of recent publications on fathers from Europe and the United States, and makes some concrete and progressive recommendations on recognizing the role of fathers, extending paternity leave and flexible work arrangements, and establishing support services for fathers. These recommendations are likely to become part of Labour Party policy in the near future.[14] The report also stresses a point beginning to be recognized by employers in both the private and public sectors—that family-friendly policies have largely been tailored to the needs of women employees, on the assumption that it was only women who would want to avail themselves of the flexible working arrangements such policies offer.

Just as important as conditions in the workplace, however, is the psychological framework within which men choose to embark on experiments in domestic democracy, the attitudes, beliefs and fantasies that inform their decisions. Here we can say with some certainty that a shift has taken place that has given men's emotional involvement with their children greater prominence, and made fathering a higher priority than has previously been the case in pre-industrial and industrial Western societies. How has this come about? Not only through a re-evaluation of men's relationships with their children—but also through a new emphasis on their relationships with their own fathers.

FATHER HUNGER OR EATING DADDY

> From our father we want validation for our ideas, dreams. I didn't get that from mine, so I just tried harder and harder . . . he died 20 years ago and I was there, just trying harder all the time.
>
> Bill, Circle of Men, Lismore

For many men like Bill, coming to terms with a 'damaged' relationship with his father has been central to his attempts to explore and re-define his masculinity and his relationships with other men. The lack of 'validation' and love from their fathers was something nearly all the men in the Circle mentioned as a reason for becoming involved with men's groups or other men's movement activities, and for their experience of some kind of deep crisis or upheaval in their emotional lives. Interestingly, fathers also figured prominently in the life stories of many men in anti-domestic violence groups, who often described their fathers' violent behaviour towards their mothers or themselves as having had a powerful effect on shaping their own attitudes.

The search for a new relationship with one's father is what we might call the defining narrative of the therapeutic or mythopoetic men's movement, the story men tell to explain how they got to where they are in their lives and where it is they are trying to go. For men like Martin, it is also a story of forgiveness and reconciliation, even though his father has been dead for many years:

> I've worked hard to come to grips with my relationship with my father. I'm now old enough to pass some of the milestones he passed through when he was doing things to me I wish he hadn't done.
>
> I had a lot of troubles with police as an adolescent, and I think in some ways they were an expression of my inchoate searchings for the attention of a wise, elderly authority figure—my father was dead by that time.
>
> I have the maturity now to see where he came from, and to see that, given the tools he had, he was doing the absolute best he was able to—so I've come to accept him and forgive him—but now I'm looking for other wise, older men.

Interestingly, Martin sees this journey as being closely linked with the journey he has made in becoming a full-time father—a re-visiting of the sources of masculine identity within himself so that he can be a better father to his son. The journey Martin describes is a central motif in the men's movement, driven by what Robert Bly describes as 'father hunger'. Bly describes this hunger as an almost physical craving:

> As I've participated in men's gatherings since the early 1980s, I've heard one statement over and over from American males, which has been phrased in 100 different ways: 'There is not enough father'. The sentence implies that father is a substance like salt.[15]

This notion has permeated the language and mythology of the therapeutic men's movement in Australia. Many of the members of the Circle of Men spoke of the nourishment they received from the presence of the older men, some of whom were invested with the title of elders.

Steve Biddulph has played a large part in popularizing the notion of father hunger in Australia, declaring in one newspaper article that the 'devaluing of the father' is '*the* 20th century disaster'.[16] Biddulph, like Bly, sees the emergence of father hunger as a relatively recent phenomenon, with its roots in the Industrial Revolution. At this time, Biddulph tells us, 'for the first time in half a million years of human existence, men stopped working alongside wives and children . . . and went to work apart, in factories and mines'.[17] At the onset of the Industrial Revolution, 'in a break with eternal tradition,' he informs us, 'boys began being raised by women'. Deprived of contact with their fathers during the working day, boys became estranged and alienated from them, with the result that the 'lack of male input to growing boys created a huge break in the social fabric'.

In pre-industrial Europe, according to both Biddulph and Bly, boys enjoyed a close relationship with their fathers and spent the day alongside them as they went about their daily work. This is a touching portrait. Historically, however, it is nonsense. In fact, by far the most common experience for most boys was to be effectively exiled from the household where they were born, often at a tender age. Children of both sexes were sent away from the home and into domestic service, sometimes at only eight or nine years of age, and continued as servants in a number of different households until they were married. This occurred at all levels of society, even in rural households of modest means, where the servants often came from the same social level as their masters.[18] This was not quite as brutal as the British upper class's practice, which continues until this day, of sending its sons away to boarding school at an early age. Nevertheless, there is very little historical evidence to support the view that, in pre-industrial Europe, sons (or daughters, for that matter) enjoyed any kind of close and constant emotional relationship with either of their parents after the early years of childhood.

Bly's and Biddulph's notion of traditional fatherhood is a modern fantasy rather than a pre-modern reality. Both of them attempt to ground their claims about father hunger in a historical narrative that tells us that we have lost something that we need to recover, something that, in fact, never existed—in Western cultures, at any rate. To attribute modern men's alienation or confusion to the loss of some purely imaginary pre-industrial idyll does no-one any service—in fact, it infantilizes men.

To be fair, Bly also has a lot to say about the role older men other than the father play in the raising and education of boys in traditional societies, and about their particular role in initiating boys. Bly sees a boy's relationship with his father as one that will inevitably involve conflict. 'It is possible,' he tells us, 'that we will never have the closeness we want from our fathers.' The young man who wants the same affection or nurturing from his father that he received from his mother is barking up the wrong tree: 'Whatever our father gives us, it will not be the same kind of closeness that our mother offered.'[19] The message of his book is the need for the son to break away from the world of the mother and enter the world of men, with the assistance of the father and other older men, so that he can take into himself 'the King', the archetypal male principle.

The 'King' has both creative and destructive attributes,

and he is also embodied in actual male rulers, so, for example, Bly sees in Churchill a manifestation of the 'Blessing King' and in Stalin the 'Twisted King'. He bemoans the fact that present-day political kings have lost their 'radiance', and seems to lament the loss of real kings, dating from the American War of Independence and the French Revolution. Without them, or political leaders who can emulate them, he says, our fathers too become diminished in our imaginations.

It's at this point that *Iron John* ceases to be a literary meditation and turns into a rather tawdry tract expounding the virtues of strong leaders and respect for authority, both paternal and political. Accompanying this is a strong undercurrent of mistrust and suspicion of women. Sons who do not have appropriate models of paternal strength and authority, says Bly, fall into a 'secret despair', adopting their mother's view of their fathers 'by the time they are six. By twenty, they will have adopted society's critical view of fathers, which amounts to a dismissal.'[20] Both Bly and Biddulph whistle the same tune: fathers have been given a raw deal by society, and more particularly by mothers, whom they have allowed to dominate them. This makes a bad impression on boys, who subconsciously become angry with their fathers for not standing up to their wives. At the other extreme, they may be angry with fathers who were too dominating, distant and disapproving, who never gave them enough encouragement or respect. Either way, the adherents of the cult of father hunger offer men a simplistic narrative of personal redemption. 'Make sure you fix it with your father,' Biddulph tells us, 'if you are at war with him in your head, you are at war with masculinity itself.'[21] There is no suggestion that a man might also need to 'fix it' with his mother (whatever 'it' is), nor consideration that there may be aspects of our lives we cannot 'fix'.

Not far beneath the surface of Bly's concept of father hunger is a deep anxiety about what happens to boys when they are 'raised by women'. This anxiety, a recurrent theme in the psychological and sociological literature of the past century, is now well on the way to becoming a full-blown moral panic in the collective imagination of societies such as ours. Remarking that between 20 and 30 per cent of American boys now live in a house with no father present, Bly tells us that 'the demons there have full permission to rage'[22]—demons, as he sees it, of suspicion and mistrust towards older men, and towards authority in general. Yet, in many of these American households, there is a much more elemental problem than father hunger, namely, hunger itself—ordinary, banal poverty. It is now common in both US and British politics to blame the rise in levels of violence, crime and drug addiction on the collapse of paternal authority or the absence of fathers from poor or deprived households.[23] It is much less common to discuss the reasons why so many families break up or fathers desert their children: chronic structural unemployment and low wages, particularly among America's urban blacks.

However facile we may find Bly's and Biddulph's account of father hunger and its historical origins and social consequences, we still have to explain why it is that fathers have become such a central preoccupation with the men's movement. As we've seen with Bill and Martin, men involved with men's groups tend to express a very complex set of emotions when talking about their fathers, from anger and a sense of betrayal through to forgiveness and remorse. One might speculate that father hunger is a self-generating phenomenon—men discover it retrospectively in themselves when they become involved in the men's movement.[24] While I think there is strong evidence that this happens, the reverse is also true—many of the men already feel that their relationship with their fathers is problematic, and experience a powerful feeling of recognition when they hear other men talk about similar experiences. It's also clear, as in Martin's story, that becoming a father causes men to reflect on the way their own fathers raised them.

In my view, there are a number of ways in which we can account for this preoccupation with fathers. One relates to the emergence of an idea of the human self and its development that sees our adult identities as largely shaped by the primal experiences of early childhood. This idea originates in psychoanalysis, but has become widely accepted in popular consciousness. Put simply, we assume that whatever is wrong with us now is the product of some trauma in our earliest years, usually to do with one or other of our parents. The assumption that underlies Steve Biddulph's injunction to 'fix it with your father' is a belief that by confronting whatever it was that our parents did to us, or failed to do in the past, we can liberate ourselves from its effects in the present. The cathartic journey of self-discovery is part of a whole set of methods of self-help and self-therapy that have become popular in the second half of this century. In many ways, in our largely secular society, they fulfil the function organized religion did in earlier times. Once men begin to feel an unease in their manhood, it is hardly surprising that the 'journey through the past' presents itself as a way of exploring whatever it is that is bothering them.

However, no similar narrative of 'mother hunger' has arisen as a dominant motif in the women's movement. We can hardly be surprised at this either, since women have on the whole been much more concerned with inequality and sexism than with questions of the nature of femininity. Femininity has not been seen as under threat in the same way as masculinity. Women have been struggling to gain power while men feel that they are losing it. At the same time as men's power is being challenged by women, many of the things which have sustained masculine identity in the industrial age—lifelong employment, pride in a particular skill or craft, solidarity within groups such as trades unions—are disappearing. In an increasingly privatized and fragmented society, we are thrown back on the search for an individual narrative that explains why we are alienated from ourselves—in Bly's and Biddulph's view, a story about the 'wound' we've received from our fathers.

Once we open up the space for men to begin a journey of self-discovery, all sorts of competing stories will spring up to fill that space. Father hunger will be with us for a while. Striving to create better relationships between fathers and sons cannot be a bad thing, especially since so many of those relationships seem to be filled with anger and resentment. 'The old men can't leave the young men alone,' was the way a close male friend of mine put it to me, 'they have to cut them down to size.' Whether there is a way out of this for fathers and sons is another question. Many of the men who write and speak most glowingly about the joys of child-rearing (and in particular, son-rearing) are bringing up small children who have not yet turned into adolescents who will challenge and reject them. However, recourse to some concocted historical fiction about a 'golden age' of relations between fathers and sons will not help us to change relationships between them in the present. In many ways, the notion of father hunger is a strategy of avoidance: it deflects men from confronting what is far more likely to be the real source of their discomfort, the challenge to their power from women. Nowhere is men's reaction to that challenge expressed more forcefully than in the movement for 'fathers' rights'.

FATHERS' RIGHTS

Among the many different areas of men's activity and activism in Australia, by far the most emotionally charged and politically organized relates to the custody of children after divorce or separation. Every state now has one or more support groups for men involved in custody battles, and many of these groups are also politically active, lobbying for changes to the Family Law Act and better services for divorced men and non-custodial fathers. There is a strong feeling among the men who run these groups, and the men who come to them for support, that current laws discriminate against men and favour women in awarding custody of children. Typically, they argue that men are just as able to be competent and caring parents as women, yet, in their view, the courts consistently demonstrate an implicit belief that children will be better off with their mother.

We are regularly confronted, in a very public way, with the intensity of emotion custody disputes can generate. I have already mentioned the case of Hoss Majdalawi, who shot his estranged wife Jean outside the Family Court in Parramatta. On previous occasions, men have directed similar acts of violence against the Court itself: one Family Court judge has been shot dead and another seriously injured, the wife of a judge was killed by a home-made bomb, and the Parramatta Court building was blown up in 1984. Sometimes, men direct the anger and frustration generated by custody disputes against themselves. It is not uncommon for men to commit suicide when they fail to gain the access to their children that they seem to desire so desperately.

It might seem naive or gratuitous to ask where these emotions come from. Men, it could be said, have a natural affection for their children, and experience natural feelings of loss and grief when they no longer see them and have contact with them every day. Yet, in many ways, this natural affection seems to have become much more prominent in men over the last 20 or 30 years. As Peter Jordan points out, 50 years ago custody disputes were almost unknown. Men either vanished, leaving their wives and children to fend for themselves, or, in cases where the 'fault' was found to lie with the women, the children were automatically awarded to the husbands.

Jordan puts his finger on two vital historical points that help to illuminate fathers' feelings about the custody of children, and the whole issue of fathers' rights, and place them in a broader context. The notion that fathers might have to fight for a right to custody of their children has only entered our legal system quite recently. The British historian Lawrence Stone argues that one of the reasons why divorce rates were so low in early modern Britain was the existence of powerful deterrents against women initiating divorce, not the least of which was 'the strong probability of losing all contact whatsoever with her children'.[25] However cruel, abusive or adulterous the husband might have been, 'the common law still granted him absolute control of the children'. This situation only began to change in the late nineteenth century. However, vestiges of this legal attitude, which saw children primarily as property and the property of the man in all but exceptional circumstances, survived well into the twentieth century. 'No-fault' divorce was only introduced in Australia in the 1970s—and interestingly, some conservative social policy lobbyists are now arguing that this was a mistake, and that notions of fault should be reintroduced.[26]

Historical records also show that, in British and Australian society at least until the mid-twentieth century, it has generally been much more common for husbands to desert wives and children than it has for wives to desert husbands and take the children with them. The reasons for this appear to have been both legal and economic, with poverty playing a central role in men's decision to leave their families and women's reluctance to leave their men. Lawrence Stone speaks of a drifting underclass in British society in the early industrial age, within which marriages were unstable and often did not last long. Husbands tended to leave because they could no longer support their families, often deserting them in time of war, while deserted women, with very little prospect of employment, were thrown back on poor relief provided by the churches. 'For most poor women,' Stone concludes, 'marriage was an economic necessity for survival,'[27] while for poor men it could easily become an economic prison.

These historical portraits may seem far away from the realities of late twentieth-century urban Australia.

However, they help to throw into sharp relief just how radically different the present situation of fathers, mothers and children is from the situation existing even in our grandparents' time. As we have moved away from notions of parental property rights over children, towards an idea of the rights of children and the responsibility of parents, men have lost an unprecedented degree of control.

It is often argued that men undergoing divorce channel their feelings of grief and anger over the loss of their former partner into a battle over custody of their children. The wish to have primary care of the children represents a need for an emotional focus to replace the one previously supplied by the relationship and an attempt to reassert power at a time when men feel particularly powerless. However, this explanation seems to me not to go far enough. We can understand this better if we look more closely at the shift that has taken place in the notion of fathers' rights. As we've seen, fathers' rights have traditionally been conceived of as property rights. However, this did not mean that when a marriage broke up and the father gained possession of the children, he would become responsible for their care. Typically, this was delegated to another female relative—his own mother, an aunt or sister—or to a housekeeper or governess, depending on the social class he came from. By contrast, the advocates of fathers' rights in Australia today argue for a right to nurture, to be involved directly in the care and upbringing of their children. This represents a radical shift in rhetoric, at the very least.

This shift, in my view, is one more manifestation of the processes of deep social change I have been talking about in this book, part of the 'transformation of intimacy', which is also a transformation of the power relations between men and women. We now live in a world in which marriage is no longer 'an economic necessity for survival' for poor women—a world in which men's primary responsibilities towards their partners and children are defined less and less in economic terms and more and more in terms of emotional and practical care. Much of the pressure for this latter trend has come directly from women themselves, struggling at the everyday, micro-political level of domestic life for greater co-operation from their male partners. Yet there is also a sense in which the wider social consensus has changed. With the dethronement of 'rightful patriarchy' as the dominant form of the Australian family,[28] a space has opened up for the creation of a new ideology of the father. However much this ideology is manufactured and manipulated by media and advertising, and other forms of fantasy in popular culture, it is also part of the lived experience and the rational choices of men from a wide range of social backgrounds, as Carol Grbich's research shows. As we've seen, there is less and less space for fathers as breadwinners in Australian society, not least because, increasingly, the breadwinner cannot win enough bread on his own. A family structure in which both parents work is now not a matter of choice on the woman's part, but a product of economic necessity. In these circumstances, men must increasingly seek a new role in the family, one that involves them in nurture as well as bringing home the bacon.

Indeed, one reasonably common complaint from men who have been denied custody of their children is that they would have liked a closer involvement with their children before the break-up of the marriage, but were hindered by the breadwinner role. I think we need to take this complaint seriously: many men do feel trapped into a life of long working hours and reduced contact with their partners and children. Interestingly, some men tell a story of being imprisoned just as much by their own attitudes as by financial realities. Richard, an engineer whose wife left him after a violent incident, began attending an anti-domestic violence group and began to see his life in a new light:

> I'm a workaholic . . . I'd say I'd be home at five, and then roll up at 7.30, when the kids were all bathed and put to bed.

> I've got my own business, own company, engineering supplies. It was no problem for me to start at 4 a.m., and finish at nine at night. I always had that pattern, to do more than I needed.
>
> For the last 18 months we led separate lives. I didn't want to go home, and when I did I'd be half drunk.
>
> There was no communication, no sex. I was a complete arsehole.
>
> Now I start at eight, come home at four, but I haven't got a wife.

Richard explained that he'd rationalised his long hours at work by telling himself that 'everything I was working for was for us'. He now has two of their children living with him, while the third child lives with his wife, with whom he hopes to be re-united. He's proud of the fact that he is looking after his teenage children, and says he's learned to 'work smarter'. Interestingly, Richard denies that he felt any pressure to be a breadwinner, and says he 'always earned good money, however many hours I worked'.

Richard's story suggests that where men are given the opportunity to explore their feelings and reassess the history of their relationship with their former partner, they may progress more easily beyond anger and begin to see their own attitudes and beliefs in a new way. Many men, however, do not have this opportunity. While the Family Court does provide counselling services for men involved in custody disputes, the extent of these services is severely limited by funding.

One important change has taken place recently in Australia in the laws governing what happens to children after divorce or separation. In 1996, the Family Law Act was amended to shift the emphasis away from a parent's right of acccss to a child, towards a notion of the child's right of contact with both his or her parents. By so doing, the framers of this change are seeking to move even further away from the traditional notion of children as property, and to strengthen a conception of the rights of children and the obligations and responsibilities of parents. Fathers' rights groups were by no means unanimous in their support of this shift, arguing in some cases that it represented a further erosion of men's ability to claim custody.

At present, around 95 per cent of couples who divorce or separate come to an agreement on which partner will have the primary care or custody of children without the matter going to a final judicial hearing. As discussed in Chapter 3, Peter Jordan reports that 'we don't see the middle classes much in the Family Court any more, they tend to be able to afford lawyers and to work things out between themselves'. Thus, the predominantly working-class couples whose custody disputes end up in litigation are those who can least afford it, and probably have least access to expensive private counselling and support services. Among these couples, the man gains custody of the children in around 37 per cent of cases, that is to say, slightly more than a third. Whether the fathers' rights groups would be satisfied with an even split is uncertain. On the whole, their criticisms tend to focus on what they perceive as the structural disadvantage of men within the Family Court system and its ancillaries such as legal aid.

Typical complaints are that legal aid workers and social workers are dismissive of men's requests for help and that the majority of Family Court counsellors are women who are felt to be unsympathetic to the arguments and aspirations of men. Outside of the immediate context of the Court, men also complain about what they see as inequities in the operation of the Child Support Act, and the burden child support payments place on men who are trying to 'rebuild' after the breakup of a relationship. Men particularly resent paying child maintenance to an ex-wife or partner who has started a new relationship with another man (though statistically, men tend to 're-partner' more quickly and more often after separation than women). Interestingly, too, men's rights groups such as the Queensland-based Men's Rights Agency, which claims in the region of 1000 members, have many active women members who are partners of divorced men paying child support. These women feel that an unfair financial burden is placed on the new relationship by the man's payments to his former spouse.

There is no doubt that many individual men can relate convincing cases of vindictive behaviour by a former spouse, and unfair treatment by one or more government agencies or the courts. Whether this amounts to systemic discrimination by the law or the state is much harder to establish. Each case tends to involve a long and complex narrative on both sides, and no two cases are the same. However, it seems to me that the fathers' rights groups, in concentrating so exclusively on the disadvantage suffered by men under the present system, actually weaken their case to be heard, because they have so little to say about the larger structural constraints affecting men's participation in the nurturing and raising of children.

In my view, if as a society we decide that we want men to share the responsibilities of child-rearing with women on an equal basis, we cannot reasonably deny them equal participation in that process after a relationship breaks up. Ultimately, a truly fair and gender-neutral approach to custody issues would involve moving towards a system of joint custody or co-residence, where children spend equal amounts of time with each parent and each parent has equal financial responsibility for each child. There is a number of obvious practical obstacles to such a system, such as income differentials between men and women, and what happens to a child's schooling when parents live a long way from each other. But there are also political and philosophical obstacles to a shared custody model, obstacles not often addressed by either the fathers' rights groups or their critics.

To begin with, it's by no means clear that there is yet a broad social consensus for 'equality parenting', or that the majority of women would necessarily support such a model once its full consequences become clear. It is even less clear that men will support it. If, indeed, equal participation and equal responsibility is what men want, they too will have to live with the consequences. For the fathers' rights groups, this means a number of things. They must, logically, begin to devote as much time to lobbying for family-friendly workplaces, increased funding for child-care, more flexible working arrangements and extended paternity leave as they currently do to campaigning for changes to the Family Law Act. They must also be willing to acknowledge that once a right is acknowledged in law, responsibilities and obligations will flow from it. In other words, after separation men may become responsible for the care of their children for two weeks out of every four whether they like it or not. Whether the fathers' rights groups will be able to persuade the broad mainstream of male voters that this is in their interests is debatable. I believe such a model could be beneficial to both men and women, and also achievable, but not without a great deal of struggle and inevitable conflict. There is a political question here for women, too. Legal changes over the last 50 years have vanquished the belief that men are the natural owners of their children, and have given women much greater autonomy and control over their lives when a marriage ends. Put bluntly, women now have more power in a situation where previously they had almost none. Moving towards a model of shared custody does mean that women will have to be prepared to give up some of that power. In a sense, this is the price that women will have to pay for greater equality in parenting, greater 'co-operation from men', as Beatrix Campbell puts it. Whether or not they will want to do this is another question, especially as they will also be asked to do so in the area of reproductive rights.

THE NAME OF THE FATHER

> People are looking for different things, that's why they have the opportunity to view the videotapes we make of the various families and, of course, the families get to see the videotapes of our applicants.

> We often suggest to a young gentleman or a middle-aged gentleman that he experience a wide range of kinds of families.
>
> We have certain package programs where an individual can experience over the course of a 12-month period a sort of sampler . . . Often this will inform that individual of the kind of family he wishes to participate with on a long-term basis.
>
> Joe Franks, *Rent-a-Family*[29]

We are listening to a radio documentary made in San Francisco. The speaker is a bright, articulate American, a businessman who has discovered a profitable niche market: men without families. Acting on a flash of inspiration, he's set up *Rent-a-Family*, a service that puts single men in touch with single women with children. Hopefuls of both sexes have to pass a stringent interview, and then submit a videotape in which they talk about themselves and their lives and interests. For a handsome fee, the men get to choose a family from a selection of tapes. They can take the family for picnics on the weekend, go away on holidays with them, and perhaps even strike up a sexual or romantic relationship with the mother. What becomes increasingly clear as we listen is that these men are not searching primarily for a partner, or even necessarily for love: they are looking for a family, and if necessary they will pay to have one, in much the same way that men pay for sex with a sex worker.

As it happens, *Rent-a-Family* is a fiction, a docu-drama, which nevertheless manages to keep many listeners convinced that what they are hearing is real for most of its three-hour duration. It is a fantasy of nostalgia for the nuclear family, one in which the male characters quite clearly have a greater investment than the women. Yet this fantasy is double-edged; it allows men the experience of family life 'on approval', without any commitment other than a weekly payment, which can be terminated at any time they choose.

In many ways, *Rent-a-Family* is an allegory of modern

relationships, yet one that specifically embodies many of the conflicting and contradictory attitudes men have to families and fatherhood. Increasingly, these attitudes are being played out not just within the confines of the nuclear family, but in the broader social arena, as the case of the fathers' rights movement makes plain. As I've suggested, in certain ways the fathers' rights movement exemplifies a tendency implicit in much of the current rhetoric about men and fatherhood—a retreat away from the problematic nature of men's relationships with women, into an area of emotional life that is less threatening, and offers more immediate and unconditional emotional rewards: the nurture of children.

We can see this tendency writ large in the emerging debate about men's relationship to reproductive technology and reproductive rights. Until very recently, there has been almost no discussion of men's involvement in this area. The signs are there, however, that reproduction will become an area of intense contest between men and women.

Another example from the United States, this time factual rather than fictional, helps to illustrate this tendency. Recently, a men's rights group submitted draft legislation to the Wisconsin state legislature seeking to deny the provision of donor sperm to unmarried women. The express purpose of the draft bill is to prevent the conception of 'fatherless children', that is to say, children who will not necessarily enjoy the presence of a father in the home where they grow up. However, a number of other, less explicit motivations are at work here.

One concrete purpose of this bill may be to deny the possibility of conception using donor sperm to lesbian couples who want to have children. This is already an extremely contentious issue in the United States, and it is likely to take on similar dimensions in Australia as the result of a legal test case in Queensland. The plaintiffs in this case are a lesbian couple who claim they have been discriminated against by a fertility clinic that refused to inseminate one of them. The clinic maintains it is simply following guidelines laid down by the Queensland government and the National Health and Medical Research Council, according to which donor insemination should be restricted to heterosexual couples.[30]

While the familiar conservative moral objections to homosexual marriage and homosexual parenting doubtless play a role here, in the case of the Wisconsin legislation I believe two other motives are paramount. One is the argument we have already encountered in the context of father hunger, namely, that the absence of fathers is a source of social disintegration, alienation, crime, and violence. This argument is not the sole preserve of the men's movement; it is also popular with social conservatives and is gaining credence with sections of the liberal Left. Fathers, it is maintained, provide a source of firm discipline that mothers are either incapable of exerting or disinclined to do so. A less conservative version of this argument suggests that when boys grow up without strong, positive male role models, they are inclined to compensate with hypermasculine behaviour: excessive aggression, highly competitive attitudes towards other males, and hostility towards all forms of authority and control—typified by the behaviour of youth gangs.

Interestingly, recent research on teenage girls and girl gangs is starting to show similar behaviours and attitudes among them, irrespective of the presence of mothers or fathers as role models—which suggests that the link between absent fathers and anti-social behaviour in boys (or girls!) is a tenuous one.[31] However, quite apart from its dubious basis in fact, the 'absent father' argument fulfils a particular political purpose for its exponents. It allows them to advance the view that women on their own are not fully competent to bring up children. In its more extreme form, this argument paints single mothers as irresponsible agents of social decay.

The second, less familiar element at work in the Wisconsin legislation is a desire on the part of the men who framed it to assert a level of control in the use of reproductive technology. Ultimately, what is at stake here is men's control over the male contribution to reproduction: sperm. While the legislation may appear to represent no more than the views of a marginal activist group, issues to do with men's right to control what happens to their sperm, both before and after the conception of a child, are beginning to be discussed more widely in Australia, especially in relation to abortion.

A number of men active in the men's movement are beginning to argue that the rights of fathers have been ignored in public debates about abortion. The argument runs like this: if society as a whole expects men to take a greater responsibility for children, that responsibility also entails rights. Thus, if a man and woman have sex and an unplanned pregnancy results, both the man and the woman should have some say in whether or not the pregnancy is terminated or carried to term. In many cases, of course, both of them may agree on one or other course of action. But if they do not agree, we can imagine two possible situations may arise. In one, the woman may want to have the baby, but the man may not wish to, because he does not want to accept the financial or emotional responsibility of caring for a child. In the other scenario, the woman may wish to have an abortion, while the man may want to become a father. Here the argument is advanced that, if the man is willing to take full responsibility for the raising of the child, and undertakes to make no further demands on the mother after the birth, there ought to be no objection to the woman carrying the pregnancy to term.[32]

Arguments such as these represent a radical challenge to the classical feminist position on abortion, the bedrock of which has been the principle that it is a woman's right to decide what happens to her own body. Indeed, the struggle to end men's control over women's bodies has been crucial to feminist politics in a whole range of areas, extending far beyond the context of abortion. Thus, any argument that suggests that women should not have complete autonomy in their choices about carrying through a pregnancy is profoundly disturbing to many women.

Some fascinating research on these questions has been carried out by Erika Haubold at the University of Wollongong. She interviewed a group of 37 men from a wide range of backgrounds on their attitudes to abortion.[33] Each of the men was asked a series of questions about how they would respond to a regular or casual sexual partner having an unexpected pregnancy. Among the group was a number of men who were involved in men's groups or other aspects of the men's movement. In their cases, Haubold believes that their responses were strongly influenced by men's movement rhetoric about the importance of fathers' involvement in their children's lives as 'spiritual guardians and mentors'. She links this with the more overtly political rhetoric of the fathers' rights groups about social and judicial bias against fathers in custody disputes, and the emergence of arguments that children have a 'right' to a relationship with their fathers.

So, for example, one of the men argued that if he did not want to have the child, the mother should be made to have an abortion, because the child might turn into a derelict without his emotional support. But he also felt that the mother should be able to choose to have an abortion if she did not want a child.

Another man argued that if the pregnancy occurred in a non-committed relationship he would be in favour of abortion. However, if the woman refused to terminate the pregancy, he would apply to the courts for full custody of the child at birth. He saw the relationship with the mother and the child as 'two very, very different things'.

Other men, by contrast, expressed a primary concern for the well-being of their partner. Overall, though, they saw themselves as having an equal right to decide on what should happen with the pregnancy, and argued generally that women should not be able to make autonomous decisions about child-rearing or abortion. If a woman did—for example, to keep a child against the wishes of the man—the men argued that she should forfeit the right to financial support from the man.

According to Haubold, the men's responses are informed by a belief in 'reproductive equality'. This sounds simple and obvious: both a man and a woman contribute an equal amount of genetic material to the conception of a child, and hence should have an equal say in what happens to it. But as Haubold points out, this view leaves 'the mother's body', and the fact that she will have to carry and bear the child, totally out of the picture. 'There is a long way between producing an embryo and delivering a healthy baby: two processes which obviously depend on the biological differences between women's and men's bodies'.[34] The rise of modern genetics, the advent of reproductive technologies such as donor insemination and IVF, and the emergence of practices such as surrogate motherhood have helped to blur this difference, increasingly transforming the mother's body into a 'container for the biological symbiosis of semen and egg'. Haubold sees a clash here between notions of biological and 'social' fatherhood, with the men she studied opting for an emphasis on biological fatherhood as the basis for their right to reproductive equality.

There are some fundamental legal, moral and political questions raised by this clash—questions that are likely to be hotly debated in the years to come. As with many of the questions we've been considering in this book, they are about power and control. The dilemmas thrown up by the issue of reproductive rights in many ways mirror those raised by custody disputes, and the history of legal and philosophical thinking that underpins them is the same history.

We've already seen that, until recently, children were considered to be the legal property of their fathers. With this legal fact went two further broad principles: that wives were considered to be the legal property of their husbands, and that a husband had the right to enjoy exclusive sexual access to his wife. To a greater or lesser extent, these two principles were also enshrined in law. If we have any doubts about the extent to which women were actually considered, in practice, to be the property of their spouses, we might consider an example from the civil courts of eighteenth-century England. From around 1700 onwards, husbands whose wives had committed adultery began to sue the co-respondent—that is to say, the wife's lover—for trespass. The legal thinking behind this was that 'by using the body of the wife, the seducer had damaged the property of the husband'.[35] In effect, this meant that the husband could sue for monetary compensation: his monopoly right over the body of his wife was given a price-tag.

As Lawrence Stone points out, over the two centuries preceding 1700, there had been a major shift in attitude to the crime of adultery and its punishment. Previously, the adulterer was forced to make a public confession of his sin before God and the ecclesiastical court, carrying a candle and clad only in a white smock. It was also thought perfectly acceptable for the wronged husband to take violent revenge on his rival or challenge him to a duel. By the eighteenth century, by contrast, adultery had become a business transaction, and the cuckolded husband made no bones about publicly revealing the injury he had suffered in order to gain compensation. With the rise of the middle-class family, yet another shift occurred: 'the concept of wifely adultery as a breach of male property rights . . . was replaced by the concept of wifely adultery as a violation of the ideal of Victorian domesticity'.[36]

Hand-in-hand with the notion that wives were the property of husbands went the notion that husbands should have a sexual monopoly over their wives. The principal practical reason for this was to ensure the paternity of their children, a crucial consideration for the inheritance of property and rights of succession. Since men could not physically prove that a child was theirs, not having borne it in their bodies, they had to be sure that no other man had the chance to impregnate their wives. The converse of this emphasis on a *biological* notion of fatherhood was that men could be made responsible for the maintenance of children they had fathered, so, for example, an unmarried woman could bring a paternity suit against a man who had got her pregnant and then deserted her. Plainly, anxiety about this aspect of biological fatherhood underlies the statements of some of the men interviewed by Erika Haubold, who argue that they should have the right to request the abortion of a child they do not wish to support.

Now DNA testing has given us a means of determining the paternity of a child with almost total certainty. It is interesting to reflect on how this unprecedented technological development might affect our notions of fatherhood. On the face of it, DNA testing would seem most likely to reinforce a strictly biological idea of fatherhood, cementing the 'natural' biological link between father and child. Yet it is also conceivable (I hope the reader will forgive the almost unavoidable pun) that quite different and unexpected consequences might follow. If the motive behind men's insistence on wifely fidelity was the need to be able to demonstrate unequivocally that they were the father of their children, effective contraception and DNA testing make wifely fidelity redundant.

Let me make this clearer: suppose a man and woman, Ivan and Mary, agree to have a child together, a child for which they will both be responsible, emotionally and financially. Let us further assume, for the sake of argument, that it is important to Ivan to know that he is the biological father of the child. It is quite possible for Mary to have sex with other men, providing she uses reliable contraception, and still be able to prove that the child she conceives is the genetic progeny of Ivan. Of course, Ivan may still be jealous of Mary, but the historical and social underpinnings of that jealousy have begun to crumble. Geneticists, of course, might argue that this jealousy is in fact inspired by the logic of evolutionary biology. The male wants to ensure that his genetic material survives and is reproduced, and beats off other competitors. But even if this were true—and the example of human cultures where 'wifely fidelity' is not the rule and the paternity of a child is not considered significant suggests that it is not—the genetic facts would still be the same. Mary would still be able to ensure that she did not fall pregnant to anyone other than Ivan (assuming, of course, that the means of contraception she used was reliable), and Ivan would, in any case, still be able to be sure that it was his DNA that was passed on to the child, no matter how many other sexual partners Mary had.

This is, of course, a hypothetical case, but it is well within the realm of possibility. Much less hypothetical is the converse case, that of men who are infertile and whose partners are impregnated with donor sperm. This is now a common practice among infertile couples in Australia. Between 1000 and 2000 children are born as a result of donor insemination every year. As yet, there are no long-term studies of the emotional effects on men of their fathering a child who is not their biological offspring. However, there is no evidence, so far, that it is any more traumatic than adoption. Ultimately, donor insemination appears to challenge the primacy of biological fatherhood.

DNA testing and donor insemination seem, on the face of it, to have radically opposed implications for biological fatherhood, one reinforcing it and one undermining it. Yet this need not necessarily be the case. If the practical grounds for men's sexual control over women begin to disappear, it is also possible that the rule of the monogamous pair bond as the dominant form of heterosexual relations may also begin to waver. This may well prove to be a development that suits both men and women. Yet, as I shall argue in Chapter 10, it can only succeed as an arrangement that grants equal rights and responsibilities to both sexes if it goes hand-in-hand with a fairly radical change in the way we think about fatherhood and parenthood, one that would place a much greater emphasis on a shared social responsibility for children. What is essential to grasp in the immediate context is that the *meaning* of paternity (or maternity, for that matter), the significance we give to it as social beings, is not fixed or immutable. Even when we are arguing for the importance of biological fatherhood, the 'bond of blood', we are doing so in a social context, within the framework of a whole set of laws, religious beliefs and institutional practices. Not only do these laws and beliefs vary from culture to culture, they are also susceptible to historical change, most notably in our own time through the impact of new technologies.

FANTASIES OF FATHERHOOD

> All his [the son's] instincts, those of tenderness, gratitude, lustfulness, defiance and independence, find satisfaction in the single wish *to be his own father.*
>
> Sigmund Freud[37]

There is one further way in which reproductive technology may change the way we think about fatherhood: it may, ultimately, make mothers redundant. This is the fantasy brought to life in Arnold Schwarzenegger's 1994 release *Junior*. Schwarzenegger plays Dr Alex Hesse, a scientist who has developed a new drug, Expectane, which guarantees successful, healthy pregnancies. When funding for his research is cut, Dr Hesse decides to prove that anything a woman can do, a man can do as well. He has a fertilized egg injected into his own abdomen and carries the pregnancy to term.

In many ways, *Junior* is a parody of motherhood, using the familiar device of a world turned upside down to satirize aspects of women's behaviour during pregnancy (or more accurately, male perceptions thereof). Thus Dr Hesse becomes moody and emotional, he has morning sickness and food cravings, and gets all clucky when he sees other infants. Schwarzenegger reported that working on the film had helped him to get in touch with his feminine side.

But *Junior* is also a male fantasy of fatherhood, a fantasy about being able to bear children independently of women. As such, it belongs to a long lineage of literary and mythological fantasies of male self-reproduction, stretching back to the ancient Greeks. The most famous of these, one of the great modern myths, is the story of Frankenstein—written, of course, by a woman. However, in the vast majority of these fantasies, male self-reproduction is metaphorical—a man brings forth life in his own image, rather than by actual procreation. Thus, in the Pygmalion legend, a man who is both a sculptor and the king of Cyprus falls in love with his own ivory statue of the ideal woman and persuades the goddess Aphrodite to bring the statue to life, whereupon he marries her, much to the chagrin of his mortal wife. In this story, Pygmalion still depends on the intervention of a woman, albeit a goddess, to bring the statue to life. Dr Frankenstein brings forth life from brute matter by his own ingenuity, for which act of hubris he is ultimately punished when his own creature destroys him. There is a rich vein of feminist writing on Frankenstein that sees it as an archetypal story of the fatal pride of male reason, an allegory of science's striving to transcend the limits of nature. Linked with this is men's striving to free themselves from the body and biology—which, for some feminists, is evidence of male hostility towards the female body that gave birth to them.[38] Recently, some writers have drawn connections between the Frankenstein myth and the development of reproductive technology, arguing that technologies such as IVF represent an attempt by scientists to bring reproductive processes under the control of male technical expertise and thus to make themselves the 'masters of creation'. Yet, the sense in which the developers of IVF technology (who include a not-inconsiderable number of women) are 'fathers' to the children produced thereby is ultimately still metaphorical. What is interesting about *Junior* is its emphasis on the male body: it's not a metaphorical pregnancy, but a physical one. As if to ensure that the edifice of masculinity would not begin to tremble too violently at the image of a pregnant man, the makers of *Junior* cast the hypermasculine Schwarzenegger in the role of Alex Hesse, rather than a more Sensitive New Age actor. In many ways, however, Schwarzenegger's character is a refracted image of the new father taken to his logical conclusion.

There is, of course, a world of difference between the idea of male self-reproduction in the literary and filmic imagination and the current state of technology. Interestingly, though, at the same time as *Junior* was released in Australian cinemas, an article appeared in the Melbourne *Age* outlining the serious scientific consideration that had already been given to the possibility of producing a successful male pregnancy.[39] Dick Teresi, a prominent American science writer, described a Kinsey Institute symposium he had attended in 1984, at which a professor of paediatrics at Johns Hopkins University and a professor of anatomy and cell biology at UCLA discussed how existing techniques could be used to create the hormonal environment in a man's body that would be necessary for an embryo to grow and flourish in his abdomen. Their conclusion, subsequently supported by a number of other eminent scientists (all of them male) working in areas such as IVF and evolutionary biology, was that there was no insurmountable obstacle to a man carrying a baby to term.

As with other areas of technology, just because it can be done does not mean it will or should be done. It is more than likely that *Junior*, like the Pygmalion and Frankenstein myths, will remain a fantasy. Moreover, even if men were one day able to gestate a child in their own bodies, they would still need women to supply eggs. In this sense, they will never be capable of autonomous self-reproduction—and nor, for that matter, will women. However, the emergence of surrogate motherhood as a means whereby childless couples can have a child suggests another potential strategy of male self-reproduction. There is no reason why a man who wishes to become a father, but does not want to do so in the context of a marriage or close emotional relationship, could not contract with a woman to conceive and give birth to a child. In line with the contractual arrangements currently entered into by couples and surrogate mothers, the child would then become the sole property and responsibility of the man, to raise and care for as he wished.

My purpose in discussing this and other aspects of reproductive technology is to make one thing clear: if we really want to understand what is at stake in the current re-definition of fatherhood, we need to think through these possibilities to their logical end. They are simply extreme cases of more everyday and concrete political questions raised by men's greater involvement in caring for children. Hiding behind these questions, but constantly rearing its head in our deliberations about them, is the question of what we consider to be 'natural'—from Signor Gaspare's invocation of 'a man's natural love for his offspring' in the *Book of the Courtier* to the rhetoric of fathers' rights groups today. Yet, at the same time, nature and what is natural are also undergoing re-definition, a process in which, once again, technology is playing its part.

Let me sum up the broad outlines of the trends I see emerging from this discussion. Men are seeking a closer and more active relationship with their children. For some, this involves a decision to give up the conventional male role of provider altogether and become a full-time care-giver, usually as part of a couple in which the woman works full-time. Others combine child-rearing with part-time work or study. Common to both groups is a feeling that they are in uncharted territory, embarking on an experiment in which there are no clear guidelines or rules as to how they should behave. Their experiment, however, takes place in a social context where it is increasingly seen as desirable that men have this greater involvement with their children, and where images of the 'new father' have become a commonplace part of the cultural landscape. Moreover, during the first half of the 1990s, a re-evaluation of fathers and fathering has occurred, to the point where sections of the men's movement and conservative social commentators maintain that the absence of paternal care and influence from children's lives is responsible for a broad spectrum of social problems, from crime to drug use and youth suicide.

These developments immediately present a dilemma for women. On the one hand, at a practical, everyday level, women have expressed and continue to express a strong desire for men to participate and co-operate more in looking after their children. It would not be too much to say that this is one of *the* crucial questions for active feminists and the broad mass of heterosexual women. Yet, for these women, the question of autonomy is also a crucial one: the everyday freedom of choice to work, to be educated, to participate fully in all areas of public life, and to make their own decisions about their sexuality, their bodies and their relationships with other people. One aspect of this autonomy may be the choice to raise children independently of a man. The rhetoric of absent fathers represents a challenge to that autonomy, implying that women cannot fulfil the emotional needs of children on their own, and are socially irresponsible if they choose to do so.

At the heart of this dilemma is the question of control. This question repeats itself in a whole range of everyday social contexts, some of which I've explored in this chapter. If, indeed, equality parenting does become the norm, it is difficult to see how we can avoid adopting shared custody, and reproductive equality as well—that is to say, equal rights for men and women in reproductive decisions. This is likely to be an even more controversial area than that of custody. Feminists have been pondering on these questions for two decades, and a number of different and often conflicting perspectives have emerged. Put very simply, the feminist dilemma is as follows: the bearing and raising of children is one area, perhaps the only one, in which women have enjoyed a degree of relative autonomy from men—an autonomy now strengthened by women's increased control over their own fertility and their decreased dependence on men to support them financially and materially. Some feminists have gone so far as to argue that reproduction is the one arena in which women have ultimate power, since they can bring forth life while men cannot, and that they should not surrender this power lightly.

An interesting counter-argument is advanced by Marge Piercy in her science fiction novel *Woman at the Edge of Time*. Piercy imagines two future worlds, one a Utopia of small co-operative communities in which men and women live in harmony and equality with each other and the natural world. The other is a dystopia, a polluted hell where patriarchal capitalism reigns triumphant and women are reduced to powerless sex slaves. The distinctive feature of her green Utopia is a surprising one: women no longer bear children. Instead, children are conceived by a version of IVF and grown in artificial wombs. After 'birth', they are cared for and nurtured by the entire community. The inhabitants of this ideal future have an interesting rationale for their reproductive regime. In order for women and men to become truly equal, they argue, it was necessary for men to give up a great deal of power. For men to assent to this, women had to give up something in return—their monopoly on the conception of children. Instead of following the course mapped out in *Junior*, they decided to break the link between women's bodies and reproduction, creating a technological Utopia of reproductive equality.

Piercy's vision of the reproductive future, heavily influenced by the writings of the radical 1970s feminist Shulamith Firestone, is sharply at odds with the arguments of most contemporary feminist thinkers on this topic. Moira Gatens, for example, argues that the 'technologization' of reproduction, intended in Firestone's model of 'cybernetic communism' to make reproduction gender neutral, actually amounts to a 'masculinization', an imposition of the 'norm'—the inability of men's bodies to produce children—on the bodies of women.[40] The one common theme that emerges from the growing field of feminist writing on reproduction is that what is ultimately at stake is power—and that our political and philosophical debates over reproduction reflect a struggle over power, in which the interests of women and the interests of men are sometimes diametrically opposed.

There can be no clearer example of this than the suggestion that men should have the right to prevent a woman having an abortion, touched on in Erika Haubold's research, and made publicly in a recent letter to the *Australian* by the editor of *Certified Male* magazine, who 'await[s] with interest a class action to challenge the right of a woman to abort a man's child even if he is prepared to take full responsibility for its upbringing'.[41] The language here is interesting: the author speaks of 'a man's child'. Is this simply an attempt to reassert the property rights that men once held over their children? Not entirely, I think. The rhetoric of fatherhood in the men's movement is not primarily about property. Rather, it focuses on the father–child relationship as part of a man's project of self-realization. This is perhaps at the core of what is genuinely new about the current redefinition of fatherhood, and in a sense it follows logically from a whole series of shifts in the way we think about ourselves as individuals. Increasingly, we see the self as a project to be worked on in different ways, whether through education, the reading of self-help manuals, therapy, meditation or other forms of self-cultivation. Psychoanalysis has taught us to regard 'coming to terms with' our sexuality and our relationship with our parents as crucial to this process. As we've seen in Chapter 5, our intimate relationships also are seen more and more as a project, in which we assist each other in working on ourselves. The re-definition of fatherhood is merely the latest stage in this progression.

It seems to me, however, to be a profoundly ambiguous development. In some ways, the focus on fathering as a core element of men's project of self-realization amounts to a strategy of avoidance, a retreat from the difficulties and complexities of relationships with women. Relationships with children, at least until they become adolescents, are largely unthreatening, and offer a source of emotional affirmation and reward a great deal less problematic than a partnership. We get a sense of this in the words of Paul, one of the men Erika Haubold interviewed, who argues that his relationship with mother and child are 'two very, very different things'.[42]

However positive it may be in terms of encouraging greater care and regard for our offspring, viewing our relationship with them as part of a project of self-realization also has a profoundly individualistic, even narcissistic element to it. There is something of this in the images of naked fathers holding babies that have become so popular in recent years. Anthony McMahon describes the male 'engrossment' in babies these images and stories reveal as 'a fantasized male bonding ritual', but points out that these fantasies appeal strongly to women also, since most of them appear in women's magazines.[43] Thus even the AFL grand final is now an occasion for magazines to publish photos of star footballers gazing into the eyes of their infants, as if seeing themselves reflected there.

'I just love being with him,' confides Richard Osborne, who plays for Melbourne team Footscray, 'there is nothing I love more than to get home and be with him. I see little changes in him all the time, and I don't want to miss any part of him growing up . . . When Mitchell gives me that smile, I just melt.'[44]

It would be churlish to question the honesty or authenticity of Richard's feelings for his son, or of his subsequent statement that footballers are 'not just a bunch of meatheads', but rather 'family men playing football for a living'. However, we should also acknowledge that the re-definition of fatherhood, and the re-definition of masculinity that makes it possible for footballers to admit to such emotions, is taking place in the context of a much larger tendency towards increasing individualism, the destruction of a whole range of forms of association and social solidarity linked to industrial society. The men's movement might appear to represent a contrary tendency, an attempt to build a new form of solidarity and civil society, yet many aspects of its notion of fatherhood seem to me imbued with individualism. One possible antidote to this tendency, and to some of the conflicts between men's and women's interests that are likely to arise out of the re-definition of fatherhood, might be to begin building an alternative conception of social parenting. What this would involve, and what benefits it might bring, is outlined in the concluding chapter of this book.

10

What does a man want?

> The great question that has never been answered and which I have not been able to answer, despite my 30 years of research into the feminine soul, is 'What does a woman want?'[1]

Freud's famous question, plaintive in its perplexity, is emblematic of the history of gender relations in the twentieth century. Historically, a great deal of male energy has gone into attempting to elucidate what it is that men think women ought to want. In the course of this century, the tables have been turned. Women have begun to state clearly what it is they want, and to fight for it, whether at the micropolitical level of their everyday sexual and domestic relations with men, or in the broader arena of social action. Yet, in a sense, as more of women's basic demands for equality of opportunity in the workplace, access to education, and economic autonomy from men have begun to be met, the question of what it is women want in their intimate relations with men has become more elusive and more complex.

As I've argued throughout this book, women have grown more and more unsatisfied with the industrial nuclear family as a way of living their lives with men and children. A part of this dissatisfaction arises from what they experience as men's continuing lack of co-operation in domestic life—yet this is by no means the whole story. Women are seeking new forms of intimacy, a kind of democracy in their relations with men that is not just domestic but also emotional. Moreover, this democracy is not a fixed, stable condition; it is a narrative, an unfolding project—what Anthony Giddens calls the pure relationship or 'confluent love'.[2]

A large part of my own narrative in this book has revolved around men's responses to women's new demands and desires. Overall, we have seen a picture of men reacting, running to keep up with women, struggling for clues and hints to lead them through a new territory in which there are no maps and few points of orientation. The challenges of the pure relationship are, if anything, more confusing and discomfiting than women's incursion into the workplace and the corridors of institutional power. There is no emotional log of claims for men to respond to, no manifesto of intimate democracy. Women, too, are exploring, feeling their way ahead. Whatever it is they 'want' is shifting, contingent, and from men's point of view, often contradictory.

Much of this book has explored what will be necessary in order for men to follow women on their journey. I've argued that in a variety of ways, they will need to be prepared to move in the direction of women's aspirations, making compromises, giving up customary power and privilege, opening themselves up to new forms of emotional experience along the way. The question of what it is that men really want has remained, to a certain extent, in the background. It seems to me that it is time to ask this question in a serious and unprejudiced way.

Let me put this another way. A great deal of what is currently written about relations between men and women amounts to a kind of rescue operation for marriage, or as it is sometimes known, the 'heterosexual pair bond'. Most writers are agreed that this bond is in crisis. Most believe that the way out of the crisis lies in extending the reach of domestic and intimate democracy in the kinds of ways I've discussed in this book. Implicit in this view is the belief that men's interests and women's interests can somehow be reconciled, and that what will be needed for this to happen is co-operation and commitment from men. Yet very few writers entertain the possibility that it may be the pair bond itself that is the problem—or that men's and women's interests may be irreconcilable, at least within the confines of the nuclear family.

In order to see how this might be so, let us imagine for a moment a future in which heterosexual marriage and long-term sexual relationships between men and women no longer exist. Men and women lead largely separate lives. Australia has become a republic with two heads of state, one male and one female. The dominant parties in the parliament are the Men's Party and the Women's Party, each with a certain guaranteed number of seats in the legislative assembly and an additional number that are competitively elected. Western Australia has seceded and become an autonomous men's republic, while Tasmania, under the domination of a radical faction of the Women's Party, rumbles continually about forming a break-away gynocracy—an independent women's state.

At an everyday level, men largely choose to live with other men for mutual support and companionship, and women do the same. Men and women come together for sex, but there is a great deal less emotional significance attached to it than in our time. Sex is for mutual pleasure and recreation, and sexual knowledge and expertise are regarded as valuable and socially useful skills. Hence many men and women make their livings as professional sex workers, a prestigious and sought-after occupation. Of course, men and women still choose to have sex for reproductive purposes. Before doing so, they make a contract for having a child, which spells out their mutual responsibilities, the amount of time each parent will care for their offspring, the part they will play in the child's education and so on. However, the contract contains no financial obligations between the woman and the man, only between parents and child. On entering into a parental contract, both parents immediately begin compulsory contributions to a child-support fund, some of which are state-run and owned, and some private. These contributions continue until the child is 25 years old, and are means and income tested. For the time of pregnancy and breast-feeding, the man's contributions are higher, in recognition of the woman's special labour in carrying the child in her own body and nursing it. Health, education and child-care are financed by the child-support funds and delivered by local authorities. However, the non-childed also pay a social parenting contribution, since children are seen as a collective resource and responsibility.

Indeed, 'non-childed' is something of an anachronism in this Australia of the future, since biological parenthood is becoming less and less significant. Because of men's and women's separate co-operative living arrangements, both 'childed' and 'childless' men live together and share the pleasures and responsibilities of parenthood between them, as do women. Generally, both men and women work an average of 30 hours a week, since 'work' is shared a great deal more evenly than it is now, and much of the distinction between paid and unpaid work has disappeared. It goes without saying that 'economic rationalism' and the 'user-pays' principle are regarded as forms of collective insanity, which have been consigned to the compost-bin of history.

Men's and women's separate lives bring great emotional benefits, too. Men can enjoy the companionship of other men and share mutual interests and pastimes without feeling guilty. They find that other men understand them better, and they are no longer so dangerously and terrifyingly dependent on one other person for emotional succour and support. Instead, they are able to enjoy sex free of the fear of vulnerability and the horror of commitment that plagued so many of their grand-fathers, and rely on other men for close friendships and validation—though many men also carry on warm and cordial friendships with women. Women, too, find these arrangements liberating. They no longer have to carry the burden of doing men's emotional labour for them, and they can enjoy close and supportive relationships with other women without the need to compete with them for the attentions of men. No longer tied to the double standard of monogamy, they enjoy an unprecedented degree of sexual freedom. Like men, they regard it as entirely natural to pay a sex worker. The cult of the body begins to recede as imagination, play and sensuality become the touchstones of desire and sexual satisfaction.

Of course, there will still be rebels and renegades in this egalitarian sexual Utopia, men and women who choose to live as couples, aspire to the ideals of romantic love, and raise children in a 'family'. There will also be a proportion of both male and female populations who will choose to have sex exclusively with others of their own sex, though whether the cohabiting couple will continue as a common form among gay men and lesbians is less certain. Perhaps the most dramatic change in sexual culture will be the considerably larger percentage of the population who will lead openly bisexual lives. It will no longer be necessary, for example, for men who currently live in heterosexual marriages but have sex with other men to hide the fact, since heterosexual marriage will no longer be the norm. Indeed, bisexuality may ultimately come to be seen as a mark of sexual 'normality', with heterosexuality regarded as a historical compromise, entered into for reasons of child-rearing, but ultimately obsolete as biological paternity and maternity become less and less tightly linked to parenting, and the household based on male/female cohabitation becomes a thing of the past.

This vision of the future is unlikely to find much favour with current champions of family values, from John Howard to Tony Blair and Bill Clinton. However, if it were to become reality in Australia, in say, 100 years from now, the historians of that time would doubtless point to the last two decades of the twentieth century, with their relentless waves of economic modernization, rationalization and globalization, as the period that sealed the fate of the industrial nuclear family. By a strange paradox, the governments that have set these 'modernizing' processes in motion— the Conservative government in Britain, the Republican administrations of the 1980s in the United States, and the Hawke/Keating government in Australia—are often those who also bewail most loudly the decline of family values and call for their restoration. Yet it is they who have done most to bring about their demise. In Australia, we are currently confronted by the perplexing spectacle of a conservative government which regularly declares that it wants to strengthen 'the family', while pursuing economic policies that put the traditional nuclear family under greater and greater strain. As I've stressed in earlier chapters, the kind of family which John Howard wants to 'strengthen' is fast becoming obsolete; his government is simply helping to accelerate this process.

Having said this, I am not suggesting that the kind of society outlined above will become a reality, or that it is an achievable or desirable solution to the problems faced by the pair bond. It is a fantasy, but one intended to throw those problems into clearer relief. It's not inconceivable that, rather than trying to solve these problems within the confines of the cohabiting couple, men and women might decide to opt out of it altogether, particularly once men do start to pose the question of what it is they really want. If, however, they choose to continue living in couples, how might warmer relations between the sexes be achieved? What are the necessary conditions for this to occur?

Firstly, we will need to radically transform our ideas about work and its place in men's and women's life cycles. As we've seen, there is a major contradiction between current trends in the economy and the changing structure of work, and creating the conditions for 'domestic democracy'. Men who are working longer and longer hours are less and less likely to be able to contribute equally to child-rearing and home duties. In core professional areas of the job market, most men and women admit that there are still enormous pressures against taking time off to care for children, or even choosing to work a 38-hour week and to collect one's children from child-care at 5 p.m. every day. A person is simply regarded as not being serious about their career if they do so.

Conversely, in the increasingly peripheral world of blue-collar employment, men who are excluded from full-time work appear to be very reluctant to move into the new areas of part-time and casualized work that women have taken on. Nor is there much encouraging evidence that they are motivated to take on 'women's work' in the home if they have been made involuntarily redundant.

Until now, much of the pressure for family-friendly workplaces and more readily available child-care has come from women. However, there's a strong case for believing that workplaces will only become family-friendly when men begin a concerted campaign in support of such workplaces, and when men begin to refuse to collude in the work ethic of long hours and unswerving devotion to career. At present, the prospects for this do not seem all that bright. However, it's possible that a number of factors associated with current working patterns may start to push men, and society as a whole, in this direction. The changes in the labour market I've described have also produced growing income inequality in Australia and entrenched, intractable structural unemployment. Five per cent unemployment is now regarded as the natural rate, and no economist seriously believes that the jobless rate is likely to fall much below 8 per cent in the foreseeable future. Increasing globalization and opening up of the Australian economy will tend to produce even more hollowing out of our middle class, with those in the upper income brackets earning more and lower-paid workers earning even less.

Whether we choose to continue living with these trends will have a vital impact on the future of relations between men and women. One obvious way out of the dilemma of fewer and fewer employees doing more and more work is to share the work around more equally, and in so doing, we will also begin to reverse the trend of income inequality. Such suggestions have often been regarded as Utopian, yet, as the French economist Alain Lipietz points out, we've already achieved a major redistribution of work this century with the introduction of the 40-hour week, and there is no reason why we should not do so again.[3] The campaign for a 40-hour week was a long and difficult one, fought in most of the industrial economies by strong and determined trades unions. The fact that a new set of economic changes has begun to undo their work does not mean the campaign cannot be fought again, if trades unions have the will to do so.

Of course, there's another issue here, the strength and relevance of trades unions in the post-industrial economy. In the United States, one of the most de-regulated low-wage economies in the Western world, trades unions are beginning to revive, and there is no reason why they should not do so in Australia.[4] Until now, unions have also tended to be highly suspicious of part-time work and job-sharing arrangements. However, if they do wish to remain relevant and important to workers, they must recognize that new forms of work and work-sharing will increasingly be part of the everyday reality of workers' lives. In my view, trades unions could gain in the long term by making a redistribution of work, family-friendly workplaces and better work-based child-care central parts of their industrial goals. Most importantly, they should begin to engage men directly on issues of domestic democracy, and achieving a more even balance of paid work and family life. This, in turn, will only be possible within the context of a philosophical commitment to 'social parenting'. By this, I mean a notion of parenting which sees the care and education of children as the responsibility of the community and the state, and not just 'individuals and their families', to repeat Mrs Thatcher's phrase. Such a notion might seem so self-evidently desirable as not to be worth stating; yet the whole thrust of the present government's policies in the areas of child care and, in much more subtle ways, in the education system, is to privatise as many of those responsibilities as possible. It is fashionable now to regard education as a commodity whose value accrues to the person being educated, and not the society to which he or she belongs. A movement which embraces the idea of social parenting might take a leaf from the book of some of the newer social theorists and argue that education is part of the social capital in which we need to invest and accumulate in order to maintain a healthy society and a healthy economy. Similarly, a social investment in affordable and accessible child care and flexible working arrangements should be seen as contributing to this stock of social capital, in the same way as some private companies (especially in the United States) are beginning to recognize that providing these things for their employees increases their productivity.[5] Trades unions can be leaders in pushing for and implementing these changes: it won't be easy, but ultimately both trades unions and workers will benefit.

It would be unrealistic, however, to expect the trades union movement to become a major engine of social change in Australia in the near future, the vanguard of the men's revolution. Is there any other kind of broadly based men's movement that might play this role? No men's movement of this kind, with a commitment to social and economic change exists at present, nor is there any sign that the disparate groups of men we've encountered in this book have enough in common to create one. Groups such as the Circle of Men, and the larger therapeutic or mythopoetic men's movement to which they belong, show no signs of wanting to confront these larger questions. If there is such a thing as a men's movement at present, I'd argue that it resides in the anti-domestic violence groups, which are confronting concrete issues of power and inequality in the everyday lives of men and women, and which are starting to generate a momentum for broader social action among their members.

Having said this, it seems to me that a more cohesive men's movement, which might come into being in the future, would need to focus not only on the 'larger questions'—the social and economic obstacles to greater democracy in men's relations with women. It would also need to build a bridge between these questions and those more personal aspects of men's emotional experience, their desire for a richer, more expressive emotional life and closer relationships with other men—and women. We can see why this should be necessary from the example of men's violence groups and their evolution over the decade they've existed in Australia. In the past, there has been a great deal of resistance from many of the men who run them to giving 'therapy' a place within the groups. This was seen as dealing with the symptoms rather than the causes, giving men permission to legitimize their feelings of anger and frustration, instead of confronting their violence and the attitudes that led them to use it. Recently, some men have begun to question the usefulness of such a hardline approach. Once men have begun a process of changing attitudes and behaviour, they argue, they begin to feel the need for a new emotional vocabulary, new ways of coping with their fears and insecurities—a language of vulnerability rather than power and control. Not to offer them ways of discovering such a language is to fail them, to abandon them halfway on the journey they are seeking to make.

Obviously, the men in these groups are not a representative sample of men in the broader population. They come to the groups because of behaviour that is not typical of the majority of men or the majority of relationships, behaviour that is often criminal. In most of their cases, their violent or abusive behaviour has brought about a crisis in their relationships and a crisis in themselves. We should be wary of drawing larger conclusions on the basis of their experience. Yet many of the men in therapeutic groups like the Circle of Men have also undergone some crisis, involving the loss of a relationship, which has made them question their feelings about who they are and how they behave as men. It is precisely this experience of crisis that has led them to seek the 'validation' of other men, and perhaps a new kind of solidarity with them.

My point here is that we need to take the dimension of emotional experience seriously when talking about any transformation of men or masculinity. This doesn't mean that we have to endorse tiresome clichés about men being unable to express emotion or get in touch with their feelings, clichés that put men under the emotional tutelage of women. Women do not want to have to teach men how to get in touch with their feelings, nor is it their business to do so. Anthony Giddens makes a useful distinction here. It's not so much that men don't know how to express feelings, he says, but that they are unable to tell stories about them, to construct an emotional 'narrative of self' that connects their feelings to the broader framework of their lives.[6] Learning how, when and in what language to express our emotions, when to press for our needs to be met and when to temper them or place them behind the needs of others is a part of becoming adult, a difficult, wearisome and often painful process, for both men and women.

The powerful sense of emotional isolation a great many men described to me suggests that any men's movement that hopes to speak to 'the whole man' will have to deal with men's feelings. Quite how it might do so is hard to imagine: we cannot put a whole society into therapy, nor would this necessarily be a good thing even if we could. For too long, however, men have been expected to simply 'keep buggering on', in the famous words of Winston Churchill, when faced with emotional or spiritual crisis. Many of the men we've met in the course of this book are plainly hungry for guidance, support, or simple recognition that they are not alone in times of trouble. A men's movement which encourages greater solidarity between men may provide some of these things in a practical way. Such a movement could also learn some important political and personal lessons from gay men. At present, there is very little communication between straight men involved in groups such as the Circle of Men, and gay men who are active politically. Indeed, the men's movement in Australia preserves a deafening silence on gay issues, all the more surprisingly since this country has what is surely one of the most visible, vocal and well-established gay cultures of any country in the world. Gay culture is not without its own internal divisions and conflicts; yet it presents a concrete example of a community of men living with and caring for each other which has no real parallel among heterosexual men—except, perhaps, in the armed forces. The central role which friendship plays in gay culture suggests that it is not so much the case that men lack the aptitude or desire for close friendships with other men, but rather that heterosexual male culture de-skills them in this area.

There seems to me to be another good reason why a democratic and egalitarian men's movement should pay attention to the question of men's emotions.

The cult of father hunger propounded by Robert Bly and popularized in Australia by Steve Biddulph has obviously touched a nerve in many men, a fact attested to not only by the sales figures of their books but the centrality given to fathers and relationships with fathers in the therapeutic men's movement. I would not argue for a minute that it's not a desirable thing for men to have better relationships with their fathers, or for fathers to have better relationships with their sons. Plainly, this is something that many men desire. But the language in which this is clothed, especially in Bly's work, should make us suspicious, if what we want is more democracy and equality in our relationships with other men and women. Bly talks about the need for men to be able to look up to figures of authority, to respect leaders, to 'honour the King'. This is not pure symbolism—Bly genuinely believes that we lose something when we lose respect for authority.

I believe that the opposite is true. We do not need more authority. We need more solidarity, and solidarity is, by its very nature, anti-hierarchical and egalitarian. At a time when the whole pressure of economic modernization and its accompanying ideology is to produce a society that is more and more individualistic, fragmented and narcissistic, forms of solidarity such as those that could arise in a men's movement are very important. It would be a tragedy if they were hijacked by social conservatives who want to reinstate paternal authority and family values. For perhaps the first time in Western history, there is a quite real possibility that the 'law of the Father' is beginning to crumble and fracture. Men too will be the losers if they attempt to restore a despot who is in the process of being deposed.

This brings us back to the question of what it is that men want, and whether it is compatible with whatever it is that women want. It would be nonsense to pretend that there is any one answer to these questions. However, I have tried to show that there are indeed some common threads running through what men in Australia today perceive as their needs, desires and aspirations. There seems to be good evidence to suggest that a sizeable proportion of men do want more equal and democratic relationships with women, a greater involvement in the raising of their children, and a way out of the emotional isolation in which many of them live their lives. Whether the route they wish to travel in order to arrive at these goals is the same one women choose to take is another matter. In many ways, it is easier to draw up a manifesto for alleviating the economic obstacles to 'intimate democracy', than it is to confront our much more intangible and often ambiguous feelings about democratizing our sexual and emotional relationships with each other.

As I've argued, achieving 'intimate democracy' is not

simply a matter of men giving up power, either in the public or the private spheres of their lives. In some areas, they are already being compelled to do so, whether through force of economic circumstance or because women will no longer recognize or tolerate the kinds of authority men have been accustomed to exercise in the past. However, in the area of intimate relationships in which women have held power and exercised authority, the sphere of the emotions, the picture is much less clear. In this domain, men do not necessarily have power to give up. It seems fairly clear that women will no longer provide the same kind of emotional support to men they have in the past—not, at least, without much greater emotional reciprocity from their male partners. Women have less and less investment in doing so. They no longer need men in the way they have done, as providers and protectors. What they do appear to need and want from men is something men have not always been accustomed to provide: companionate friendship, emotional literacy, someone to talk to and listen, willingness to work on the 'project' of a relationship, which will change and evolve through time, as friendships do.

There are questions here about whether men really want these things too. Certainly, it seems that some men do—but not all men necessarily want to spend a lifetime working on a relationship or series of relationships as a project or projects. The kind of emotional commitment required in this kind of relationship—in the sense of a willingness to struggle, to be patient, compromise, to look to long term goals and to respect the other's need to change and grow—may simply be more than many men want. Many men, if they are honest with themselves, may recognize that they are happier in the company of other men than they are with women. Some men may wish to make raising children, rather than a relationship with a female partner, the primary emotional focus of their lives. We should not censure them for feeling so, or for choosing not to enter into the emotional world of the pure relationship. We should, however, be honest about the consequences of these choices. The nuclear family cannot survive these consequences in its present form. Perhaps the sort of future world I've outlined above would suit people better than one in which both sexes struggle to fulfil an ideal of attachment and association between men and women in which neither really believes.

Of course, it would be foolish to imagine that men as a group will choose one form of relationship with women. Their choices are likely to be even more diverse and improvisatory than they are now. I do not believe that men will travel down the path of separatism, nor do I think it would be a good thing if they did. Certainly, creating greater solidarity among men may help to reduce their emotional dependence on women, and thus enable them to engage with women on a more equal emotional basis. However, I think we should be wary of assuming that men will share women's aspiration for 'confluent love'. Professor Higgins' exasperated refrain in *My Fair Lady*—'Why can't a woman/Be more like a man?'—has, to a certain extent, been turned on its head. One thing that seems clear is that those men who do want change do not want to become more like women, nor do women appear to want them to, either. Creating a new culture of masculinity and new forms of relationships will be a difficult, painful process. Along the way, men may begin to assert new interests and new demands, which will not necessarily be the same as women's. If anything, the sexes are likely to move further apart before they begin to come together, if they ever do.

In this book I have tried to stress both the positive and tangible areas in which men are changing and responding to the changes made by women, as well as the many intractable obstacles to change. I am not as optimistic as Ron, whom we met in Chapter 1. As Ron put it, women had 'had their revolution in the 1960s and 1970s'. Men, according to Ron, are following them down that path now with their own revolution, and in 20 years 'we will all be equal'. I suspect it will take much longer for this to happen, if indeed it ever does. Revolutions are about power, and history tells us that there are few revolutions in which the transfer of power is not accompanied by a measure of conflict and retribution. The war between men and women is likely to continue for some time.

Its outcome, moreover, will depend to a very large extent on the trajectory of the large social and economic changes I have referred to throughout my narrative. These changes, which signal the end of the industrial era of modern Western capitalism, have been accompanied by the ascendancy of a particularly virulent form of individualism and an economic ideology that is deeply suspicious of the state, and of most forms of collective action and solidarity. The society that these forces are shaping is a society without sociality, a mass of narcissistic individuals interested only in the fulfilment of their own needs and the expansion of their ability to consume. In some ways, such a society may offer women—and men—some freedoms they have not had in industrial capitalism or its predecessors, but they will be choices bought at the cost of solidarity and the common weal.

However, despite the apparent triumph of economic rationalism (or neo-liberalism as it is also known) in Australia, there are signs that challenges to its orthodoxy are beginning to emerge, both in the world of ideas and the arena of political action. Interestingly, these signs are emerging both in the private sector, where managers are beginning to acknowledge that the slash-and-burn policies of the last two decades and the cult of 'downsizing' have actually damaged the productivity of many companies, and in countries such as Britain which have contracted out or privatised public services, and discovered that the result is higher costs and a lower standard of service. However, these recognitions can only be the beginning of a real intellectual and political challenge to neo-liberalism. Wherever that challenge comes from, if it is to be successful, it cannot consist simply in a return to the mechanisms for social and economic justice which were the foundation of the post-war welfare state, and which survived largely untouched in Australia until the mid-1980s. Creating a just and human society in the conditions of the early twenty-first century will require new ideas, new strategies and, above all, a new kind of moral vision of the possibilities of the human person.

The question of how to create more democratic relations between men and women, both in everyday life and the larger social and economic order, will be absolutely central to any new political and moral vision of this kind. If this is what men want, they must begin now to think about how it might be achieved.

Notes

In my text I have quoted from a substantial number of personal interviews undertaken in the course of my research. In general, these quotes have been transcribed directly from tape recordings of those interviews, and are not sourced in footnotes.

1 THE MEN'S REVOLUTION

1 See the *Sydney Morning Herald*, 16 December 1996, *Agenda* p. 11. The figures are based on research by Andrew Hede of the Sunshine Coast University, and Elizabeth O'Brien of the Australian Catholic University.

2 THE POWER PARADOX

1 The edition quoted here is the German translation: *Die Töchter Egalias. Ein Roman uber den Kampf der Geschlechter*, von Gert Brantenberg, Berlin, Olle und Wolter, 1979. The passage quoted is my own translation of the opening lines of the novel.
2 I am quoting from publicity material released by the Men's Rights Agency in 1994. The Men's Rights Agency can be contacted at: Men's Rights Agency, PO Box 28, Waterford, Queensland, Australia,Telephone 07–38055611. Most Australian states now have active fathers' rights organizations.
3 See *The Age*, 6 March 1992, p. 3. The Brunswick baths

case received regular coverage in *The Age* in the early months of 1992.

4 I am grateful to Mrs Lorna Mobbs of the Randwick and Coogee Ladies Swimming Club for supplying these details to me.

5 Some two years and a change of government later, the results and recommendations of this inquiry were published as *Girls and Boys at School: Gender Equity Strategy 1996–2001*. To the chagrin of the Carr Labor government, the strategy was criticised by the Parents and Citizens Federation and attacked by activists. *Certified Male*, a magazine on men's issues published in New South Wales, described it as a 'miserable failure' and claimed that the boys' education strategy envisaged by the previous government had been replaced by a 'repackaged girls' strategy' which did not address the needs of boys. See *Certified Male*, Winter 1995 and Winter 1996, pp. 8–9 and 6–7 respectively.

6 See Eva Cox, *Leading Women*, Random House, Sydney, 1996, p. 221.

7 Warren Farrell, *The Myth of Male Power: Why Men are the Disposable Sex*, 1994, Random House, Sydney, p. 97.

8 Robert Bly, *Iron John: A Book about Men*, Element, Brisbane, 1994, p. 234.

9 David Morgan calls this the penitential mode in the men's movement, which 'may include recognition of the wrongs that men have done to women, both in general terms and often in particular terms with reference to the experiences or past practices of the writer'. In *Discovering Men*, Routledge, London and New York, 1992, p. 38.

10 See for example Ian Law, 'Adopting the Principle of Pro-Feminism', in *Accountability: New Directions for Working in Partnership*, Dulwich Centre Newsletter 1994 Nos 2 & 3, published by the Dulwich Centre, Hutt Street, Adelaide, pp. 40–3. The problems faced by profeminist men are also discussed by Bob Connell in his *Masculinities*, Allen & Unwin, Sydney, 1995, pp. 128–39.

11 Michael Ondaatje, *In the Skin of a Lion*, Picador, London, 1988, pp. 10, 15.

12 The main Promise Keepers Website is at http://www.promisekeepers.org.
13 This quote is from material broadcast as part of the *Male Matters* series on ABC Radio National in January 1995. Interviews with men from the Shoalhaven Men's Group were collected by Nick Rushworth.
14 Quoted in Badinter, Elisabeth, *XY: On Masculine Identity*, tr. Lydia Davis, Columbia University Press, New York, 1995, p. 19.
15 ibid. See the section of Badinter's book entitled 'Earlier Crises in Masculinity' for a fuller account.
16 ibid., p. 14.
17 See Elaine Showalter, *Sexual Anarchy: Gender and Culture at the Fin de Siècle*, Virago, London, 1992, p. 41. Much of my description of the 'crisis of masculinity' in the the late nineteenth century is based on Showalter's brilliant and entertaining book, especially Chapters 1 and 3.
18 ibid., p. 41.
19 ibid., pp. 42, 43.
20 From Sandra M. Gilbert and Susan Gubar, *No Man's Land*, New Haven, Yale, 1986, quoted in Showalter, *Sexual Anarchy*, p. 7.
21 See *Australian Social Trends*, Australian Bureau of Statistics, 1996, Catalogue No. 4102.0, p. 31.
22 See Farrell, *The Myth of Male Power*, Chapter 3.
23 See Cox, *Leading Women*, pp. 28–9.
24 David Ireland, *The Glass Canoe*, Macmillan, Sydney, 1976, p. 30.
25 George Klein is a behavioural scientist, counsellor and therapist based at the University of Sydney. I discuss his concept of the 'gender contract' in more detail in the following chapter.

3 THE END OF THE GENDER CONTRACT

1 See Beatrice Gottlieb, *The Family in the Western World from the Black Death to the Industrial Age*, OUP, Oxford and New York, 1993, p. 7. Gottlieb's book is a lucid and readable synthesis of the very large body of research on the history of the family which has been

published over the last 20 years. There are lively debates among historians about the nature and composition of the 'pre-industrial family', and Gottlieb stresses the importance of recognizing that there was no single model, while drawing out the features that we can reasonably assume were common to households and families across Europe. My account of the pre-industrial household draws primarily on Gottlieb's text, and is necessarily general. I have dispensed with further references to her book for the sake of simplicity.

A useful introduction to the debates among historians about families in the pre-modern era can be found in Michael Gilding, *The Making and Breaking of the Australian Family*, Allen & Unwin, Sydney, 1991, Chapter 1.

Interested readers are referred to Lawrence Stone's *The Family, Sex and Marriage in England 1500–1800 (London, 1977), and Mitterauer, Michael and Reinhard Sieder, The European Family—Patriarchy to Partnership: From the Middle Ages to the Present* (Oxford, 1982).

I have also drawn on a summary of German historical research on the family: Brunner, Conze, Koselleck (Hg.), *Geschichtliche Grundbegriffe*, Bd. 2, Stuttgart, 1975, pp. 269–73.

2 As a general rule, historians agree that households in Northern Europe tended to be smaller than those in Southern Europe, and were less likely to include multiple members of the extended family group.

3 The question of whether or not the Industrial Revolution produced a decisive break or rupture in family structures is now a matter of some contention amongst historians. In recent years, some have argued that there was more continuity in the size of families and the nature of family relations from the pre-industrial period (that is, roughly, prior to 1750) through to the middle of the nineteenth century, than I've allowed for in my account. See for example Hugh Cunningham, *Children and Childhood in Western Society since 1500*, Longman, London and New York, 1995, p. 88.

However, while there was certainly great variation in the speed of the process by which the industrial nuclear family came into being across countries, and particularly across different class groups, the essential changes I've described in the nature of the family and what people thought and felt about it (what historians call the 'aspect of representation') are well entrenched among the European middle classes by the middle of the nineteenth century and become more and more prevalent amongst working-class people in the latter half of that century.

4 Quoted in Tom Burton, *Words, Words, Words*, University Radio 5UV, Adelaide, 1995, p. 14.

5 Anthony Giddens, *The Transformation of Intimacy: Sexuality, Love and Eroticism in Modern Societies*, Polity, Cambridge, 1995, p. 26.

6 So for example Olwyn Hufton, in the first volume of her recent book *The Prospect Before Her: A History of Women in Western Europe. Volume One: 1500–1800*, (HarperCollins, 1995), argues that the heroines of highly successful novels such as *Clarissa Harlowe* and *Pamela* were seen by women readers as 'civilising agent[s] imposing right standards upon a man'. (Quoted in the *Times Literary Supplement*, December 15, 1995, p. 8.)

7 Giddens, ibid., p. 43.

8 ibid., pp. 46–7.

9 See Wolcott, Irene and Glezer, Helen, *Work and Family Life: Achieving Integration*, Australian Institute of Family Studies, 1995, pp. 7ff.

10 See *Australian Social Trends 1996*, Australian Bureau of Statistics, Catalogue No. 4102.0.

11 *Future Labour Market Issues for Australia*, EPAC Paper No. 12, Australian Bureau of Statistics, Catalogue No. 6203.0 *The Labour Force*, August 1995, p. 105. Unless otherwise indicated, all statistical information and analysis of social trends quoted in this section is from this publication.

There is a broad consensus among Australian demographers now that the traditional single-income family is only likely to survive in upper-income brackets. See the *Sydney Morning Herald*, 29 January 1997, *Agenda* p. 9.

12 See *Future Labour Market Issues for Australia*, p. 105.

13 Women now represent about a third of self-employed people in Australia, the number of businesses run by

women is increasing at a faster rate than those run by men, and the survival rate of women's businesses is better. These are some of the results of a study entitled *Women in Small Business: A Review of Research*, published by a team from Flinders University in Adelaide. See *Flinders Journal*, Vol. 7 No. 16, September/October 1996.

14 See the *Economist*, 28 September 1996, pp. 23–8. All of the figures and information quoted in the following paragraphs are drawn from this source.

15 See Probert, Belinda and Wilson, Bruce W. (eds), *Pink Collar Blues: Work, Gender and Technology*, Melbourne University Press, Melbourne, 1993. p. 14.

16 Anna Hetzel was interviewed for the Radio National series *Male Matters*. Her impressions are borne out by some unpublished research done by Juanita Muller, Assistant Professor of Psychology at Bond University, who interviewed a number of blue-collar unemployed men and found that those who had adjusted best to being out of work were those who'd become involved in child care and 'home duties'.

17 The *Economist*, 28 September 1996, pp 23–8.

18 See for example Rose, S., 'Gender antagonism and class conflict: Exclusionary strategies of male trade-unionists in nineteenth-century Britain', in *Social History*, 1988 vol. 13, no. 2.

19 See Michael Gilding, *The Making and Breaking of the Australian Family*, Allen & Unwin, Sydney, 1991, especially pp. 53ff.

20 Quoted in Showalter, *Sexual Anarchy*, p. 20.

21 A term coined by Anthony McMahon, a sociologist at La Trobe University. For a further exposition of this term, and McMahon's work, see Chapter 9.

22 See Michael Bittman, *Juggling Time: How Australian Families Use Time*, Canberra, Australian Government Publishing Service, 1992, and Bittman's follow-up study, *Recent Changes in Unpaid Work*, ABS Occasional Paper Catalogue No. 4154.0, 1995.

23 Bittman, *Recent Changes in Unpaid Work*, p. 15.

24 See Peter Moss and Julia Brannen, 'Fathers and employment', in *Reassessing Fatherhood, New Observations on*

the Modern Family, Charlie Lewis and Margaret O'Brien (eds), London, 1987, pp. 40ff.

25 See Alison Lewis, *Subverting Patriarchy: Feminism and Fantasy in the Works of Irmtraud Morgner*, Berg, Oxford, 1995, Chapter 4.

26 Beatrix Campbell was speaking in an interview with Phillip Adams on the Radio National program *Late Night Live*, broadcast on Monday 29 April 1996.

27 See Lynne Segal, *Slow Motion: Changing Masculinities, Changing Men,* Virago, London, 1994, p. 48.

28 See Peter Jordan's two studies, conducted in 1984 and 1994: 'The effects of marital separation on men', in *Journal of Divorce*, Vol. 12(1) 1988, pp. 57–126, and: *The Effects of Marital Separation on Men—10 Years On*, Family Court of Australia, Research Report No. 14, November 1996. Jordan reports that there's been little change in the 'key indicators' of divorce over the last ten years. The one significant difference is that more men now blame their former wives for the breakdown of the relationship than did in 1984.

29 Jordan, 'The effects of marital separation on men', (1988) p. 78.

30 'Even Bastards Care' was first published in the *Australia and New Zealand Journal of Family Therapy*, Vol. 10, No. 4, 1989.

31 See Funder, Kathleen, Harrison, Margaret and Weston, Ruth (eds), *Settling Down: Pathways of Parents after Divorce*, Australian Institute of Family Studies Monograph No.13, Melbourne, 1993, especially pp. 57–65.

32 See Umberson, D. and Williams, C.L., 'Divorced fathers: parental role strain and psychological distress', *Journal of Family Issues*, No. 14, quoted in Jordan (1996) p. 7: 'The family is an important locus of control for men in our society. Men lose control over their families following divorce in several ways that are conducive to distress'.

33 George Klein was interviewed for the Radio National series *Male Matters*.

34 Giddens, *The Transformation of Intimacy*, p. 58.

35 ibid., pp. 117, 130.

4 REPORTS FROM THE FRONTLINE

1 Although most of them did not request it, all the names of the men quoted in this chapter who are members of men's violence groups have been changed. Quotations are verbatim, from interviews conducted in Melbourne at the Doveton and Box Hill men's violence groups, and at the Campbelltown group run by Centacare in Sydney. Material from the Melbourne interviews was broadcast in *Disarming Daddy*, on ABC Radio National's Background Briefing, in February 1994.

Quotations from Alison Newton, Dallas Colley, Alan Jenkins, Rod Greenaway, Harvey Tuck, Jenny Nunn and Justice Sally Brown are all from personal interviews broadcast in the same program.

2 This summary is drawn from a discussion paper entitled *Programs for Perpetrators of Domestic Violence*, prepared by Lynne Townsend for the New South Wales Domestic Violence Strategic Plan, and published by the NSW Women's Co-ordination Unit, July 1991. See especially pp. 17ff.

3 An analysis not dissimilar to that of George Klein, quoted in the previous chapter, who has worked with violent men in a variety of contexts, including prisons, for the last ten years.

4 This summary of Jenkins' approach is drawn from a personal interview in January 1994.

5 Dale Hirst, from Melton Community Health Centre in Victoria, received a Churchhill Fellowship to study men's violence groups and ways of evaluating their success in the US and Britain. According to Hirst, studies in both these countries indicate strongly that men in 'voluntary' rather than 'mandated' programs are more likely to change their behaviour and become violence-free. See Hirst's interview on ABC Radio National's *Life Matters*, May 16th 1996.

6 According to Dale Hirst, evidence from around 30 American studies shows a success rate of between 50 and 80 per cent. The primary criterion used to assess success was whether the man's partner reported that he was 'violence-free' a year after joining the group.

7 At the time of writing, Ruth Frances' study had not yet been published. It was undertaken for her doctoral thesis

in the Department of Criminology at the University of Melbourne. My summary of her findings is based on two personal interviews. I am grateful to Ruth Frances for her time and generosity, and for subsequently providing me with a copy of her thesis on disc.

8 Shew's case, and the failure of his complaint was also reported in the Brisbane *Courier-Mail*, on 10 February 1996.

9 See 'All Men are Bastards', by John Coochey, in the *Independent Monthly*, November 1995, pp. 48–51.

10 See especially Beatrice Faust, *Backlash? Balderdash! Where Feminism is Going Right*, University of NSW Press, Sydney, 1994.

11 See Straus, M.A., Gelles, R.J., and Steinmetz, S.K., *Behind Closed Doors: Violence in the American Family*, New York, 1980, and also Straus M.A. and Gelles, R.J., *Physical Violence in American Families: Risk Factors and Adaptation to Violence in 8,145 Families*, New Brunswick, 1990.

12 This figure, and those quoted in the following paragraphs, are drawn from a research report entitled 'Domestic Violence', by Virginia Routley and Jenny Sherrard and published in the Journal of the Monash University Accident Research Centre, *Hazard*, No. 21, December 1994.

13 See Anne Campbell, *Out of Control: Men, Women and Aggression*, Pandora, London, 1993, p. 180. Campbell's views are supported by the very intelligent discussion of masculinity and violence in Segal, *Slow Motion*, pp. 261–71.

14 Sheree Lee Seakins comments are quoted here from an interview broadcast on ABC Radio's PM program, December 1993.

15 See Campbell, *Out of Control*, pp. 121, 183, footnote 63.

16 ibid., p. 104.

17 ibid., p. 121.

5 INTIMATE EXPERIMENTS

1 See Anthony Giddens, *The Transformation of Intimacy: Sexuality, Love and Eroticism in Modern Societies*, Polity, Cambridge and Oxford 1992, p. 8.

2 See *New Woman*, June 1994.
3 Lyrics from 'Fake that Emotion', (Perkins/Dormand, Polygram Music/Control) from the album *Tex, Don and Charlie—Sad but True*, Polydor, 1993, are reproduced by kind permission of Tex Perkins.
4 Lyrics from 'I Must Be Getting Soft' (Perkins, Polygram Music), from the album *Tex, Don and Charlie—Sad but True*, Polydor, 1993, are reproduced by kind permission of Tex Perkins.
5 See Elisabeth Badinter, *XY: On Masculine Identity*, tr. Lydia Davis, New York, 1995, pp. 142–3.
6 ibid., p. 128.
7 Quoted in Badinter, ibid., p. 152.
8 Badinter, ibid., p. 143.
9 Quoted in Badinter, ibid., p. 229.
10 ibid., p. xi.
11 ibid., p. 5.
12 See Peter Looker, 'Doing it with your mates', in *The Abundant Culture: Meaning and Significance in Everyday Australia*, David Headon, Joy Hooton and Donald Horne (eds), Allen & Unwin, Sydney, 1994, pp. 215–19, here pp. 211–12.
13 ibid.
14 See Raymond Evans, 'A gun in the oven: masculinism and gendered violence', in *Gender Relations in Australia. Domination and Negotiation*, Kay Saunders and David Evans (eds), Harcourt Brace Jovanovich, Sydney, 1992, pp. 197–218, here pp. 203ff.
15 Such forms of sexual etiquette are much more clearly visible in French culture, for example, where pre-Revolutionary aristocratic values have, paradoxically, permeated the middle classes and proved much more tenacious than in Britain or other northern European countries.
16 Baldesar Castiglione, *The Book of the Courtier*, tr. George Bull, Penguin, 1995, p. 268.
17 ibid., p. 222.
18 ibid, p. 270.
19 See Giddens, *The Transformation of Intimacy*, pp. 58ff.
20 Quoted in Naomi B. McCormick, *Sexual Salvation: Affirming Women's Sexual Rights and Pleasures*, London/Connecticut, 1994, p. 35.

21 ibid.
22 See Steve Biddulph, *Manhood: A Book About Setting Men Free*, Finch Publishing, Sydney, 1994, p. 70.
23 ibid., p. 19.
24 Giddens, *The Transformation of Intimacy*, p. 130.
25 ibid., p. 131.
26 Kerry Riley, with Diane Riley, *Sexual Secrets for Men*, Random House, Sydney, 1995, p. x.
27 ibid., p. 90.
28 Olivia St Claire, *Unleashing the Sex Goddess in Every Woman*, Bantam, New York and Sydney, 1996, p. 147.
29 Giddens, *The Transformation of Intimacy*, p. 3.
30 See *Unsafe Sexual Practices in the Sexual Behaviour of Female and Male Sex Workers: A Study Conducted in the School of Sociology, University of New South Wales*, by Frances Lovejoy, Roberta Perkins and Meredith Jacobsen, UNSW, 1995.
31 ibid., p. 2.
32 See Segal, *Slow Motion*, p. 213.
33 ibid.
34 ibid., p. 215.
35 ibid. p. 212.

6 THE END OF SEX?

1 Helen Garner, *The First Stone: Some Questions About Sex and Power,* Picador, Sydney, 1995, p. 16.
2 ibid., p. 113.
3 This clearly does not apply to prostitution, the most clearly economic form of sexual transaction, which continues to be tightly controlled and regulated by the state, and subjected to social and moral discrimination.
4 This quote is drawn from the transcript of a report by Judith Kampfner on the ABC Radio National program *The Law Report*, broadcast on 25.2.96. All details of the Normal case, and all quotes from interested parties in the following account, are taken from the transcript. I am grateful to Judith Kampfner for her kind permission to quote from her report.
5 This is a provision of the American Employment Discrimination Statute.

6 Garner, *The First Stone*, p. 93.
7 See the *Sydney Morning Herald*, 25 January 1996, p. 5; 26 January 1996, p. 6; 11 April 1996, p. 5; and 28 June 1996, p. 17.
8 See the *Australian*, 17–18 August, 1996, p. 53.
9 This seems to me a somewhat surprising assertion, given that France has both a long history of Protestantism and an extensive literature which portrays petit bourgeois puritanism—in the novels of Georges Simenon for example.
10 Lynne Segal, *Straight Sex: The Politics of Pleasure*, Virago, London, 1994. The passage quoted here is from pp. 246–7, in the chapter 'Rethinking heterosexuality'.
11 Quoted in Moira Gatens, *Imaginary Bodies: Ethics, Power and Corporeality*, Routledge, London and New York, 1996, p. 78.
12 Garner, *The First Stone*, p. 112.
13 The story is 'Harrison Bergeron', in: Kurt Vonnegut Jr., *Welcome to the Monkey House*, Panther, St Albans, 1976, pp. 19–25.
14 All the passages quoted in this section are from Garner, *The First Stone*, pp. 89 and 99.
15 ibid., p. 89.
16 See Camille Paglia, *Sex, Art, and American Culture: Essays*, Penguin, London, 1993, p. 72. 'I do feel that women have to realize their sexual power over men. That is part of our power.'
17 Quoted in Wright, Robert, *The Moral Animal: Evolutionary Psychology and Everyday Life*, Abacus, London, 1994, p. 30.
18 As I point out in the following chapter, some influential contemporary thinkers in the biological sciences and related areas, which might be grouped under the heading of 'sociobiology', are now doing their best to reinforce those stereotypes.
19 Quoted in Giddens, *The Transformation of Intimacy*, p. 7.
20 Castiglione, *The Book of the Courtier*, pp. 241–2.
21 I refer to the PM interview with Seakins quoted in Chapter 4.

7 THE CASE AGAINST MASCULINITY

1 *The Age*, 21 May 1996, p. A13.

2 See for example Caroline Walker Bynum, *Jesus as Mother: Studies in the Spirituality of the High Middle Ages,* University of California Press, Berkeley & London, 1982.
3 In a sense, as the novel itself makes plain, Foster's objection to masculinity is equally an objection to sexuality itself, which he regards as a distraction from the spiritual life, a burden, and something which should not be separated from procreation. In this sense, he seems to be espousing views not dissimilar to those of some of the early Church fathers.
4 See the summary of the principles of eco-feminism given by Karen J. Warren, and quoted in Luc Ferry, *The New Ecological Order*, tr. Carol Volk, University of Chicago Press, Chicago and London, 1995, p. 116.
5 See Mies, Maria and Shiva, Vandana, *Ecofeminism*, Spinifex, Melbourne, 1993, p. 5.
6 ibid., p. 14.
7 See Plumwood's analysis of the interlocking dualisms in Western thought, quoted in Ferry, *The New Ecological Order*, p. 118.
8 See Gatens, Moira, *Imaginary Bodies: Ethics, Power and Corporeality*, Routledge, London, 1996, especially Chapters 2 and 5. Gatens argues that the 'body politic' is 'based on an image of a masculine body which reflects fantasies about the value and capacities of that body' (*Imaginary Bodies*, p. 25).
9 See Ferry, *The New Ecological Order*, pp. 121ff.
10 The recent announcement of the cloning of a sheep in Scotland is only the latest in a series of developments in contemporary genetics—which suggest this tendency.
11 See Rita Felski, *The Gender of Modernity*, Harvard University Press, Cambridge and London, 1995, p. 17.
12 ibid.
13 By another curious twist of the narrative, the rescuer John Connor sends back through time to protect his mother from the Terminator also becomes his father—yet another variant of the Frankensteinian fantasy of male self-reproduction.
14 Ferry, *The New Ecological Order*, p. 118.
15 ibid., p. 124.
16 ibid., p. 126.

17 See Reinhart Koselleck, *Kritik und Krise: Eine Studie zur Pathogenese der bürgerlichen Welt*, Suhrkamp, Frankfurt am Main, 1979.
18 ibid., pp. 107–11. Koselleck himself was of a conservative cast of mind, and saw the intrusion of morality into politics as a kind of dangerous virus spreading through the body politic, one whose ultimate goal could only be the destruction of the host—in this case, the absolutist state by the French Revolution.
19 See Connell, R.W., *Masculinities*, Allen & Unwin, Sydney, 1995, pp. 84–5.
20 ibid., pp. 231, 235–8.
21 ABC-TV Evening News, Saturday 18 May, 1996.
22 See, for example, Gatens, *Imaginary Bodies*, pp. 77–9, 86–8.
23 See, for example, Matt Ridley's *The Origins of Virtue* and Robert Wright's *The Moral Animal*, Abacus, London, 1996.
24 Wright, *The Moral Animal*, p. 96.
25 ibid., pp. 72ff.
26 This does not mean that we have to revert to a position which says that human behaviour, sexuality, and moral development are purely the products of nurture. It means, rather, giving much more careful scrutiny to what it is that writers like Wright believe they can infer from the 'evidence' of evolutionary biology, and demonstrating that their interpretative framework is itself coloured by their own assumptions about what is 'natural'.
27 See Rita Felski, *The Gender of Modernity*, p. 211.

8 THE CIRCLE OF MEN

1 See the *Sydney Morning Herald*, 20 April 1996, *Spectrum*, p. 11.
2 Robert Bly, *Iron John*, p. 32.
3 See Richard Sennett and Jonathan Cobb, *The Hidden Injuries of Class*, Knopf, New York, 1972.
4 Of course, post-war working-class culture was built on women's sacrifice as well; the sacrifice of women's aspirations on the altar of the nuclear family. My point here is simply that choices and opportunities have opened up for women to move beyond this ethos of sacrifice and

find new sources of identity and a sense of self-determination. The range of new sources of identity for men is much more limited; the primary one consists in a new affirmation of men's role as fathers, a topic I discuss in Chapter 9.

5 This, at least, is the conclusion of a study of attitudes to retirement across generations commissioned by Anglican Retirement Villages in NSW and released in October 1996.

6 See Bly, *Iron John*, p. 169.

9 FATHERHOOD

1 See Badinter, *XY: On Masculine Identity*, p. xii.

2 This is a 1991 Australian Bureau of Statistics figure. All of the statistics quoted here are taken from Carol Grbich's paper 'Male primary caregivers and domestic labour: involvement or avoidance', in *Journal of Family Studies*, Nov/Dec 1995, p 3.

3 ibid., p. 17.

4 See Grbich, Carol, 'Women as Primary Breadwinners in Families where Men are Primary Caregivers', in *ANZJS* Vol. 30, No. 2, August 1994, p. 111.

5 Grbich, 'Male Primary Caregivers and Domestic Labour: Involvement or Avoidance', p. 18.

6 Grbich, Carol, 'Women as Primary Breadwinners in Families where Men are Primary Caregivers', p. 112.

7 See Grbich, Carol, 'Societal response to familial role change in Australia: marginalisation or social change', in *Journal of Comparative Family Studies*, Canada, Vol. XXIII, No. 1, Spring 1992, pp. 83ff.

8 All three quotes are from Grbich, Carol, 'Societal response to familial role change in Australia: marginalisation or social change', p. 91.

9 See Giddens, *The Transformation of Intimacy*, p. 182.

10 Carol Grbich made this comment to me in a personal interview.

11 See Anthony McMahon, 'Taking care of men: discourses and practices of everyday life', PhD thesis in the Department of Sociology and Anthropology, La Trobe University, January 1994.

12 McMahon also points out that images of the 'new man' and 'new father' have been manufactured by the advertising industry, which sees them as a lucrative new target market—and a way of selling products to women. See 'Taking Care of Men', pp. 141–9.

However, Carol Grbich's study seems to suggest that there is some element of reality behind these images. In the couples she surveyed, 46 per cent of all tasks were done by men alone, 24 per cent shared, 16 per cent by women alone and 6 per cent by persons employed as home help. See 'Male primary caregivers and domestic labour: involvement or avoidance', pp. 16 and 22.

13 See Ilene Wolcott and Helen Glezer, *Work and Family Life. Achieving Integration*, Australian Institute of Family Studies, Melbourne, 1995.

14 See Adrienne Burgess and Sandy Ruxton, *Men and Their Children: Proposals for Public Policy*, Institute for Public Policy Research, London, 1996.

At the time of writing, Adrienne Burgess's book *Fatherhood Reclaimed: The Making of the Modern Father* (Vermilion, London, 1997) had not yet been published. Adrienne Burgess was kind enough to provide me with an advance copy of *Fatherhood Reclaimed* while I was making the final revisions to this book. Her conclusions—drawn primarily in a British context, but making use of a very wide body of research from around the world—are similar in many areas to my own.

15 See Bly, *Iron John*, p. 92.

16 See the *Sydney Morning Herald*, 2 September 1995, *Spectrum* p. 3.

17 Biddulph, *Manhood*, pp. 24–5.

18 See Beatrice Gottlieb, *The Family in the Western World from the Black Death to the Industrial Age*, pp. 7ff.

19 Bly, *Iron John,* p. 121.

20 ibid., p. 99.

21 See Biddulph, *Manhood*, p. 38.

22 Bly, *Iron John,* p. 96.

23 See for example the *Economist Review*, 14 September 1996, p. 4, review of *The Essential Neo-Conservative Reader*.

24 This is an argument advanced by Erika Haubold in an unpublished paper 'Feminist Utopia and the New

Fathers', part of a PhD thesis for the Department of Sociology at the University of Wollongong.
25 See Lawrence Stone, *Broken Lives: Separation and Divorce in England 1660–1857*, Oxford, 1993, p. 14.
26 See Barry Maley, *Wedlock and Wellbeing: What Marriage Means for Adults and Children*, Centre for Independent Studies Monographs No. 33, 1996.
27 Stone, *Broken Lives*, p. 6.
28 See Gilding, *The Making and Breaking of the Australian Family*, p. 120.
29 From Joe Franks, *Rent-a-Family: Work in Progress*, produced for National Public Radio (USA) and first broadcast in Australia on *Radio Eye*, ABC Radio National, 2 January 1994.
30 See the *Sydney Morning Herald*, 23 September 1996, p. 11.
31 See for example Anne Campbell, *Out of Control*, Chapter 8, 'Street Gangs' and Anne Campbell's other work on girl gangs. Similar research is now beginning to be published in Australia.
32 See for example letters published in the *Australian* by Peter Vogel and Gavin Dimery, 23 September 1996, p. 10.
33 The following material is quoted from Erika Haubold, 'Feminist Utopia and the New Fathers' (see note 24 above). I am extremely grateful to Ms Haubold for permission to quote from her research.
34 See Haubold, 'Feminist Utopia and the New Fathers', p. 8. Haubold draws here on work by Françoise Laborie, who believes that current trends in genetics have helped to reinforce a 'naturalist' paradigm which grounds 'reproductive equality' in biology.
35 See Stone, *Broken Lives*, p. 23.
36 ibid., p. 25.
37 Quoted in Gatens, *Imaginary Bodies*, p. 53.
38 It could be argued that the attempts to create artificial intelligence and conscious machines are the most interesting contemporary manifestation of this tendency.
39 See *The Age*, 14 December 1994, p. 17.
40 See Gatens, *Imaginary Bodies*, p. 17.
41 The *Australian*, 23 September, 1996, p. 10.
42 As we would hope they would be; what seems unspoken

but implicit here, though, is that the woman is somehow incidental, peripheral to the man's primary relationship with the child. Haubold also make the point that men are shifting their emotional focus onto children, though she argues that 'for both partners, the child very often becomes the field onto which closeness and continuity are projected'.

43 See McMahon, *Taking Care of Men*, pp. 141, 192.

44 *New Idea*, 28 September 1996, p. 16.

10 WHAT DOES A MAN WANT?

1 Quoted in Shoshana Felman, *What does A Woman Want? Reading and Sexual Difference*, Johns Hopkins University Press, Baltimore & London, 1993, p. 21.

2 See Giddens, *The Transformation of Intimacy*, p. 61.

3 See Alain Lipietz, *Towards a New Economic Order*, Polity, Cambridge, 1992, p. 84. 'In the French case, calculations based on a reduction of working hours during the period 1968–78 show that one hour a week less created, *all other things being equal*, 250,000 jobs over a five-year period.

4 See *Business Week*, 16 September 1996, pp. 74–80 and the *Sydney Morning Herald*, 2 December 1995, *Employment* Section, p. 1.

5 See *Business Week*, 7 April 1997.

6 See Giddens, *The Transformation of Intimacy*, p. 117.

Bibliography

Australian Bureau of Statistics, *Australian Social Trends*, Catalogue No. 4102.0, 1996

Badinter, Elisabeth, *XY: On Masculine Identity*, tr. Lydia Davis, Columbia University Press, New York, 1995

Biddulph, Steve, *Manhood: A Book About Setting Men Free*, Finch Publishing, Sydney, 1994

Bittman, Michael, *Juggling Time: How Australian Families Use Time*, Australian Government Publishing Service, Canberra, 1992

Bittman, Michael, *Recent Changes in Unpaid Work*, ABS Occasional Paper Catalogue No. 4154.0, 1995

Bly, Robert, *Iron John: A Book about Men*, Element, Brisbane, 1994

Brantenberg, Gert, *Die Töchter Egalias: Ein Roman uber den Kampf der Geschlechter*, Olle und Wolter, Berlin, 1979

Brunner, Conze, Koselleck, (Hg.), *Geschichtliche Grundbegriffe*, Bd. 2, Stuttgart, 1975, pp. 269–73

Burgess, Adrienne, *Fatherhood Reclaimed: The Making of the Modern Father*, Vermilion, London, 1997

Burgess, Adrienne and Ruxton, Sandy, *Men and their Children: Proposals for Public Policy*, Institute for Public Policy Research, London, 1996

Burton, Tom, *Words, Words, Words*, University Radio 5UV, Adelaide, 1995

Bynum, Caroline Walker, *Jesus as Mother: Studies in the Spirituality of the High Middle Ages*, University of California Press, Berkeley and London, 1982

Campbell, Anne, *Out of Control: Men, Women and Aggression*, Pandora, London, 1993

Castiglione, Baldesar, *The Book of the Courtier*, tr. George Bull, Penguin, London, 1995
Connell, R.W., *Masculinities*, Allen & Unwin, Sydney, 1995, pp. 128–39
Coochey, John, 'All men are bastards' *Independent Monthly*, November 1995, pp. 48–51
Cox, Eva, *Leading Women*, Random House, Sydney, 1996, p. 221
Cunningham, Hugh, *Children and Childhood in Western Society since 1500*, Longman, London and New York, 1995
Evans, Raymond, 'A gun in the oven: masculinism and gendered violence', in *Gender Relations in Australia: Domination and Negotiation*, Kay Saunders and David Evans, eds, Harcourt Brace Jovanovich, Sydney, 1992, pp. 197–218.
Farrell, Warren, *The Myth of Male Power: Why Men are the Disposable Sex*, Random House, Sydney, 1994
Faust, Beatrice, *Backlash? Balderdash! Where Feminism is Going Right*, UNSW Press, Sydney, 1994
Felman, Shoshana, *What Does A Woman Want? Reading and Sexual Difference*, Johns Hopkins University Press, Baltimore and London, 1993
Felski, Rita, *The Gender of Modernity*, Harvard University Press, Cambridge and London, 1995
Ferry, Luc, *The New Ecological Order*, tr. Carol Volk, University of Chicago Press, Chicago and London, 1995
Foster, David, *The Glade within the Grove*, Random House, Sydney, 1996
Franks, Joe, *Rent-a-Family: Work in Progress*, produced for National Public Radio (USA) and first broadcast in Australia on *Radio Eye*, ABC Radio National, 2 Jan. 1994
Funder, Kathleen, Harrison, Margaret and Weston, Ruth, eds, *Settling Down: Pathways of Parents after Divorce*, Australian Institute of Family Studies Monograph No. 13, Melbourne, 1993
Future Labour Market Issues for Australia, EPAC Paper No. 12, Australian Bureau of Statistics, Catalogue No. 6203.0, *The Labour Force*, August, 1995
Garner, Helen, *The First Stone: Some Questions About Sex and Power,* Picador, Sydney, 1995

Gatens, Moira, *Imaginary Bodies: Ethics, Power and Corporeality*, Routledge, London and New York, 1996

Giddens, Anthony, *The Transformation of Intimacy: Sexuality, Love and Eroticism in Modern Societies*, Polity, Cambridge, 1995

Gilbert, Sandra M. and Gubar, Susan, *No Man's Land*, New Haven, Yale, 1986

Gilding, Michael, *The Making and Breaking of the Australian Family*, Allen & Unwin, Sydney, 1991, Ch. 1

Gottlieb, Beatrice, *The Family in the Western World from the Black Death to the Industrial Age*, OUP, Oxford and New York, 1993

Grbich, Carol, 'Societal response to familial role change in Australia: marginalisation or social change' *Journal of Comparative Family Studies*, Canada, Vol. XXIII No. 1, Spring 1992

——'Women as primary breadwinners in families where men are primary caregivers' *ANZJS* Vol. 30, No. 2, August, 1994

——'Male primary caregivers and domestic labour: involvement or avoidance' *Journal of Family Studies*, Nov./Dec., 1995

Haubold, Erika, 'Feminist Utopia and the new fathers', unpublished paper, part of a PhD thesis for the Department of Sociology at the University of Wollongong

Hufton, Olwyn, *The Prospect Before Her: A History of Women in Western Europe, Vol. 1: 1500–1800*, HarperCollins, London and New York, 1995

Ireland, David, *The Glass Canoe*, Macmillan, Sydney, 1976

Jordan, Peter, 'The effects of marital separation on men' *Journal of Divorce*, Vol. 12(1) 1988, pp. 57–126

——*The Effects of Marital Separation on Men—10 Years on*, Family Court of Australia, Research Report No. 14, November, 1996

Koselleck, Reinhart, *Kritik und Krise: Eine Studie zur Pathogenese der bürgerlichen Welt*, Suhrkamp, Frankfurt am Main, 1979

Law, Ian, 'Adopting the principle of pro-feminism' *Accountability: New Directions for Working in Partnership*, Dulwich Centre Newsletter, Nos 2 & 3, The Dulwich Centre, Hutt St., Adelaide, 1994, pp. 40–3.

Lewis, Alison, *Subverting Patriarchy: Feminism and Fantasy in the Works of Irmtraud Morgner*, Berg, Oxford, 1995

Lipietz, Alain, *Towards a New Economic Order*, Polity, Cambridge, 1992

Looker, Peter, 'Doing it with your mates', in *The Abundant Culture: Meaning and Significance in Everyday Australia*, David Headon, Joy Hooton and Donald Horne, eds, Allen & Unwin, Sydney, 1994, pp. 215–19

Lovejoy, Frances, Perkins, Roberta and Jacobsen, Meredith, *Unsafe Sexual Practices in the Sexual Behaviour of Female and Male Sex Workers: A Study Conducted in the School of Sociology, University of New South Wales*, UNSW Press, 1995

Maley, Barry, *Wedlock and Wellbeing: What Marriage Means for Adults and Children*, Centre for Independent Studies Monographs No. 33, 1996

McMahon, Anthony, 'Taking care of men: discourses and practices of everyday life', PhD thesis in the Department of Sociology and Anthropology, LaTrobe University, January 1994

McCormick, Naomi B., *Sexual Salvation: Affirming Women's Sexual Rights and Pleasures,* London and Connecticut, 1994

Mies, Maria and Shiva, Vandana, *Ecofeminism*, Spinifex, Melbourne, 1993

Mitterauer, Michael and Sieder, Reinhard, *The European Family—Patriarchy to Partnership: From the Middle Ages to the Present*, Oxford University Press, Oxford 1982

Morgan, David, *Discovering Men*, Routledge, London and New York, 1992, p. 38

Moss, Peter and Brannen, Julia, 'Fathers and employment', in *Reassessing Fatherhood: New Observations on the Modern Family*, Charlie Lewis and Margaret O'Brien, eds, London, 1987

Ondaatje, Michael, *In the Skin of a Lion*, Picador, London, 1988

Paglia, Camille, *Sex, Art, and American Culture: Essays*, Penguin, London, 1993

Pateman, Carol, *The Sexual Contract*, Polity, Cambridge, 1988

Probert, Belinda and Wilson, Bruce W., eds, *Pink Collar Blues:*

Work, Gender and Technology, Melbourne University Press, Melbourne, 1993

Riley, Kerry and Riley, Diane, *Sexual Secrets for Men*, Random House, Sydney, 1995

Rose, S., 'Gender antagonism and class conflict: exclusionary strategies of male trades-unionists in nineteenth-century Britain' *Social History*, Vol. 13, No. 2, 1988

Routley, Virginia and Sherrard, Jenny, 'Domestic violence' *Hazard*, No. 21, Monash University Accident Research Centre, December, 1994

Segal, Lynne, *Straight Sex: The Politics of Pleasure*, Virago, London, 1994

——*Slow Motion: Changing Masculinities, Changing Men*, Virago, London, 1994

Sennett, Richard and Cobb, Jonathan, *The Hidden Injuries of Class*, Knopf, New York, 1982

Showalter, Elaine, *Sexual Anarchy: Gender and Culture at the Fin de Siècle*, Virago, London, 1992

St Claire, Olivia, *Unleashing the Sex Goddess in Every Woman*, Bantam, New York and Sydney, 1996

Stone, Lawrence, *The Family, Sex and Marriage in England 1500–1800*, London, 1977

——*Broken Lives: Separation and Divorce in England 1660–1857*, Oxford University Press, Oxford, 1993

Strathern, Marilyn, *After Nature: English Kinship in the Late Twentieth Century*, Cambridge University Press, Cambridge, 1992

Straus M.A., and Gelles, R.J., *Physical Violence in American Families: Risk Factors and Adaptation to Violence in 8,145 Families,* New Brunswick, 1990

Straus, M.A., Gelles, R.J. and Steinmetz, S.K., *Behind Closed Doors: Violence in the American Family,* New York, 1980

Townsend, Lynne, *Programs for Perpetrators of Domestic Violence*, prepared for the New South Wales Domestic Violence Strategic Plan, and published by the NSW Women's Co-ordination Unit, July 1991

Umberson, D. and Williams, C.L., 'Divorced fathers: parental role strain and psychological distress' *Journal of Family Issues*, No. 14

Vonnegut, Kurt Jr., *Welcome to the Monkey House*, Panther, St Albans, 1976

Winton, Tim, *The Riders*, Pan Macmillan, Sydney, 1994
Wolcott, Irene and Glezer, Helen, *Work and Family Life: Achieving Integration*, Australian Institute of Family Studies, 1995
Wright, Robert, *The Moral Animal: Evolutionary Psychology and Everyday Life*, Abacus, London, 1994

Index